CHURCHILL WANTED DEAD OR ALIVE

CELIA SANDYS is a granddaughter of Sir Winston Churchill. Her mother was Churchill's eldest daughter, Diana, and her father was Lord Duncan-Sandys, the former Cabinet Minister and member of his father-in-law's wartime government. She is married, has four children and lives in Wiltshire. She is the author of *From Winston With Love and Kisses: The Young Churchill*, and has lectured in America, Canada, Japan and Britain.

From the reviews of *Churchill Wanted Dead or Alive*:

'A thrilling early life and a thrilling read'
ALAN JUDD, *Spectator Books of the Year*

'This excellent short book, covering the years 1899 to 1902, shows how all-consuming was Churchill's lust for fame, glory and medals . . . well-researched and compelling . . . Sandys attempts, on the whole successfully, to defend her grandfather against long-standing charges of having behaved disgracefully towards his comrades during the escape . . . [She] goes deeply into the issue, uncovering new evidence and concluding that her grandfather was right when he said that he had acted "with perfect comradeship and honour the whole way through" . . . This well-written, fast-moving narrative is a fine portrait of a young man in a hurry, albeit one who occasionally cut corners to reach his glorious destination' ANDREW ROBERTS, *Literary Review*

'Thankfully, it is clear from the start that Sandys is not going to paper over the cracks in the young Churchill's character ... a cracking good yarn about a cocky young Victorian lad whose jingoistic adventures in a far-flung colony nearly cost him his life ... For those who like history without cobwebs, this is an absorbing, down-to-earth read'

ELIZABETH CLARKE, *Independent on Sunday*

'Churchill's granddaughter, Celia Sandys, has successfully captured the vitality of the young Churchill. Her understanding of the African terrain and the campaigns is admirable ... a very special and charming addition to all that has already been written about the colossus of the twentieth century'

HILARY PRATT, *Irish Independent*

'A story of refreshing intimacy, illuminating events of 100 years ago with the humble testimony of history's bit-players'

STUART WAVELL, *Sunday Times*

'The book paints a vivid picture of a bumptious, supremely self-confident young man, determined to make his mark on the world. Doubling as soldier and war correspondent, he made friends and enemies with equal facility. Sandys has not only re-examined all the relevant letters and papers, but visited South Africa and spoken to many of the descendants of those involved in the fighting. An old tale is thus freshened by many new anecdotes'

The Week

CHURCHILL
Wanted Dead or Alive

CELIA SANDYS

HarperCollins*Publishers*

HarperCollins*Publishers*
77–85 Fulham Palace Road,
Hammersmith, London w6 8jb

The HarperCollins website address is:
www.**fire**and**water**.com

This paperback edition 2000
1 3 5 7 9 8 6 4 2

First published in Great Britain by
HarperCollins*Publishers* 1999

ISBN 0 00 653084 2

Set in PostScript Linotype Janson by
Rowland Phototypesetting Ltd,
Bury St Edmunds, Suffolk

Printed and bound in Great Britain by
Omnia Books Limited, Glasgow

For Ken

CONTENTS

ILLUSTRATIONS

Section Two

Section Three

MAPS

ACKNOWLEDGEMENTS

I would like to thank the many descendants, and their families, of those who were involved with Winston Churchill during the Anglo–Boer War who responded to my request for information. Without their help and guidance as I retraced my grandfather's footsteps around South Africa this book could not have been written. I am grateful to them for sharing with me the stories told to them by their parents or grandparents, for allowing me to reproduce diaries, letters and photographs, and for their friendship and hospitality. They include: Jim and Barbara Bailey, Martha Bam, Lette Bennet, Anthony Berlein, Joan Bromley, Molly Buchanan, John Burnham, Liz Burrow, Angela Caccia-Lloyd, Max Van Cittert, Stewart and Jenny Clegg, F L. Hugh de Souza, Dr Jonathan de Souza, Johanna de Wet, Errol Dewsnap, Daniel du Plessis, Joy Fourie, Vera Gallony, Ken Gibson, Dr Alexander J.P. Graham, Jay Haggar, John Haldane, Ian Hamilton, Dr F.E. Hofmeyr, Nancy Horsfall, E.N. Howarth, Yvonne Knowles, Karl Kohler, Mike McKenna, Doris Maud, E.P. Mitchell, Jill Osborne, Tessa Power, Molly Pringle, Dr Willem Punt, Alan Raubenheimer, Becky Smit, Alexander M. Stewart, Charles Wagner and Judge Louis Weyers.

I am most grateful to my cousin Winston S. Churchill for permission to quote from works of Sir Winston Churchill and to reproduce certain documents and photographs.

I am indebted to the directors and staffs of the following libraries, museums and archives, many of whom have allowed me to reproduce material from their collections: Thomas B. Smyth of the Black Watch Museum; Marcell Weiner and Diana Madden of the Brenthurst Library; Dr Piers Brendon, Keeper of the Archives, Churchill Archive Centre, and his staff; Sir John Boyd, Master of Churchill College, Cambridge; Brian Spencer of the Don Africana Library; Lieutenant Colonel J.J. Hume of the Durban Light Infantry Museum; George Goodey of Fort Durnford Museum; the director and staff of the Killie Campbell Africana Library; Gilbert Torlage of the KwaZulu-Natal Museum Service; Marjorie Heron and Brian Kaighin of the Ladysmith Historical Society; Maureen Richards and Elizabeth Sprit of the Ladysmith Siege Museum; Clive Kirkwood of the National Archives Repository, Pretoria; the Trustees and Sheila Mackenzie of the National Library of Scotland; Philip Hirst, editor of the *Oldham Chronicle*; John G. Entwhistle of Reuters Archive; John Montgomery of the Royal United Services Institution; Piet Westra of the South African Library, Durban; Hester Nel and Mona Niemand of the Staats Model School, Pretoria; Barbara Conradie of the Standard Bank, Johannesburg; the staff of the MOTH Museum, Johannesburg.

It is with great gratitude that I acknowledge the assistance of the many people who helped by providing information and material from which I have quoted: Dr Paul Addison, W.H. Atteridge, Eric Bingham, David Blem, Eric Boswell, George Chadwick, the late 'Pitch' and Eileen Christopher, Minnie Churchill, Peregrine S. Churchill, Liz Clark, Elliott Costas, Brian Dodds, Ambassador du Buisson, Steve Forbes, Robin Fryde, John Gaunt, Sir Martin Gilbert, Ken Gillings, Jill Gowans, Dr Ryno Greenwall, Peter Grindal, Clive Hatch, Sheila Henderson, Marjorie Heron, Raymond and Lynette Heron, Dr Fay Liesling, Brian Logan, Keith Lyon, W.H. Mackay, Jimmy McLachlan, Alastair Martin, Peter and Fiona Martin, the late Clive Mennell, Jessel Molin, Professor Fransjohan Pretorius, David Rattray, Taffy Shearing, Peter Stockil, Mary Swan, Audrey Densham Tanner, Ann Tyrrell, Graham Viney, Errol Wilson, Fred and Jo Woods.

I am indebted to Jim Miller of SAMCOR and Nic Griffin of AVIS, who kindly provided me with vehicles for my travels around South Africa.

I wish to thank Bridget and Harry Oppenheimer for their kindness and hospitality, and for introducing me to South Africa more than thirty years ago.

My greatest thanks must go to Mary Slack for her help, advice and encouragement, and for giving us such a wonderful home from home in South Africa, but above all for her unswerving friendship since we first met at school when we were twelve years old.

I am most grateful to my agent Araminta Whitley, my publisher Richard Johnson and my editor Robert Lacey for their enthusiastic encouragement, sensitive guidance and friendly support.

Finally I must thank my husband Ken Perkins for his help and guidance throughout the research and writing of this book. His military knowledge has been invaluable and his patience endless.

Celia Sandys
Savernake Forest
March 1999

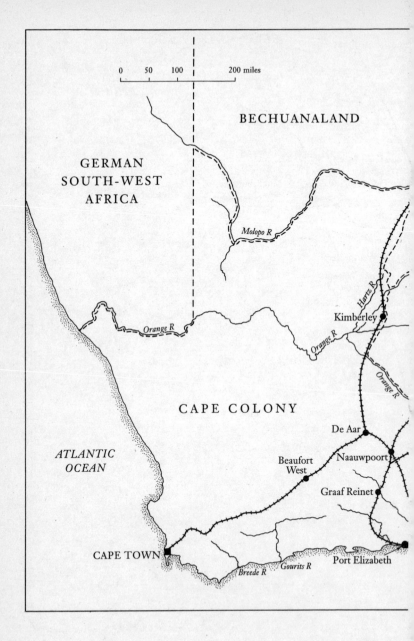

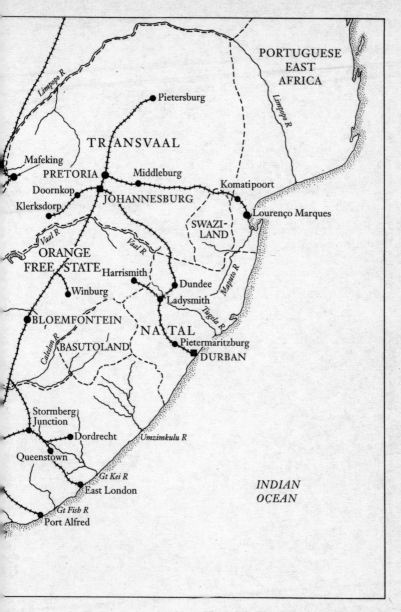

The Scene of Conflict – South Africa 1899

PREFACE

Winston Churchill's heroic escapades during the Anglo–Boer War propelled him overnight onto the international stage. In 1994 I went to South Africa to research what I thought would be two or three chapters of a book I intended to write about my grandfather from 1895 to 1908. I chose to go there partly because I loved the country and already had great friends there, but mainly because that was the period of Churchill's life which interested me most.

Retracing his footsteps through South Africa during what was unquestionably the greatest adventure of his life was the most exciting journey I have ever made, even though there was no danger for me of death or capture – I only risked being killed by the kindness and hospitality of new friends eager to help me in my voyage of discovery.

Although I knew there would be some people in South Africa with stories to tell, I expected my research to be mostly geographical. But during a television interview shortly after my arrival I appealed for anyone whose parents or grandparents had been involved in any way with Churchill during his time in South Africa to come forward. The response was incredible. Before the programme had even finished the telephone started to ring, the fax machine poured out constant messages, and letters arrived by every post. Encouraged by this, and with the cooperation of the South African media, I spread my request all around the country, on television, radio and in the newspapers. I found myself swamped with information, and it was at this point that I realised I was researching not just a chapter or two, but a whole book.

The expedition soon became a family pilgrimage as, with my husband and our two young children, I travelled from place to place to check out information and meet those who had contacted me.

We were welcomed with open arms by the descendants of Churchill's friends and foes alike, who enthusiastically told us the stories they had heard while sitting on their grandparents' or, occasionally, their parents', knees.

There was nothing orderly about the way the information came in, and therefore there was no efficient way for me to follow it up. We simply zig-zagged our way from place to place, with no idea where we would be the next day. From Johannesburg to Pretoria, from Vereeniging to Witbank, south to Ladysmith and Estcourt, on to Durban, north to the very edge of the Kruger National Park, back to Natal and down to the Cape. So it went on. It was not only we who travelled: some people came long distances to meet us.

Wherever we went we were welcomed with great warmth, enormous interest in and huge enthusiasm for our search. We were wined and dined, shown treasured letters, diaries and photographs while at the same time making a host of new friends in a beautiful country we had all grown to love. This is the sort of research I enjoy most. Of course I visited libraries and archives, where people took endless trouble to help me find anything of relevance, but there is nothing to equal the experience of hearing living history passed down directly from those who were actually there.

I experienced moments of highly charged emotion: discovering the place where my grandfather surrendered to the Boers, and being hugged by the descendants of men who had risked their lives for his safety and freedom. There were also amusing incidents, like the day we were told how Churchill chased a chicken round a farmyard because he wanted it for his dinner.

One small mystery remains. Following his return to England in 1900, Churchill sent eight inscribed gold watches to people who had helped him during his dramatic escape as a prisoner of war. This story attracted a lot of attention when I mentioned it during my South African interviews, and as a result I now know where six of those eight watches are. Maybe the last two will come to light as a result of their present owners reading this book.

Intrigued as I had always been by my grandfather's time in South

Africa, it was only as I retraced his footsteps of a century before that I realised with awe how thrilling were his adventures, and how great were the dangers which he often treated so lightly. It has been a wonderful experience to make this journey with my younger children, and to show them where their great-grandfather had adventures which any modern-day hero would have been proud to share.

PROLOGUE

'Twenty to twenty-five. Those are the years!'

WINSTON CHURCHILL, *My Early Life*

THUS WROTE MY GRANDFATHER WINSTON CHURCHILL more than a quarter of a century after his breathtaking adventures during the Anglo–Boer War. As a young man in his early twenties his escapades on India's North-West Frontier and with Kitchener in the Sudan had earned him the respect, though not always the approval, of the British military hierarchy. He also proved himself as a journalist and writer, earning more by the pen than by the sword. Members of Parliament had noticed him not just as the son of the late Lord Randolph Churchill, a leading political figure of his day, but as a budding politician in his own right. But it was his exploits in the Anglo–Boer War, during which he became a national hero, which set him on the road to fame. I had always been fascinated by this meteoric overnight leap onto the international stage, a position Churchill would occupy for over a half a century. What, I asked myself, were the circumstances in which a young journalist and aspiring politician so suddenly became a household name?

As the Anglo–Boer War provided the springboard, I decided I had better first understand its origins. I started with my grandfather's own words, from Volume IV of *The History of the English Speaking Peoples*:

> Two landlocked Boer Republics, owing a vague suzerainty to Britain, were surrounded on all sides, except for a short frontier with Portuguese Mozambique, by British colonies, protectorates, and territories. Yet conflict was not inevitable ... even

in the Transvaal, home of the dourest frontier farmers, a considerable Boer party favoured cooperation with Britain ...
But all this abruptly changed during the last five years of the
nineteenth century.

The Cape of Good Hope had originally been settled by Europeans in 1652, when the Dutch East India Company founded a
shipping station there. The early Dutch settlers brought with them
an innate resentment of any attempt to interfere with their Calvinist
traditions and customs. From the outset they were heavily out-
numbered by their black and 'Coloured' (mixed-race) servants and
slaves, not to mention the existing inhabitants of the region. The
poorest and most independent of the settlers were itinerant farmers,
known as Boers, who moved progressively northwards into the
interior, in search of better grazing and of freedom from the authority of the local officials.

In 1806 the British established a naval base at the Cape and, by
conquest and a payment of £6 million to the Netherlands, took
possession of the colony. The motive at this time was purely strategic – to facilitate the sea route to India. Potential British settlers
were deterred by the climate, so the colony's white population
remained predominantly Afrikaner, a minority of whom, particularly the Boers, were resentful of British rule. United in their determination to deny political rights to blacks and Coloureds at a time
when slavery was being banished within the British Empire, some
five thousand Boers, with a similar number of Coloured servants,
moved north in the Great Trek of 1835–37. They crossed the
Orange and Vaal rivers to set up the independent republics of
Transvaal and the Orange Free State. In 1843 Britain annexed
Natal, to the east of the new republics, which thus found themselves
unhappily surrounded by British-controlled territory on three sides,
while their only access to the sea was through Lourenço Marques
in Portuguese East Africa.

The Transvaal was soon in difficulties, threatened from within
by bankruptcy and internal dissent, and from without by the Zulus,
whose territory was being impinged upon by the newcomers and
their livestock. In 1877 Britain, with the formation of a union of

South African white communities in mind, annexed the Transvaal – whose independence it had recognised since 1852. No sooner had order been restored than the Boers revolted, under the leadership of Paul Kruger. This conflict, the first Anglo–Boer War, ended after only three months when a small British force was cut to pieces at Majuba Hill in early 1881.

The British government now reversed its policy. Declining to commit the forces necessary to restore its authority in the Transvaal, it granted the colony self-government. These contradictory actions of recognition, annexation, and abdication were reflections of the negative and ambivalent British policy in South Africa generally, which inevitably caused relations between the opposing sides to fester. On the one hand, jingoists in Britain and the Cape dreamed of avenging Majuba. On the other, Kruger, firmly ensconced as President of the Transvaal, was intent on escaping British domination.

Kruger's policy went hand in hand with the newfound prosperity of his country. The rich seams of gold discovered in the Rand in 1886 brought such wealth and economic influence to the Transvaal that it began to threaten British supremacy in Southern Africa. A plan to counter this was hatched by Cecil Rhodes, Prime Minister at the Cape and the multi-millionaire creator of de Beers, as well as of the Chartered Company which administered the new British colony of Rhodesia, to the north of the Boer republics.

Gold may not have been the root cause of the quarrel, but it played a considerable part. The gold rush had attracted thousands of immigrants, called 'Uitlanders', of whom a large number were British. Their presence – they were thought to outnumber the Boers – was a potential threat to the independence of the Transvaal which Kruger sought to remove. In 1890 he tried to block the enfranchisement of the Uitlanders by increasing from five to fourteen years the residential qualification for voting in central government and presidential elections. Rhodes believed that the Uitlanders' political plight offered a pretext for once more annexing the Transvaal.

His intention was to unseat Kruger by means of an Uitlander

rebellion in Johannesburg and a simultaneous invasion by Rhodesian mounted police and Cape volunteers. The invasion, which began on 30 December 1895, was led by Dr Leander Starr Jameson, with troops from Rhodes' British South Africa Company, from the Bechuanaland Protectorate, which provided a suitable base from which to strike. The Jameson Raid, as it became known, went disastrously wrong. The Uitlanders failed to rise, Rhodes having grossly overestimated the strength of their opposition to Kruger. Jameson's force was subjected to a running battle and surrendered after four days at Doornkop, twenty-five miles short of Johannesburg.

Kruger published secret documents captured from the raiders and, saving Jameson from summary execution in Pretoria, embarrassed the British by sending him to London for trial. Rhodes, forced to testify, cut a wretched figure in the witness box. Having been exposed as a plotter and bungler who had attempted to shift the blame on to Jameson, he was forced to resign as both Chairman of the Chartered Company and Cape Prime Minister.

Following the failure at Majuba, the fiasco at Doornkop left Britain's Southern Africa policy in tatters. The Colonial Secretary, Joseph Chamberlain, advised patience, saying that the Jameson Raid had placed Britain in a 'false position'. Military action was out of the question, as it would leave a legacy of bitterness inimical to Britain's long-term aim of a union of South Africa. It would also be unpopular in Britain, unless Kruger were to put himself flagrantly in the wrong. Chamberlain considered that time was on his side, and that Kruger, given enough rope, would eventually hang himself.

After 1898 it was the British High Commissioner at the Cape, Sir Alfred Milner, rather than the Colonial Secretary, who was driving British policy. Milner, who saw himself as the protagonist of a South African federation under the British flag, was determined to annex the Transvaal, which he recognised as the main impediment to his plans. In his view, time was on Kruger's side. Milner needed to raise the stakes.

He found a willing ally in Percy Fitzpatrick, the foremost political activist among the Uitlanders. Fitzpatrick was employed by Alfred

Beit, who had partnered Rhodes in the foundation of Rhodesia. The profitability of Beit's mining operations, in common with those of other magnates on the Rand, was at the mercy of Kruger's industrial policies, which pushed up the cost of labour and dynamite, and imposed a profits tax. On Beit's instructions, Fitzpatrick was negotiating for less onerous policies with the Transvaal Attorney, Jan Christiaan Smuts, and a new arrangement, called the Great Deal, was virtually on the table. However, Fitzpatrick had no interest in seeing the Great Deal go through. He was more concerned with his own political ambitions, which he regarded as not inconsistent with those of his employer, and which, incidentally, ran parallel to Milner's. All the problems, he believed, would be solved if the franchise issue could be settled in favour of the Uitlanders, and control of the Transvaal thus transferred into British hands. But something was needed to raise the Uitlanders' enthusiasm for politics.

The opportunity came when uproar among them followed the acquittal of a South African policeman for the over-hasty shooting of a young British boilermaker, Tom Edgar, during a drunken brawl. Having engineered the last-minute failure of his negotiations with Smuts, in April 1899 Fitzpatrick was able to present Milner with a petition to Queen Victoria, signed by twenty-one thousand British subjects on the Rand, calling for British intervention on their behalf.

Milner's recommendation for intervention had actually been agreed by the British government when leading Cape Afrikaners proposed a meeting between Milner and Kruger. President Martinus Steyn of the Orange Free State offered a venue at Bloemfontein. Milner promised Chamberlain that he would be 'studiously moderate', but he was bent on war, and had no intention of reaching any compromise. Yet after three days the gap between the two sides was so narrow that Milner became alarmed. He brushed aside Kruger's offers, describing them as a 'Kaffir-bargain', and cabled Chamberlain that the negotiations might have to be broken off. Chamberlain, who was still seeking a settlement, replied: 'I hope you will not break off too hastily . . . you should be very patient . . . before you finally abandon the game.'

The cable arrived too late. Kruger had sensed Milner's true intentions – to annex the Transvaal. 'It is our country you want,' he had said, with tears in his eyes. Milner had closed the negotiations with an icy response: 'This conference is absolutely at an end, and there is no obligation on either side arising from it.' It was 5 June 1899.

The talks having broken down, Milner now convinced the government in London that the British Army in Natal should be reinforced. He disingenuously assured them that a show of strength would force Kruger back to the negotiating table, and war would be averted. The obsession of Milner, the High Commissioner, with imperial expansion, the ambitions of the Irish political adventurer Fitzpatrick, and the financial interests of the 'gold bugs' had, together, taken charge of British policy. Events were leading inexorably to war.

Although there was much sympathy for the Boers among the Continental states of Europe, who also shared a general inclination to exploit Britain's difficulties to their own advantage, no country was prepared to incur British displeasure by committing itself to open support of the Boers. In any event, Britain's naval supremacy enabled her to implement her policies in South Africa without fear of foreign intervention. Seasoned regiments with ample stores and artillery were sent to the Cape from India and the Mediterranean, and by the end of September 1899, fifteen thousand British troops were ranged in a threatening manner along the borders of the Transvaal and its ally, the Orange Free State. In London, thought was given to mobilising General Sir Redvers Buller's 1st Army Corps and cavalry division as an indication that Britain meant business, but few preparations were made. The War Office was firmly of the view that Buller's thirty-five thousand men would not be needed, and it was widely believed if war came, the Boer commandos would be chased from the field by Britain's professional army.

The Boers thought differently, and with reason. Thanks to the wealth of the Transvaal they could, within a week, mobilise a force of some twenty-five thousand men, equipped with modern small arms and artillery. To this could be added a further fifteen thousand men from the Orange Free State. Apart from the artillery, who were professional soldiers, this was a civilian army of burghers commandeered to fight when their country was threatened. The Boer forces were organised into commandos, each of some five hundred mounted riflemen, their mobile tactics of hit-and-run well suited to operations across the local terrain, of which they had intimate knowledge. Their effectiveness would so impress Churchill that more than forty years later, as Prime Minister during the Second World War, he would order the formation of commandos for raiding purposes.

Kruger's final words at the Bloemfontein conference had correctly summed up Milner's intentions: to annex the Transvaal. Assuming, reasonably enough, that Milner was pursuing the British government's policy, Kruger issued an ultimatum on 9 October 1899. It demanded that all points of difference be settled by arbitration, and that the British troops be withdrawn from the Transvaal's border. Failure to accept these terms would be regarded as a formal declaration of war. Milner had succeeded in his plan to brand Kruger as the aggressor, and the British government was more than content to ignore the ultimatum.

War began two days later. Ill-conceived and uncoordinated policies had embroiled Britain in a conflict it had hoped to avoid, but which, now joined, it was convinced could be speedily and successfully concluded.

It was a conviction that the young Winston Churchill shared as he set sail for the Cape from Southampton on 14 October. It was a conviction that would soon be shattered.

ONE

Gateway

> 'War service was the swift road to promotion and advancement.
> It was the glittering gateway to distinction. It cast glamour
> upon the fortunate possessor alike in the eyes of elderly gentle-
> men and young ladies.'
>
> WINSTON CHURCHILL, *My Early Life*

BY THE AGE OF TWENTY-FOUR, Winston Churchill was already
a seasoned campaigner. Leaving the Royal Military Academy in
December 1894, a fortnight after his twentieth birthday, he had
been commissioned into a fashionable cavalry regiment, the 4th
Hussars, on 20 February. He was impatient to make an immediate
impact, but found the army almost entirely occupied with the chores
and pleasures of peacetime soldiering. The usual pursuits of the
cavalry officer during his five months of winter leave, pursuing
foxes across the English Shires or young ladies through London
drawing rooms, were not for the young Churchill, and he looked
around for some scene of active service which would provide experience and perhaps medals. The world was largely at peace, but in
Cuba a guerrilla war between indigenous rebels and the island's
Spanish rulers was reaching a conclusive stage.

Within eight months of joining his regiment, Churchill set off
for Cuba. He had used his family connections to good effect. Not
only had his father been a national figure, but Lady Randolph
Churchill, his beautiful and talented mother, numbered Edward,
Prince of Wales among her many admirers. Little wonder that in

Churchill's pocket was an introduction to the Spanish Captain-General. For company he had Reggie Barnes, a fellow officer who had been persuaded that an adventure in Cuba would be more beneficial and less expensive than a season fox-hunting. To defray the expense of this private venture Churchill had secured his first journalistic contract, having arranged with the *Daily Graphic* that he would be paid five guineas for each 'letter from the front' he dispatched to the paper.

On his way to Cuba he stopped off in New York. Here he was looked after and introduced around by Senator Bourke Cockran, another admirer of Lady Randolph. Cockran, a distinguished lawyer and politician, was probably the first person to recognise the young man's vast potential, and admitted himself profoundly impressed with the vigour of Churchill's language and the breadth of his views. The two men were to strike up a friendship and maintain a long-standing political correspondence. Years later Churchill was to say of Cockran's political oratory, 'He was my model – I learned from him how to hold thousands in thrall.'

After a week in New York, a thirty-six-hour train journey to Tampa, Florida and a short sea-crossing, Churchill and Barnes arrived in Havana on 20 November. They lost no time in setting out by train and coastal steamer for the war zone, where they attached themselves to the Spanish General's staff. There followed days in the saddle, advancing through 'endless forests and undulations of a vast, lustrous landscape dripping with moisture and sparkling with sunshine'.

Having researched even thus far into Churchill's adult life, I could already see that he always made the very best of whatever cards he held. A winter of idleness was being put to the best possible use. His mother's sponsorship, which others might have used simply to enhance their social life, provided him with a passport to New York and Cuba. His contract with the *Daily Graphic* was no doubt obtained largely on the strength of his father's reputation with that paper for which he had written from South Africa in 1891. Lord Randolph would have been agreeably surprised, having only a year before his death in January 1895 expressed his concern that his son would become 'a mere social wastrel, one of the handful of public school failures'.

The cards were not always to be so favourable. In the next few years Churchill would be dealt hands which others would have thrown in without hesitation. Somehow he always turned them into winners.

Churchill did not celebrate his twenty-first birthday on 30 November 1895 with a ball at Blenheim Palace, his ancestral home. That would have been conventional, and he was not a conventional young man. It was not the popping of champagne corks but the crack of rifle-fire which heralded his coming of age. In Cuba, under fire for the first time, a bullet missed his head by less than a foot before fatally wounding the horse beside him. It was the first example of what would be Churchill's phenomenal luck in the face of enemy fire.

This short adventure in someone else's war brought Churchill his first medal – the Spanish Red Cross, which unfortunately he could not wear on his British uniform – and earned him a certain amount of notoriety in the British press. It also earned him twenty-five guineas, his first income as a journalist. His letters from Cuba, written while living rough, were a portent of his formidable journalistic talents.

In January 1896 Churchill returned from Cuba to rejoin his regiment, with whom it was intended he would leave later that year for an eight-year posting in India. While most young officers looked forward with keen anticipation to military life in India – polo, pigsticking and a host of servants – Churchill increasingly saw it as a political backwater he must avoid. Nine months remained before the regiment would set sail, and during this time he once more prevailed upon his mother to use her influence with those in power. He wished to be posted, as he put it, 'to scenes of adventure and excitement – to places where I could gain experience and derive advantage'. He would have liked to join General Sir Herbert Kitchener's expedition to reconquer the Sudan, but when that prospect dimmed he set his sights on Rhodesia, which, he explained in a letter to his mother on 4 August, would provide 'excitement and adventure'. Meanwhile, assiduously promoted by Lady Randolph, he used his time in England to cultivate many important people.

Having failed in his attempts to obtain a more exciting posting, Churchill sailed for India on 11 September 1896. Here, in the garrison of Bangalore, he was to endure two years of peacetime soldiering, alleviated only by polo, a great deal of reading – 'the desire for learning came upon me' – and Miss Pamela Plowden.

Pamela, seven months older than he, was the first love of Churchill's life. She was the daughter of the Resident of Hyderabad, and they met during a polo tournament. He wrote the next day to his mother, 'She is the most beautiful girl I have ever known . . . We are going to try to do the city of Hyderabad together – on an elephant.' The love affair would continue for several years at a desultory pace dictated by the demands of Churchill's main aim: to win the fame and fortune he felt he needed to launch his political career. (She would marry the Earl of Lytton in 1902, would remain friends with Churchill, and would outlive him.)

It was during his time in Bangalore that, as far as we know, Churchill first confided his ultimate political aspirations, to Captain Bingham of the Royal Artillery. Bingham was Master of the Ootacamund Hounds, and was bringing the pack home through the dusty, undulating country when a young cavalry officer out riding fell in with him. They struck up a conversation, during which the young officer, puffing on a cigar, said he would be giving up the army for politics, and would one day be prime minister.

In the summer of 1897 Churchill came home on leave. On the lawns at Goodwood, while he was enjoying the racing and improving his finances, an opportunity arose for further adventure. The news arrived of a rebellion among the Pathan tribesmen in the mountains along the North-West Frontier of India. A British expedition, the Malakand Field Force, had been formed to quell the uprising, and the General appointed to command it was none other than Sir Bindon Blood, who the year before had promised

Churchill a place on his staff should he ever command an expedition again.

As I looked through the archives, I was struck once again by the alacrity with which Churchill seized this outside chance. Abandoning his leave, he took the next boat to India, cabling General Blood to remind him of his promise. Blood was unable to find an immediate vacancy, but his reply was encouraging: 'I should advise your coming to me as a press correspondent . . . If you were here I think I could, and would if I could, do a little jobbery on your account. Yours in haste, B. Blood.'

The hint was more than enough for Churchill. Having persuaded his Colonel to grant him leave, he set off by rail for the two-and-a-half-thousand-mile journey from Bangalore to the scene of operations. He had been commissioned as a war correspondent by an Allahabad newspaper, the *Pioneer*, and had also arranged that the *Daily Telegraph* would pay him £5 a column for his letters from the front.

Within a month of arriving at General Blood's headquarters, Churchill had been attached to the force as a replacement for an officer who had been killed, had been involved in heavy fighting, and mentioned in dispatches. He had achieved all his aims. Was he lucky, or had he simply made the most of the situation? I think the latter. He continued to write for the *Daily Telegraph*, and thus got the best of both worlds – as an officer on active service and a war correspondent. Thinking he had struck an insufficiently hard bargain with the paper, he sought his mother's help in negotiating for better terms: 'When I think of the circumstances under wh. those letters were written . . . temperature of 115 degrees or after a long days action or by a light which it was dangerous lest it drew fire . . . I think they are cheap at the price.' (Greater financial reward would come with his book *The Story of the Malakand Field Force*, which he wrote in five weeks and which, on its publication in March 1898, was widely recognised as a military classic.)

His letters home spared Lady Randolph none of the details which soldiers usually conceal from their loved ones:

I rode forward with the 35th Sikhs until firing got so hot that my grey pony was unsafe. I proceeded on foot. When the retirement began I remained till the last and here I was perhaps very near my end ... I was close to both officers when they were hit almost simultaneously and fired my revolver at a man at 30 yards who tried to cut up poor Hughes's body ... Later on I used a rifle which a wounded man had dropped and fired 40 rounds at close quarters. I cannot be certain but I think I hit four men. At any rate they fell ...

In one letter to his mother, written on the eve of a battle, he expressed for the first time a sentiment he was to repeat at intervals over the next few years: 'I have faith in my star,' he wrote, 'that I am intended to do something in the world.' It was a faith that was reinforced when he emerged unscathed on the frequent occasions he recklessly exposed himself to enemy fire: 'I rode my grey pony all along the skirmish line where everyone else was lying down ...' There is no doubt he actually enjoyed the danger. 'Bullets,' he wrote to Lady Randolph, 'are not worth considering. Besides I am so conceited I do not believe the Gods would create so potent a being as myself for so prosaic an ending.'

The Malakand Field Force's successful campaign ended with punitive action against the rebellious tribes. There is little of Churchill's usual animation in his laconic description of this final action, rather a hint of disapproval: 'We were to stay in the Mamund Valley and lay it waste ... we lost for every village two or three British officers and fifteen or twenty native soldiers. Whether it was worth it, I cannot tell. At any rate, at the end of a fortnight the valley was a desert, and honour was satisfied.'

Churchill managed a second attachment in early 1898 when he joined the Tirah expedition, also on the North-West Frontier. However, negotiations brought peace, and he returned disappointed to his regiment in Bangalore. He had not given up his hope to join Kitchener in the Sudan, and he now bombarded his mother with requests for her to influence those who could help. The main stumbling block was Kitchener himself, who took exception to

Churchill's attempts to manipulate the military system for his own ends, and refused to accept him.

Due for leave, Churchill returned to England in May 1898. He had sent a copy of *The Malakand Field Force* to the Prime Minister, Lord Salisbury, who invited the author to come and see him. Five days later Churchill was notified of his attachment to the 21st Lancers for the Sudan campaign: it was obvious that Prime Ministerial influence had been successful where feminine allure had failed. The military were not amused, and instructed him to proceed to North Africa at his own expense, warning him that should he be killed or wounded, 'no charge of any kind will fall on British Army Funds'. Ignoring these barbs, Churchill set off forthwith for the Sudan and the campaign which he would call 'the River War', after the River Nile. The War Office had forbidden him to write for the press, but he arranged to send dispatches to the *Morning Post*, in the guise of letters ostensibly written to a friend.

We may imagine Kitchener's annoyance when, of all the officers who might have been sent to reconnoitre the enemy positions, it was Churchill who cantered across the shimmering desert to deliver his personal report: 'I saw the Union Jack by the side of the Egyptian flag,' Churchill was to write many years later. 'Kitchener was riding alone two or three horses' lengths in front of his Headquarters Staff. His two standard bearers marched immediately behind.'

The report given, Churchill reined in his horse to let the retinue flow past. A friendly voice invited him to lunch: 'in our path appeared a low wall of biscuit boxes which was being rapidly constructed, and on top of this wall I perceived a long stretch of white oil-cloth on which again were being placed many bottles of inviting appearance and large dishes of bully beef and pickles.' He was no doubt thinking of the cavalry charge promised for the following day when he summed up the meal as being 'like a race luncheon before the Derby'.

The battle of Omdurman, on 2 September 1898, saw the last British regimental cavalry charge. In a clash with hundreds of massed Dervishes, 'ten or twelve deep at the thickest, a great grey mass gleaming with steel', Churchill survived unscathed, although

7

the two minutes cost the regiment nearly a quarter of its strength. His survival probably owed much to the fact that, due to an injured shoulder, he was wielding a pistol instead of the traditional cavalry sword: 'I saw the gleam of [a Dervish's] sword as he drew it back . . . I fired two shots into him at about three yards . . . I saw before me another figure with uplifted sword. I raised my pistol and fired. So close were we that the pistol actually struck him.'

His book of the campaign, *The River War*, was published a year later, and would become the standard history.

Churchill's formidable abilities were already evident, but their impact on the world at large had so far been confined to his trenchant writing, as he combined the roles of cavalry officer and war correspondent. He now decided it was time for him to leave the army and enter politics. This was an audacious move for a young man with considerable debts, who would need an income if he were to pursue a Parliamentary career. He had been trained for no profession other than the army, and although he had demonstrated a rare ability to write, his pen remained an uncertain source of income.

He was, however, sanguine, and wrote explaining his decision to his grandmother, the Duchess of Marlborough:

> Had the army been a source of income to me instead of a channel of expenditure – I might have felt compelled to stick to it. But I can live cheaper & earn more as a writer, special correspondent or journalist; and this work is moreover more congenial and more likely to assist me in pursuing the larger ends of life. It has nevertheless been a great wrench and I was vy sorry to leave all my friends & put on my uniform & medals for the last time.

Courted by the Conservative Party, Churchill stood in a by-election for the Parliamentary seat of Oldham in Lancashire on 6 July 1899, but was narrowly defeated. However, fortune was about to favour the brave.

TWO

Preparing for War

'Britain entered the twentieth century in the grip of war. She placed nearly half a million men in the field, the biggest force she had hitherto sent overseas throughout her history. The conflict in South Africa, which began as a small colonial campaign, soon called for a large-scale national effort . . . the years of the Boer War saw a surge of patriotism among the vast majority of the British people, and a widespread enthusiasm for the cause of Empire.'

WINSTON CHURCHILL,
History of the English Speaking Peoples, VOLUME IV

AS BIG BEN CHIMED IN the new century, the patriotic crowds celebrating in the streets of London seemed to echo the response of Queen Victoria to one of her ministers who had tried to raise the subject of the series of military disasters in South Africa: 'Please understand that there is no one depressed in *this* house. We are not interested in the possibilities of defeat. They do not exist.' The national feeling was that Britain would triumph, as she had always done. But there was no denying, she was in the grip of war.

Yet less than six months earlier, as Winston Churchill canvassed the voters of Oldham, South Africa had not even remotely been an issue at the hustings. This was hardly surprising. The Empire had largely been at peace for a long time. The humiliation of Majuba had been almost forgotten by the public, if not by the regiments involved; there had been no rush to arms in April 1899, when Queen Victoria had received the Uitlanders' petition; and the

Jameson Raid had been disingenuously disowned by the government. The tussle between British imperialism and Afrikaner nationalism had been going on for half a century, and there was still the hope in London that war could be avoided.

Meanwhile, the Boers' economic power, and thus their influence in the region, was increasing daily, and their wealth enabled them to fill their armouries from ready suppliers in Germany and France. Churchill, still a young officer watching events from his garrison in India, had grasped this at the time of the Jameson Raid. He produced a memorandum – presumably for his own amusement, as it was never published – on the main issues involved. Entitled 'Our Account with the Boers', it is a pity it did not see the light of day, for it would have struck a chord among the public, and might well have had some influence:

> Imperial aid must redress the wrongs of the Outlanders; Imperial troops must curb the insolence of the Boers ... There must be no half measures. The forces employed must be strong enough to bear down all opposition from the Transvaal and Free State; and at the same time overawe all sympathisers in Cape Colony. There will not be wanting those who will call such a policy unscrupulous. If it be unscrupulous for the people of Great Britain to defend their most vital interests, to extend their protection to their fellow countrymen in distress and to maintain the integrity of their Empire, 'unscrupulous' is a word we shall have to face. Sooner or later, in righteous cause or a picked quarrel, with the approval of Europe, or in the teeth of Germany, for the sake of our Empire, for the sake of our honour, for the sake of the race, we must fight the Boers.

Two years after forecasting the need for a shift in Britain's Southern Africa policy, and shortly after his first, unsuccessful attempt to enter Parliament, Churchill found himself cruising in leisurely fashion along the Thames with Joseph Chamberlain, the Colonial Secretary. The two men were weekend house guests of a mutual friend, Lady Jeune. They had met before, but this was the first real opportunity for Churchill to make the acquaintance of his father's old friend, whose conversation, he found, was 'a practical political education in itself'.

The discussion which began on the river continued over dinner. Uninhibited by his inexperience in politics, and not in the least awed by Chamberlain's formidable presence, Churchill pressed for a strong line against President Kruger. Churchill's strategic instincts, which the world would one day come to know so well, were already well developed. He felt that the policy of intervention had failed at Majuba and Doornkop not because it was wrong, but because it had been irresolute or bungled. He did not believe, like the British government, that in time the Transvaal would fall of its own accord, leaving Britain to pick up the pieces. His instincts were not dissimilar to those of Cecil Rhodes, who within two years would say of him, 'He is a young man who will go far if he doesn't overbalance.'

Churchill's experience in India, to say nothing of his aristocratic background and a political philosophy inherited from his father, inclined him to the view that the British exerted a benevolent and beneficial influence wherever they imposed their rule. He remained at heart a Victorian all his life, and to him British interests and the well-being of whoever might be under British rule were virtually synonymous. Magnanimity towards the conquered was also an essential part of his philosophy. This was a concept which he had developed while campaigning on the North-West Frontier, but it required the opponent to be subdued before generosity could be extended. Kruger, he believed, should be brought to heel.

Chamberlain listened patiently to the young man's arguments. 'It is no use blowing the trumpet for the charge and then looking around to find nobody following,' he replied. His own political career having been threatened by the aftermath of the Jameson Raid, he was hesitant to follow any policy other than that of 'no war'. Neither man realised that even then Chamberlain's own appointed High Commissioner to South Africa, Sir Alfred Milner, was doing exactly what Churchill had recommended in his unpublished memorandum two years earlier: picking a quarrel.

Meanwhile, Churchill was absorbed with the proofs of his book

The River War, which ran to two volumes and almost a thousand pages. It was dedicated to the Prime Minister, Lord Salisbury, whose influence had smoothed Churchill's way to the Sudan. To ensure that Salisbury would accept the dedication, Churchill submitted to him in advance the more critical passages in the book, offering to delete anything of which he disapproved. Salisbury's reply, only three days later, was that no alterations were needed.

The constraints of military discipline had never caused Churchill to flinch from trenchant comment, although he had been well aware that his future advancement might well be determined by the very generals he was offending by his articles in the London press. (It was in fact these which gave rise in 1898 to the edict which since then has forbidden serving officers from writing in newspapers.) Now, no longer a soldier, he found himself 'able to write what I thought about Lord Kitchener without fear, favour or affection, and I certainly did'.

On the whole *The River War* contained a balanced account of Kitchener's actions and an honest appreciation of his great military abilities. However, Churchill strongly disapproved of Kitchener's punitive actions after the battle of Omdurman, and while he had muted his criticism of these in his articles, he gave full vent to his feelings when writing *The River War*. In particular he objected to the 'inhuman slaughter of the wounded', for which he held Kitchener responsible, and to the desecration of the tomb of the Sudanese leader the Mahdi, whose head was lopped from the corpse on Kitchener's orders, to be 'passed from hand to hand till it reached Cairo ... an interesting trophy'.

By the time they had become Cabinet colleagues during the First World War, Churchill and Kitchener had put their differences behind them; but for many years the antipathy would persist. This mattered little to Churchill, who was no longer a soldier. But, with his sights set on Parliament, what might have worried him was that in denouncing the desecration of the Mahdi's tomb he was going against the mood of the Conservative Party, which had looked upon the incident as 'a bit of a lark'. 'So here I was,' he later wrote, 'already out of step.' But had this bothered him greatly, he would surely have omitted the criticism from the book. His decision not to do so was an early indication of the honesty which would be a characteristic of his long political career.

The River War would be published in November 1899, but before then Churchill had been drawn to more exciting possibilities, and he was beginning to arrange his participation in the war in South Africa, which most people now regarded as inevitable. On 18 September he had written to his mother: 'Harmsworth [the owner of the *Daily Mail*] telegraphed me this morning asking if I would go as their correspondent to the Cape. I wired this to Oliver Borthwick [editor of the *Morning Post*] and made definite offer to go for M.P. for my expenses, copyright of work, and one thousand pounds – for four months shore to shore – two hundred a month afterwards. He has accepted.'

This was an extraordinarily lucrative contract, which made Churchill the highest-paid war correspondent of the day. But there was more in it for him than the immediate money. Because it left him with the copyright of whatever he wrote, he would be able to turn his dispatches from South Africa into successful books. Although *The Malakand Field Force* had become a best-seller and he had high hopes for *The River War*, he still needed every penny his pen would earn.

In acquiring Churchill's services, Oliver Borthwick would have had in mind the formidable competition. The war correspondents in South Africa included many who would become household names: Rudyard Kipling, who within eight years would be awarded the Nobel Prize for Literature; Edgar Wallace; H.G. Wells; Arthur Conan Doyle, who doubled as a doctor and a writer; Leo Amery, a friend of Churchill's at Harrow who would be a member of his government forty years on; and H.A. Gwynne, who would go on to edit the *Morning Post* for twenty-five years.

Having secured his position as a war correspondent, Churchill next pulled every available string in order that he would arrive in South Africa with access to all the important people there. He wrote to the Colonial Secretary asking for a letter of introduction.

Chamberlain replied that although he could not officially introduce a press correspondent, he would be 'most happy to give one as a private friend', adding: 'You will not need any other letter as Sir A. Milner himself will be the best person to introduce you in S. Africa & will know who are best worth seeing. I shall be very glad to see you before you go out any time when I am in London.'

Churchill lost no time in taking up this offer, and was given an appointment at the Colonial Office. It says much for the regard in which he was already held in political circles that when he was unable to get there in time for the meeting, he was invited to Chamberlain's house the following morning. His family connections undoubtedly helped, but it is unlikely that such an important Cabinet Minister would have made himself so readily available had he not valued the young man's views.

When Churchill arrived at Chamberlain's house in Prince's Gardens the Colonial Secretary was smoking a cigar. He presented his guest with another, and the two men sat reviewing the situation in South Africa. Chamberlain was due at the Colonial Office, so he invited Churchill to accompany him in a hansom cab in order that they could continue their talk.

As they clip-clopped towards Whitehall, Chamberlain took the optimistic view that if war did break out it would be over before General Sir Redvers Buller, who had been appointed as Commander-in-Chief in South Africa, even arrived at the Cape. Buller and his staff were to sail on the next available ship, the *Dunotar Castle*, which was departing from Southampton Docks on 14 October. 'He would have been wiser to have gone out earlier,' said the Colonial Secretary. 'Now, if the Boers invade Natal, Sir George White with his sixteen thousand men may easily settle the whole thing.'

'What about Mafeking?' asked Churchill, sensing the vulnerability of this strategically positioned town a few miles from the Transvaal border.

'Ah, Mafeking, that may be besieged. But if they cannot hold out for a few weeks, what is one to expect?' replied Chamberlain. 'Of course,' he prudently added, 'I have to base myself on the War

Office opinion. They are all quite confident. I can only go by what they say.'

How Churchill responded we do not know, but it is likely that, in his usual forthright way, he would have questioned the War Office's judgement. Indeed, he had already reported his misgivings in a letter to Lady Randolph: 'I fear the War Office is working vy crankily.' As usual he was remarkably well informed, tapping into different levels of the hierarchy in order to get the complete story. The complacency of the Secretary of State for War, Lord Lansdowne, was in direct contrast to the views of his Under-Secretary, George Wyndham, who had painted a far from rosy picture while dining with Churchill.

Churchill had been planning to visit Germany, where Pamela Plowden was staying. He now cancelled this trip and booked his passage on the *Dunotar Castle*. As always, he kept his mother up to date with his plans, writing on 2 October: 'It is definitely settled that I start on 14th ... I am not going to Germany. Pamela will be in England before 14th.' Had Pamela not been visiting England, he would no doubt have sailed without seeing her. In an earlier letter to his mother Churchill had admitted that he was lonely without Pamela; but, smitten though he undoubtedly was, he remained uncommitted. Not only was he somewhat inhibited in the company of the opposite sex – Pamela had once said he was 'incapable of affection' – but personal relationships were subordinated to his huge ambition.

His letter of 2 October reflects this. Having disposed of Pamela in half a line, he turns to more absorbing topics: 'The book [*The River War*] is finally finished – but my time is busy with preparations for departure. War is certain and I expect that there will be a collision in a few hours ... they [the War Office] have cheated Brabazon [who had been Churchill's commanding officer in the 4th Hussars] out of his Brigade – and appointed over his head Babington – a man who has never seen a shot fired ... if true it is monstrous.' Brabazon had seen a great deal of active service, which in Churchill's assessment of soldiers – and later even of Cabinet Ministers – always weighed heavily in their favour.

Churchill was thinking of making a documentary war film while he was in South Africa, and on 4 October he contacted a distant relative, the Member of Parliament Murray Guthrie: 'About the Cinematograph scheme: I do not expect it would require more than £700 altogether: and I am willing to join with you in the venture on the following simple terms:- Each to pay half the expenses: You to make all the arrangements & do all the business here: I all that is necessary in South Africa.'

He also continued his dialogue with Chamberlain, who wrote on 4 October: 'My dear Winston, I have your telegraph & will write to Milner tonight asking for the good offices for the son of my old friend. I am sure he will do all in his power. I shall be in London on Monday but I gather that you leave before then. If so good luck & best wishes! Yours very truly J. Chamberlain.' Chamberlain's letter to Milner described Churchill as 'a very clever young fellow . . . He has the reputation of being bumptious, but I have not found him so, and time will no doubt get rid of the defect if he has it.' Bumptious though he undoubtedly was, Churchill was careful not to let it show to someone as eminent and experienced as Chamberlain, particularly when he was being so helpful. The High Commissioner also received a letter from George Wyndham of the War Office, which enthusiastically recommended Churchill as 'a very clever fellow . . . bringing out an unprejudiced mind'.

Already a seasoned campaigner, Churchill was well aware of the soldier's maxim that any fool can be uncomfortable, and was energetically provisioning himself with all the means of easing life in the field. His contract with the *Morning Post* provided for expenses, and we can assume that the newspaper paid for the supplies which Randolph Payne & Sons dispatched to accompany him as the *Dunotar Castle* set sail: a dozen and a half bottles of whisky, two dozen bottles of wine, half a dozen each of port, vermouth and eau de vie, and a dozen of lime juice. It was indicative of Churchill's shaky finances that the account for £26.18s., dated 6 October 1899, included £10.18s. outstanding since early 1895, and was not settled until 1 March 1901.

As Churchill did not intend that the chores of the campsite would divert him from more interesting and profitable activities, he would be accompanied by his valet, Thomas Walden, whom he had inherited from his father. Walden was an experienced traveller, having attended Lord Randolph on many journeys, including one of several months in Southern Africa only a few years earlier.

A glimpse of Churchill as he bustled about London preparing for the forthcoming campaign is provided in a letter to Lady Randolph from her admirer and future husband George Cornwallis-West, a Lieutenant in the Scots Guards who was the same age as her son: 'I saw Winston today in St James Str, dont tell him I said so, but he looked just like a young dissenting parson, hat brushed the wrong way, and at the back of his head, awful old black coat and tie, he is a good fellow but very untidy.'

Churchill would be going to war as a civilian, a status to which the ambitious young man could see disadvantages. Information might not come to him as readily as it had when he was both an officer and a correspondent. Officially he would be in South Africa only as an observer, a role which would seem to provide little scope for military glory. But he had once been promised a place on Sir Redvers Buller's staff, and, confident that he could circumvent the new rule that officers could not double as war correspondents, he cast about for a way to secure a temporary commission. He wrote to Lord Chesham, the Honorary Colonel of the Royal Bucks Yeomanry, seeking his support for a commission in that regiment. The letter, however, was not sent, as on second thoughts he felt he would be more likely to obtain a commission under the auspices of his father's old friend Lord Gerard, who was sailing as an elderly ADC responsible for Buller's comfort in the field. For the present, no commission materialised, and Churchill would go to war as a civilian.

Anxious to have wider and more varied sources of information than those which might result from Chamberlain's letter to Milner, he sought help from someone who was intimately involved in the conflict between British interests and Boer independence: Cecil Rhodes's partner Alfred Beit, who had been a friend of his father. Beit replied with letters of introduction to several influential people on both sides of the South African political divide: 'I send you herewith some letters for the Cape and wish you every success in your mission. Mr Eckstein who is my partner ... He knew your father very well ... Mr Silberbauer is in touch with the Boer people and might give you an introduction to Mr Hofmeyr ... Mr Solomon is a member of the present government ... Mr Seymour is our Head Engineer ... I hope you have a very successful meeting tonight.'

The meeting Beit referred to was in Oldham, the Parliamentary constituency to which Churchill had failed to be elected three months previously. His imminent embarkation was not deflecting him from his long-term aim, and now, only forty-eight hours before he sailed, he was finding time to travel north for constituency business.

The week before his departure was also a busy one socially, with friends giving farewell dinners each evening in his honour. From one of these comes an early example of Churchillian wit. No doubt bubbling with enthusiasm over his coming adventure, he was pulled up short by a friend of his mother's, who said she liked neither his politics nor the moustache which he was, somewhat unsuccessfully, trying to grow. 'Madame,' he replied, 'I see no earthly reason why you should come into contact with either.'

Even as he travelled in the boat train to Southampton, the indefatigable Churchill wrote again to Murray Guthrie about his filming project: 'I see the American Biograph Coy have already sent out a machine ... I have no doubt that, barring accidents, I can obtain some very strange pictures. My only fear is that all the Theatres will be pledged to the American Coy. But even then I might make a lecturing tour. If you wire me Standard Bnk – Capetown "Biograph coming" I shall know business is settled ...' Unfortunately, Guthrie was less enterprising than his potential partner. The venture fell through, and the American company was left a clear field.

Churchill's main worry at this time was that the war would be over before he arrived. On 10 October he wrote to George Sandys, whom he had met on a ship homeward bound from India: 'Dear Sandys, I am sorry we missed each other. I sail on the 14th for the

Oct. 10. 1899

356, GREAT CUMBERLAND PLACE,
W.

Dear Sandys,

I am sorry we missed each other. I sail on the 14th for the Cape, but the actual fighting will begin before the week is out and may be over before the main army arrives. I shall hope to meet you again somewhere.

Yours sincerely

Winston S. Churchill

Letter from the author's maternal grandfather, Winston Churchill, to her paternal grandfather, George Sandys. (*Collection of Steve Forbes, New York*)

Cape, but the actual fighting will begin before the week is out and may be over before the main army arrives. I shall hope to meet you again somewhere. Yours sincerely Winston S. Churchill.' Their paths were to cross again later when they were both Members of Parliament, and, more significantly, when Churchill's daughter Diana married Sandys's son Duncan in 1935.*

Churchill need not have worried about missing the action. Almost three bloody years, costing well over sixty thousand British, Boer and African lives, would pass before the war's end.

* I was their youngest child.

THREE

Cruising to a Catastrophe

'I thought it very sporting of the Boers to take on the whole British Empire . . . Let us learn our lessons . . . Always remember, however sure you are that you can easily win, that there would not be a war if the other man did not think he also had a chance.'

WINSTON CHURCHILL, *My Early Life*

SUCH WERE WINSTON CHURCHILL'S SENTIMENTS as he set sail for the Boer War, and his reflections, set down thirty years later, arising from the illusions that war was to shatter.

As the *Dunotar Castle* cast off from Southampton Docks on the evening of Saturday, 14 October 1899, an impressive array of military passengers lined the ship's rails. Rubbing shoulders among them were a few civilian war correspondents, none more at home in the uniformed throng and more impatient to get going than Churchill. On the dockside a large crowd sang 'Rule Britannia'. Then, seeing the tall, imposing figure of General Sir Redvers Buller on the bridge, they struck up 'For he's a Jolly Good Fellow.' As the ship steamed out into the Solent they ended with 'God Save the Queen', the singing led, according to *The Times*, by Lady Buller.

Britain's huge confidence in the Commander-in-Chief was reflected in a contemporary ditty, though its subtle comment on his taciturn nature was probably lost on the general public.

> Redvers Buller has gone away
> In charge of a job at Table Bay;

In what direction Redvers goes
Is a matter that only Buller knows . . .
If he's right, he'll pull us through.
If he's wrong, he's better than you.

Buller himself had no illusions about the task ahead. As the ship steamed southwards he paced the deck each day, his ADC Captain Algy Trotter constantly at his side. Buller had commanded Boer troops in the Zulu War of 1878–79, defending white settlers buffeted by the tide of Bantu people migrating southward from Central Africa, and knew their stubborn character. Recognising the threat they posed in Natal, he had urged caution on the Secretary of State for War, Lord Lansdowne. He had advised that it might prove disastrous if the generals then controlling operations in South Africa, Lieutenant-General Sir George White and Major-General Sir Penn Symons, risked their forces north of the Tugela River. His words had gone unheeded, and he foresaw trouble.

Churchill lost no time in making the most of Buller's presence aboard. A thumbnail sketch by one of the other correspondents on the *Dunotar Castle*, J.B. Atkins of the *Manchester Guardian*, noted that Churchill had 'acquired no reverence for seniors as such, and talked to them as if they were his own age, or younger . . . He stood alone and confident, and his natural power to be himself had yielded to no man.' Atkins described his subject as 'slim, slightly reddish-haired, lively, frequently plunging along the deck with neck out-thrust . . . I had not encountered this sort of ambition, unabashed, frankly egotistical, communicating its excitement.'

Churchill's first letter home was posted when the ship called at Madeira, four days after sailing.

My dearest Mamma,

We have had a nasty rough passage & I have been grievously sick. The roll of the vessel still very pronounced prevents my writing much, and besides there is nothing to say. Sir R. Buller is vy amiable and I do not doubt that he is well disposed towards me. There are a good many people on board – military or journalistic – whom I know and all are vy civil – but I cannot say that I am greatly interested in any of them . . .

I won't write more – but please fire off weekly letter and
stimulate everyone else to write too . . .
Ever your loving son Winston.

Churchill was a notoriously bad sailor, which no doubt explains
the perfunctory nature of his letter. Otherwise the mere roll of a
ship would hardly deter such an avid correspondent, who had never
before allowed uncongenial surroundings to inhibit his pen.

Events would show that Buller was, indeed, well disposed towards
the young man. Churchill's sentiments towards the Commander-in-
Chief were presumably influenced both by the fact that he had
been awarded the Victoria Cross for his gallantry in the Zulu War,
and by the ambitious young correspondent's need to gain his confidence. As the ship steamed south through the Atlantic swell, Churchill seemed content to take the older man at face value and,
unusually for him, to make no comment on his character.

Thirty years later, when recounting the voyage on the *Dunotar
Castle*, the pen-portrait by a less inhibited and vastly more experienced Churchill is more illuminating:

> Buller was a characteristic British personality. He looked sto-
> lid. He said little, and what he said was obscure. He was not
> the kind of man who could explain things, and he never tried
> to do so . . . He had shown himself a brave and skilful officer
> in his youth . . . Certainly he was a man of considerable scale.
> He plodded on from blunder to blunder and from one disaster
> to another, without losing either the regard of his country or
> the trust of his troops, to whose feeding as well as his own he
> paid serious attention.

After calling at Madeira, where there was no news of the war,
the *Dunotar Castle* continued her steady passage southwards, not
even increasing her speed above the normal commercial peacetime
rate. Such a measure would have been unprecedented, signalling
an undue concern over events which the British forces expected to
take in their stride. Understandably, Churchill found the voyage
frustrating: 'I am very excited to know what will have happened
when we land,' he wrote to his mother on 25 October. 'Fourteen
days is a long time in war, especially at the beginning.' He predicted

that the British Army would be in Pretoria by the end of February, and that he might be home by March. However, he did hedge his bets: 'But it is perhaps early to make such speculation.'

The River War was about to be published, and his letter continued: 'I am all eagerness to hear about my book and I beg you to send me everything that occurs in connexion with it. I forgot to put Pamela down on the list I gave you. Please send her one of the first copies and write a line with it . . .' However much in love he was with Pamela, she flitted from his mind quite easily: he had not forgotten to send copies of his book to the Prime Minister, the Commander-in-Chief of the Army or the Adjutant-General.

Churchill's first dispatch to the *Morning Post* was datelined 'RMS *Dunotar Castle*, at sea: October 26th'. In the course of its two thousand words it left the reader in no doubt of what its author thought of sea travel: 'What an odious affair is a modern sea journey! . . . In the sixteenth century nobody minded taking five months to get anywhere. But a fortnight is a large slice out of the nineteenth century.' He went on to describe shipboard life – deck games, a fancy dress ball and 'light gusts of controversy', such as the question of who should read the Sunday service: the parson or the captain. He also reported the extremes of opinion in forecasting events: 'Speculation arises out of ignorance. Many and various are the predictions as to what will be the state of the game when we shall have come to anchor in Table Bay,' but soon returned to his original theme: 'Monotony is the characteristic of a modern voyage . . . Monotony of view . . . monotony of food . . . monotony of existence . . . all fall to the lot of the passenger on great waters.'

Churchill then offered a few thoughts on inoculation against enteric fever: 'The doctors lecture in the saloon . . . Nearly everyone is convinced . . . Others, like myself, remembering that we stand only on the threshold of pathology, remain unconvinced, resolved to trust to "health and the laws of health". But if they will invent a system of inoculation against bullet wounds I will hasten to submit myself.'

It seems incredible that the voyage could have proceeded in as leisurely a manner as it did. Even when an occasion arose to discover what was happening in South Africa, the opportunity was ignored, as Churchill's dispatch records: 'Yesterday we passed a homeward-bound liner, who made great efforts to signal us, but as she was a Union boat [i.e. from a rival line] the captain refused to go near enough to read the flags.' Had the military passengers been aware of the true situation in South Africa they would surely have objected to this petty attitude, but no one on board, Churchill included, doubted the ability of the British troops already in Natal under Major-General Sir Penn Symons to inflict a resounding defeat on any Boer incursion.

In fact, as the homeward-bound liner slipped astern of the *Dunotar Castle*, Symons was already in his grave, having died of wounds in a field hospital at Dundee, which had been abandoned to the Boers as the British troops retreated into Ladysmith. True, there had been small tactical victories, but the tide of war was running in favour of the Boers. Buller's fears had been realised, though no one on board yet had an inkling of this.

The news of Symons's death came several days later, when another ship bound from the Cape passed the *Dunotar Castle*. Churchill's dispatch, which he continued on 29 October, describes the incident:

> This morning we sighted a sail – a large homeward-bound steamer spreading her canvas to catch the trades . . . She passed us at scarcely two hundred yards, and . . . displayed a long black board, on which was written in white paint 'Boers defeated; three battles; Penn Symons killed.' What does it mean – this scrap of intelligence which tells so much and leaves so much untold? 'Boers defeated.' . . . The crisis is over, and the army on the seas may move with measured strides to effect a settlement that is both wise and just.

In the circumstances of a threefold Boer defeat, the death of a British general seemed unusual. But Penn Symons was known to lead his men from the front – and had not Nelson died at the moment of his greatest victory? Thus, no one on board doubted that the Boers had suffered a crushing defeat, and the sombre thoughts among Buller's staff at the loss of Penn Symons were matched by gloom at the thought of the war being over before they arrived in Cape Town. Buller, though, remained inscrutable. A staff officer ventured, 'It looks as if it will all be over, sir.'

Economical as ever with his words, Buller replied, 'I dare say there will be enough left to give us a fight outside Pretoria.'

With this reassurance, morale was restored. Churchill was the odd man out when he suggested that the message raised more questions than it answered. It would, he pointed out, have taken but ten minutes to stop the ship and request fuller information. The staff officers to whom he aired his views replied that a war correspondent, particularly one who had recently worn uniform, should not question the decisions of superior officers in time of war.

Churchill declared himself impenitent and unconvinced. He had often met General Symons while he was campaigning in India. The toast three years before, when the two men had dined together in Jumrood Fort, on the North-West Frontier, had been 'Our men.' Never hesitant to appear in the very forefront of battle – which was how he had been fatally wounded – Penn Symons was the sort of romantic soldier Churchill admired. The last page of his dispatch written aboard the *Dunotar Castle* was virtually an obituary, ending with the tribute: 'May the State in her necessities find others like him.'

When the ship docked at Cape Town late in the evening of 30 October, her passengers were soon made aware that they had not in fact missed the war. A series of military disasters had occurred that very day: Ladysmith, Kimberley and Mafeking had all been besieged by the advancing Boer forces. The most perilous situation appeared to be in Natal. The opening battle of the war, a mile or two north-east of Dundee at Talana Hill, where Penn Symons had fallen, had been at best a hollow victory, and not the Boer defeat which the shipborne blackboard had suggested. Having encircled General White and his forces in Ladysmith, it now seemed possible that the Boers could break through to the port of Durban, 150 miles to the south-east, and so gain their much-needed access to the sea.

Much of Buller's army corps was still at sea, and would be arriving throughout November and early December. The original plan, made before Buller left England, was to await the assembly of the entire corps of thirty-five thousand men, and then advance through the Orange Free State. Within a few days of arriving in the Cape Buller had abandoned this idea, and taken the difficult decision to dispatch the troops as they arrived, in the hope of stemming the tide of invasion. On 22 November he left for Natal to take personal command of the situation there.

Meanwhile, Churchill, not content to watch the plans unfold, had set off towards the sound of gunfire – which was at its loudest in Natal. He could have conveniently continued to Durban on board the *Dunotar Castle*, but having by now had quite enough of the ship's leisurely progress, he decided on a short-cut by rail and coastal steamer, in the hope of reaching Ladysmith before it was entirely surrounded.

Although he was in Cape Town for less than a day, Churchill managed to take up his introduction to the High Commissioner, Sir Alfred Milner. From Milner, the local newspapers and military sources, he formed a broad assessment of the situation which he used as the basis of a wide-ranging dispatch, running to two thousand words, which he had written before nightfall. This dispatch was calculated to reassure and rally public opinion at home. It appealed to emotional Victorian patriotism: 'It is a long casualty list of officers . . . all lying under the stony soil or filling the hospitals of Pietermaritzburg and Durban.' It reflected the High Commissioner's concern, as had been explained to Churchill that very day: 'it is no exaggeration to say that a considerable part of the Colony trembles on the verge of rebellion.' And it balanced the bad news by painting a picture of Imperial grandeur: 'Sir Redvers Buller landed in state . . . The ship was decked out with bunting from end to end . . . The crew and stokers of the Dunotar Castle gave three hearty cheers . . . streets bright with waving flags and black with cheering people.'

Churchill was not a man to say 'I told you so' when things were going badly because his advice had been unheeded. His positive attitude in times of adversity was reflected in his dispatches, and although he had foreseen the need to pick a fight and, in his conversations with the Colonial Secretary, had urged a tough line against the Transvaal, his readers were not to be distracted by even a hint that he had been proved right. (History was to repeat itself in the next century: in his rallying calls as wartime Prime Minister, Churchill would waste no words on those who had ignored his warnings.) Now was the time for support, not recrimination, and he took care to provide reasons for Britain's lack of military preparedness: 'A democratic Government cannot go to war unless the country is behind it. The difficulties of rallying public opinion in the face of the efforts of [the names of members of the anti-war Peace Party were listed] and others has caused a most dangerous delay in the dispatch of reinforcements.'

The dispatch gave an honest military analysis of the situation, while at the same time seeking to allay any panic over the recent disasters:

> The Natal Field Force is now concentrated at Ladysmith, and confronts in daily opposition the bulk of the Boer army. Though the numbers of the enemy are superior and their courage claims the respect of their professional antagonists, it is difficult to believe that any serious reverse can take place in that quarter, and meanwhile many thousands of soldiers are on the seas. But the fact is now abundantly plain ... that a fierce, certainly bloody, possibly prolonged struggle lies before the army of South Africa.

Churchill ended on a note designed to help cement Imperial ties:

> 'At last,' says the British colonist as he shoulders his rifle and marches out to fight, no less bravely than any other soldier (witness the casualty lists), for the ties which bind South Africa to the British Empire – 'at last they have made up their mind at home.'

Already in South Africa as Churchill disembarked was his aunt, the glamorous and strong-willed Lady Sarah Wilson. Sister of Lord Randolph and a friend of Rhodes, Jameson and others involved in the raid, she had first come out to the country in 1895, and was now acting as a war correspondent for the *Daily Mail*. With her reputation and undoubted knowledge of Southern Africa, it may seem strange that Churchill, who left no source untapped as he raced around gathering news and views, made no attempt to contact her. Her meddlesome nature was the reason. She had caused Churchill much embarrassment by concocting a tale of his 'thievish practices' when, as an impecunious cadet at Sandhurst, he had advertised a surplus pair of his own field glasses for sale. To Lady Randolph he had described his aunt as 'a cat', proclaiming, 'such a liar that woman is.'

Churchill's short-cut to Natal involved a train journey to East London, skirting enemy frontiers as the line ran through De Aar, Naauwpoort and Queenstown, and an overnight steamer to Durban. Setting out within twelve hours of his disembarkation at Cape Town, Churchill's train was the last to get through before the Boers cut the line. On 3 November, as the train approached East London, he wrote to Lady Randolph.

> My dearest Mamma,
>
> I write you a line – it can be no more [than] to tell you my plans. The rest the *Morning Post* will inform you of as well as I can. We landed on 31st and started the same night for Natal – train to E. London boat thence. I have two pleasant companions – Captain Campbell the correspondent of Laffan's Agency and a young gentleman named Atkins – who represents the *Manchester Guardian* and is an exceedingly clever & accomplished specimen of Cambridge.
>
> I hope to reach Ladysmith tomorrow or the day after and I shall remain there until the preparations for the main advance are completed. This I may tell you privately is to be straight north through the Orange Free State. I expect George [Cornwallis-West, Lady Randolph's future husband] will land at Port Elizabeth. Troops are very badly needed all along the N of Cape Colony as well as in Natal. The Boer advance southward has just begun and you will I think hear of fighting all along the line from Orange River – de Aar – Naauwpoort – Queenstown – before a week is out.

We have greatly underestimated the military strength
and spirit of the Boers. I vy much doubt whether one Army
Corps will be enough to overcome their resistance – at any
rate a fierce and bloody struggle is before us in which at
least ten or twelve thousand lives will be sacrificed and from
which the Boers are absolutely certain that they will emerge
victorious. Naturally I do not share that last opinion – but
it is well to bear it in mind. Sir Alfred Milner told me that
the whole of Cape Colony was 'trembling on the verge of
rebellion' – and this will further complicate the issue. I will
write to you from Ladysmith. We have had good luck so
far, this being the last train to get thorough from de Aar, and
we have gained four days on all the other correspondents. I
shall believe I am to be preserved for future things.

Your ever loving son Winston.

He was right to strike a note of caution. Buller's single army
corps would not be nearly enough, though it is unlikely that Churchill could have prophesied the tenfold increase which would
eventually be required. His warning of casualties was nearer the
mark. Some twelve thousand British and Boers were to be killed
in action, and at least as many again died of wounds or disease.

The final line of his letter reflected yet again Churchill's sense
of destiny. It would be echoed a number of times during the coming
months, as he survived one close shave after another.

The overnight voyage to Durban was by a small coaster of some
150 tons. Sailing a mile off the rocky shore in the teeth of a gale
was an alarming experience, but Churchill's 'misgivings were dispelled by the most appalling paroxysms of seasickness', and he spent
a miserable night in the cramped confines of the crew's quarters.
The passage left such an indelible impression on him that in his
autobiography *My Early Life*, published in 1930, he devoted over
half a page to it.

In the few hours Churchill spent in Durban he went aboard the
hospital ship *Sumatra*, where among the wounded he found a
number of friends, including Reggie Barnes, with whom he had
played polo and shared his baptism of fire in Cuba. That adventure
was pale by comparison with what Barnes had just been through.

Thirty per cent of his regiment had been killed or wounded in a single action.

Travelling onwards by rail, Churchill and his companions were soon in Pietermaritzburg, where they hired a special train to take them on to Ladysmith. However, the line had been cut by the Boers and their journey ended at Estcourt, the railhead for those troops not already besieged in Ladysmith, forty miles away. It was a small township of about three hundred tin-roofed houses, mostly single-storeyed, some lining the town's two broad streets, others straggling away into the surrounding hills.

Here, on 6 November 1899, in the centre of a reversing triangle in the railway yard, Thomas Walden unpacked Churchill's kit in an empty bell tent.

FOUR

The Station Yard

'A long and bloody war is before us – and the end is by no
means as certain as most people imagine.'

WINSTON CHURCHILL,
letter to Sir Evelyn Wood, 10 November 1899

CHURCHILL'S BASE WAS ONLY A small-town station yard, but
although it was not the centre of attention, it was certainly the hub
of military activity. While Ladysmith grabbed the headlines, its
relief depended upon the reinforcements and supplies which came
in through the railhead at Estcourt. Churchill had occupied the
centre ground.

From here he set out daily, on foot through the town or on
horseback through the green, undulating countryside, to collect
information on which to base his almost daily dispatches. Scribbled
out in a single draft with only occasional alterations, their quality
made them required reading in London. Running to at least fifteen
hundred words, and often much longer, composing them would
have occupied the entire waking time of most correspondents. Only
a master of the English language, blessed with keen political and
strategic antennae and a military background, could have carried
them off with such aplomb.

Yet to Churchill, his dispatches were simply the end-products of
days spent constantly on the move. Evoking atmosphere, conveying
information and laced with wisdom, they were intended to convince
the reader of the rightness of an Imperial strategy in which the

British flag was synonymous with protection and good government. Yet they were never jingoistic, and always showed respect for a decently behaved enemy. Nor in his writing was there any trace of the bumptiousness which the young Churchill undoubtedly displayed in ample measure. His dispatches took a humane and charitable view of men doing their best against the odds. However, he never hesitated to pour scorn on hypocrisy of all sorts, and he was unrelenting in his criticism of official ineptitude.

His first dispatch was dated 6 November, the day of his arrival in Estcourt. Among much else, it eloquently pleaded the cause of the British colonists in Natal:

> They have never for one moment lost sight of their obligations as a British colony ... The townsfolk are calm and orderly ... Boys of sixteen march with men of fifty to war ... The Imperial Light Horse can find no more vacancies, not even for those who will serve without pay ... This colony of Natal will impress the historian. The devotion of its people to their Sovereign ... should win them general respect and sympathy; and full indemnity to all individual colonists who have suffered loss must stand as an Imperial debt of honour.

The Boer War brought together a number of rising stars, with many of whom Churchill was already acquainted. At Estcourt he found the *Times* correspondent, Leo Amery, who had been in the top form at Harrow when Churchill arrived at the bottom. Amery was small of stature and, mistaking him for a boy in the lower school, Churchill had pushed him into the school swimming-pool. The tables had been immediately turned, Amery being several years older, head of his house and no mean athlete. But the incident had led to an academic alliance in which Amery helped Churchill with his Latin translations while the future Nobel Prize-winner dictated the older boy's English essays. Now Churchill invited Amery to share his tent in the station yard. Forty years on he would invite him to join his wartime government.

There were many others, mostly army officers, who had already come to the notice of the public, but in this sparkling constellation none, new or established, shone more brightly than the youthful, impetuous Churchill. Unusually for anyone except the very highest in the South African firmament, his portrait appears twice in a pictorial record of the Boer War, *War Impressions*, which was published in 1900 by the well-known British artist Mortimer Menpes. One picture shows Churchill, dressed for the fray, at his tent door. The other is more conventionally posed, with the subject wearing a suit and bow tie. In the commentary accompanying the paintings, the artist's pen is more revealing than his brush. His subject was 'quite ready to retire into the background and listen to any one's conversation – if it is interesting. If it is not – well, I think it might chance to be speedily interrupted.' Menpes thought the young war correspondent 'a man who might be unpopular because of his great cleverness. He is too direct and frank to flatter, and would never consent to efface himself in order to give added and unmerited value to the quality of others.'

A century after Churchill's arrival, Estcourt has spilled much further into the surrounding hills than had the small town of 1899, but something of its original colonial character remains, and there are still plenty of tin roofs. The Churchill connection is enshrined in his freedom of the borough, granted sixty years after he bivouacked there. That this small town should be the only place in the southern hemisphere so to honour him reflects his close association with its inhabitants.

All the women in Estcourt had been evacuated some weeks before, except for Mrs Brewitt, the doctor's wife, and Mrs Norgate, the wife of an Englishman who had emigrated to South Africa as a young man and who was now acting as a British Army guide. Nevertheless the military influx had swelled the population, and among it Churchill became very much the young man about town. Stories of his time in Estcourt abound even now.

It was at the bar of the Plough, still the local pub, that he bought the horse which would carry him around the district. The local horse trader, who asked an extortionate price for an animal of dubious quality, quickly discovered he had a customer who knew

Winston Churchill's Natal

more about horses than he did. Another regular port of call was Dr Brewitt's pharmacy in the Medical Hall. The building, where Churchill chatted daily with the manager, Mr Tuffy Brickhill, is still recognisable.

There was one man in Estcourt who boasted for years that he had been the only person to tell Churchill, 'Go to hell.' This was Signaller Owles of the Durban Light Infantry, one of the soldiers manning the Estcourt garrison heliograph station. Avid for news from Ladysmith, Churchill approached one evening as a message of little consequence was being received. The Sergeant in charge was replying, sending the letters 'AAR'.

'I know the morse code, but what does AAR mean?' Churchill enquired of Owles.

'Go to hell,' was the reply.

Churchill retreated to contemplate this rebuff, but returned shortly afterwards. 'I realise now that your messages are strictly private, but what does AAR really mean?' he asked with unusual reticence.

'It means "Go to hell," ' replied Owles.

Robert Clegg, the stationmaster at Estcourt in 1899, wrote in the *Estcourt Gazette* forty years later about Churchill's arrival in the town: 'He wanted to know all about everything. He made daily excursions over the hills towards Colenso and went as far as buying or hiring an old spider [a small horse-drawn carriage] in which he journeyed out to Frere and Chieveley to see the Boer camp which could be seen from there.'

Robert Clegg's great-grandson, Derek Clegg, told me a story, well known in their family, of Churchill beside a campfire or in the bar of the Plough, telling tales of his time in India and the Sudan. Each episode contained more excitement than most people would meet in a lifetime, and the stationmaster believed Churchill's stories to be much exaggerated. He laughed when the bumptious adventurer declared, 'Mark my words, I shall be Prime Minister of England before I'm finished.' Forty years later Robert Clegg would look up from his newspaper and exclaim to his daughter, 'By Jove, he's done it!'

The Plough and the campfire were not the only places in Estcourt where Churchill relaxed during the balmy evenings of early November. John Atkins, the correspondent of the *Manchester Guardian*, who together with Amery shared Churchill's bell tent, gives a picture of a more sophisticated form of social life: 'We had found a good cook and we had some good wine. We entertained friends every evening, to our pleasure and professional advantage and, we believed, to their satisfaction.' They would have been waited on by Churchill's valet Thomas Walden, who, having accompanied Lord Randolph on his expeditions to India and Africa, was no stranger to maintaining high standards in difficult circumstances.

Undeterred by the Boers besieging the town on all sides, Churchill was impatient to get into Ladysmith. His dispatch of 9 November indicates his frustration. It began: 'How many more letters shall I write you from an unsatisfactory address. Sir George White's Headquarters are scarcely forty miles away, but between them and Estcourt stretches the hostile army. Whether it may be possible or wise to try to pass the lines of investment is a question I cannot yet decide.' In fact he had already let it be known locally that he was looking for a guide to lead him to Ladysmith.

The dispatch goes on to describe a reconnaissance by armoured train to Colenso, a small township in no-man's-land some twenty miles short of Ladysmith. One can imagine Churchill tingling with excitement at the first prospect of action since he had charged with his regiment at Omdurman a year before: 'The possibilities of attack added to the keenness of the experience.' They started early in the afternoon, the engine pulling two trucks carrying soldiers and three with platelayers and spare rails, in case it should be necessary to repair the line.

The train slowly wound its way through the undulating grassland, a green landscape with a hazy blue backdrop of the distant Drakensberg mountains. They halted every four or five miles while the officer in charge of the train, Captain Hemsley, questioned locals and liaised with small bodies of troops, some on bicycles, who were patrolling in the vicinity of the track. Evidently there were no Boers about, no mounted men in slouch hats with Mauser rifles who might be alerted by the belching black smoke of the approaching engine into springing an ambush. By mid-afternoon the train had reached Chieveley, some five miles short of its objective. From here the occupants could see a brown speck in the sky: the observation balloon floating above Ladysmith, hidden beyond the distant hills.

The train moved on even more slowly and warily as Colenso came into view. The little town of less than a hundred tin-roofed houses was silent, and appeared to be deserted. Captain Hemsley stopped the train half a mile short of the first buildings and, accompanied by a sergeant, went forward on foot. According to his dispatch, Churchill followed. No doubt he did more than merely follow. He had, after all, a good deal more active military experience than almost all the officers around him, but in his dispatches he modestly limits his own role to that of correspondent. It is only in his private letters that he writes excitedly of the escapades he so frequently participated in or engineered.

So, the readers of the *Morning Post* followed with Churchill:

> We soon reached the trenches that had been made by the British troops before they evacuated the place . . . The streets were littered with the belongings of the inhabitants. Two or three houses had been burned. A dead horse lay in the road, his four legs sticking stiffly up in the air, his belly swollen . . . We made our way back to the railway line and struck it at the spot where it was cut . . . the damage to the lines was such as could easily be repaired. The Boers realise the advantage of the railway . . . They had resolved to use it for their further advance, and their confidence in the ultimate issue is shown by the care with which they avoid seriously damaging the permanent way. We had learned all there was to learn – where the line was broken, that the village was deserted, that the bridge was safe, and we made haste to rejoin the train . . . So we rattled back to Estcourt through the twilight.

Although he was officially a non-combatant reporter, Churchill was never content to remain a mere spectator. His fellow correspondent Atkins described an occasion when he and Churchill were entertaining the officer commanding Estcourt garrison, Colonel Long. The conversation was distracted by the cries of troops and the clanking of metal on metal, and the Colonel explained that the garrison's field guns were being loaded onto railway trucks to be withdrawn to a safer position near Pietermaritzburg. Estcourt, he said, would fall should the Boers advance against it. Churchill believed it was a mistake to withdraw the guns, and said so with some conviction, pointing out that signs of evacuation would encourage the hitherto cautious Boers to be more adventurous. Atkins envied his confidence, but as a mere correspondent and thus a spectator, was embarrassed by the way in which Churchill lectured a senior officer. However, Colonel Long was not at all put out, and shortly after he had left them, the noise, which had stopped once the guns were aboard the trucks, began again. He had decided that the guns should remain at Estcourt, and they were being unloaded. Atkins describes how Churchill beamed, and said: '*I* did that.' Then, assuming a more modest attitude, he added gracefully, '*We* did that.'

In his dispatch of 10 November, Churchill reminded London of its responsibilities, and the cost of meeting them. He had ridden out to have lunch with a farmer who for fifteen years had sunk his entire efforts and assets into his property. He had, wrote Churchill,

> bought the ground, built the house, reclaimed waste tracts, enriched the land with corn and cattle, sunk all his capital in the enterprise, and backed it with the best energies of his life. Now everything might be wrecked in an hour by a wandering Boer patrol. And this was happening to a law abiding citizen more than a hundred miles within the frontiers of Her Majesty's dominions! Now I felt the bitter need for soldiers – thousands of soldiers – so that such a man might be assured ... The military situation is without doubt at this moment most grave and critical.

That same day, prompted no doubt by his recent excursion, Churchill wrote a letter of over six hundred words to the Adjutant-General in London, Sir Evelyn Wood. He began with a tribute to Reggie Barnes, who was lying wounded aboard the *Sumatra* in Durban Harbour. Churchill used his influence with the Adjutant-General to commend his friend in the hope that, in spite of his serious wounds, 'the State may find a useful servant in the future'. The patient did indeed remain a useful servant, eventually retiring after the First World War as Major-General Sir Reginald Barnes, KCB.

Most of the letter was devoted to an appreciation of the military situation: 'here we remain at Estcourt ... in an untenable cup in the hills. Five days have however passed in safety. Four more will bring reinforcements and change the complexion of affairs. Were the Boers less ambitious they would be more formidable.'

Churchill then explained the less ambitious strategy which would

have brought the Boers more immediate success, but which, fortunately, they had not followed. They would have been better advised
to tear up the railway line from Durban and so delay the British
troops being sent for the relief of Ladysmith. But because they
themselves planned to use the line in their advance to Durban after
they had taken Ladysmith, they had done little damage to it, and
had left the bridges intact. Nevertheless, Churchill continued, the
situation hung in the balance: 'It is astonishing how we have under-
rated these people ... A long and bloody war is before us – and
the end is by no means as certain as most people imagine.'

He went on to criticise the number of British prisoners who had
been taken, and the manner of their capture: 'The Boers have
captured twice as many soldiers as have been hit – not a very pretty
proportion ... I think we ought to punish people who surrender
troops under their command.' This last remark reflected Churchill's
lifelong philosophy, encapsulated in a Second World War speech
by the words 'Never give in.' No doubt in the early stages of the
Boer War some demoralised troops had given up too easily; and
Churchill may have had in mind the abandonment of the wounded
at Dundee, who included his friend Sir Penn Symons. He would
also have been influenced by his personal experience of previous
campaigns, when tribal enemies took no prisoners, and themselves
either fought to the death or melted into the hills. But this was
war in an entirely different context, and one in which he had yet
to get to grips with the enemy. When he did, within a week, he
would have cause to remember, somewhat ruefully, his strictures
on those who had surrendered.

At this stage Churchill criticised the conduct of the war only in
private, and – in marked contrast to his frank comments on other
campaigns – his dispatches contained nothing intended to rock the
boat. It was not that there had been no serious errors of judgement
by the generals. The attempt in the first few weeks, before adequate
forces had arrived, to defeat the Boers as they invaded Natal, had
resulted in the bulk of the British forces becoming besieged in the
disease-ridden town of Ladysmith. This whole strategy, and the
inflexible tactics to implement it, had been so misplaced that Buller,

supported by the War Office at home, wanted to sack General Sir George White, the general officer commanding in Natal. But White, now trapped in Ladysmith, was more at the mercy of the Boers than of the War Office. The errors and stupidities would not have escaped Churchill's notice, but in his view there was nothing to gain by drawing public attention to them while the crisis persisted. It was more important to maintain morale.

The breadth and depth of Churchill's connections is illustrated by the confidence with which he corresponded with the highest in the land, and the frequency with which he bumped into influential friends. Throughout his time in South Africa he was to reinforce friendships already established in the military world and to forge new ones which, besides bringing personal pleasure, would assist him politically in the years ahead. Inevitably for someone of Churchill's nature, his activities would confirm the opinion of him in a few minds as impossible and incorrigible. These antipathies some-times caused temporary and local difficulties, but, as with General Kitchener, seldom had permanent ill-effects.

Kitchener's aversion to Churchill, which had begun even before the young man's arrival in the Sudan, and which was to be fanned into fury by *The River War*, was kept burning when, as Chief-of-Staff in South Africa, he bumped into him again. The fences were to some extent mended in 1914 when Churchill, as First Lord of the Admiralty, wrote to Kitchener, who had just become Secretary of State for War: 'It is a great pleasure to work with you.' When Churchill was forced out of the Admiralty in 1915, Kitchener appeared sorry to see him go. Churchill later wrote: 'When I left the Admiralty . . . the first, and with one exception the only one of my colleagues who paid me a visit of ceremony was the overbur-dened Titan whose disapprobation had been one of the discon-certing experiences of my youth.'

The River War, which was published while Churchill was at Estcourt, received almost universal acclaim. A single paper, the *Saturday Review*, carried a hostile notice: 'Only this astonishing young man could have written these two ponderous and pretentious volumes.' The reviewer was irritated by the author's 'irrepressible egoism' and 'airs of infallibility'. The *Daily Mail* also referred to an 'astonishing young man', but in praise rather than censure, calling the book 'an astonishing triumph'.

While his book was selling out in London, Churchill was scheming to get into Ladysmith. He had let it be known that he would pay £200 to anyone who would lead him through the Boer lines, and William Park Gray, an enterprising twenty-one-year-old trooper of the Natal Carbineers, took up the challenge. The grandson of a first-generation English settler, he knew the local countryside intimately. He was the regiment's rifle-shooting champion, and his stamina in the saddle was legendary. His military talents would take him to the rank of Lieutenant-Colonel in the First World War. Anxious to acquire £200 and to escape close military discipline for a few days, he was ideally suited to the task.

Many years later he recorded his impressions of Churchill, whom he found sitting in his tent:

> a lonely, young, very young, Englishman. He had a complexion that many a South African girl would envy and although four years older than I, looked to be about 17 or 18. He became very animated when I told him what I had come for and asked what plans we should adopt. I assured him the only danger we would encounter would be when we approached our outposts outside Ladysmith ... I then approached my commanding officer ... I was crestfallen when I was told he could not spare a single man, let alone me, to lead a bloody war correspondent into Ladysmith. I think that Churchill was more disappointed than I when I told him the news.

Within a day or two Churchill had found another volunteer to lead him through the Boer lines. This was Richard Norgate, the army guide whose wife had remained with him in Estcourt. Whereas Park Gray wrote of his encounter with Churchill, Norgate's account has been passed down by word of mouth, which may explain some of its inconsistencies – it is said, for example, that he agreed to undertake the perilous task for the paltry sum of £5. His wife tried unavailingly to dissuade him, and a rendezvous was agreed for the following morning. However, the venture was postponed when Churchill accepted an invitation for a second ride on the armoured train.

The officer in charge of the armoured train that day was Captain Aylmer Haldane, a friend of Churchill's from the Tirah expedition in India. Wounded in a battle at Elandslaagte the previous month, Haldane was attached to the Dublin Fusiliers in Estcourt while he awaited the opportunity to rejoin his battalion, the Gordon Highlanders, who were now cooped up in Ladysmith. He had been ordered by the garrison commander to take the armoured train on a reconnaissance.

Haldane had some misgivings about the nature of the mission he had been given. However, he was eager for adventure, and thought that Churchill, who had already accompanied the train on a reconnaissance as far as Colenso, would be an admirable companion. In the dispatch which had taken his *Morning Post* readers along on his previous mission, Churchill had called the train 'a locomotive disguised as a knight errant', pointing out that it was by no means as impressive as it looked. Nevertheless, he agreed to join the expedition, considering it his duty to gather as much information as possible for his paper, and as ever hoping for a brush with the enemy. Amery and Atkins declined his invitation to join him, the former with the excuse that it was raining, the latter on the grounds that he was being paid to follow the war, not to land up in enemy hands.

Thus the scene was set for the most exciting adventure of Churchill's first quarter-century.

FIVE

Knight Errant

'Nothing looks more formidable and impressive than an armoured train; but nothing is in fact more vulnerable and helpless ... This situation did not seem to have occurred to our commander.'

WINSTON CHURCHILL, *My Early Life*

THROUGH THE EARLY-MORNING MIST, clear across the stillness of the rolling veldt, came the unmistakable panting sound of an approaching railway engine. General Louis Botha stood in his stirrups, straining his eyes to penetrate the thin grey curtain drifting over the long grass. After a few minutes he was rewarded by a plume of black smoke rising from behind a hill, and then by the sight of the train itself – six trucks, with the engine in the middle. As it rattled across the trestle bridge spanning the rocky gorge of the Blaaw Kranz River, its fate was as good as sealed.

Botha's cavalcade, some five hundred Boers from the Krugersdorp and Wakkerstroom commandos, had been riding south for two days in order to probe the British position at Estcourt, still fifteen miles away. Theirs was a reconnaissance in force. They had no intention of getting into a serious fight, although they would seize any plums that might drop into their laps. And here, only twenty-four hours after crossing the Tugela, they had stumbled across one waiting to fall.

Botha watched the train rumble past, less than a half a mile away, on its way north. He then gave orders for boulders to be placed across the track, deployed three field guns and a quick-firing Maxim on the hill above, and settled down to await the train on its return journey. By now it was raining heavily.

The soldiers who manned the armoured train had no illusions about its limitations, and often called it 'Wilson's death trap', the identity of Wilson being lost in the mists of time. 'Hairy Mary' was another well known nickname, but this applied to a later version in which the locomotive was festooned for protection by thick rope mantling. The expedition with Captain Haldane was a more substantial reconnaissance than the one Churchill had accompanied to Colenso. At the head of the train was a flat railway truck on which was mounted a muzzle-loading seven-pounder naval gun manned by four seamen and a petty officer from HMS *Tartar*. Next came two armour-plated trucks, with slits through which the soldiers could fire their rifles, then the locomotive and tender. At the rear were two more armoured trucks, and finally a truck for a breakdown gang and the guard.

The train made regular forays along this piece of track: five had taken place in the ten days before Haldane invited Churchill to accompany him. Designed both to reconnoitre the unoccupied country as far as Colenso and to mask the weakness of the British position at Estcourt by a display of activity and strength, a more fatuous and pointless military manoeuvre would be hard to devise. Two or three men on horseback would have been more effective at reconnaissance, while the train was no more than a hostage to fortune. A force of three officers and 117 men from the Durban Light Infantry and the Dublin Fusiliers, together with five sailors and an ancient cannon, were making routine excursions along a fixed route highly vulnerable to ambush. The size, smoke and noise of their transport precluded any possibility of surprise or concealment. That the train was certain one day to be caught in a trap was the opinion of every officer in Estcourt.

The train, with Haldane and Churchill in the leading armoured truck, had left Estcourt early in the morning of 15 November. Colonel Long, the garrison commander, had instructed Haldane to reconnoitre cautiously towards Colenso, keeping out of the range of enemy guns – a curious instruction from an artillery man, who would have been well aware that guns could move anywhere at will, and could be concealed in such a way that they need only announce their presence when they opened fire.

In a dispatch for his paper written five days after the event, Churchill recorded: 'We started at half-past five and ... reached Frere station in about an hour. Here a small patrol of the Natal police reported that there were no enemy within the next few miles and that all seemed quiet in the neighbourhood.' This patrol's report was fatally misleading. At that moment less than four miles separated General Botha and the stationary train hissing and steaming in the little station which served the small community of Frere.

Normally, at this point during the reconnaissance the commander of the train would wire back to the garrison commander at Estcourt before proceeding further north. On this day Haldane did send a report to Colonel Long, but then moved on across the Blaaw Kranz River without waiting for a reply. Had he waited, Long would have told him to sit tight, as he had learned from other patrols that Boers had been spotted at Chieveley, twelve miles beyond Frere.

However, it would seem that Churchill had begun to call the tune. Captain Haldane, twelve years Churchill's senior, an experienced officer with a Distinguished Service Order already to his name, admitted as much many years later when he wrote: 'I do not wish to lay blame on anyone but myself but had I not had my impetuous young friend Churchill with me ... I might have thought twice before throwing myself into the lion's jaws ... But I was carried away by his ardour and departed from an attitude of prudence.' Churchill himself, two months after the action, would admit that they had driven confidently to within firing range of the Boers, intending to teach them a lesson. Although he was well blooded in tribal wars, he had as yet no experience of artillery bombardment or being under concentrated rifle fire.

His dispatch describes his first sight of the enemy:

> As the train reached the station [at Chieveley] I saw about a hundred Boer horsemen cantering southwards about a mile from the railway. Beyond Chieveley a long hill was lined with a row of black spots, showing that our further advance would be disputed. The telegraphist who accompanied the train wired back to Estcourt ... and Colonel Long replied by ordering the train to return to Frere. We proceeded to obey and were about a mile and three quarters from Frere when on rounding a corner we saw that a hill which commanded the line at a distance of 600 yards was occupied by the enemy.

Churchill's response, as reported by his friend Atkins in the *Manchester Guardian*, was to say, 'Keep cool, men! This will be interesting for my paper.' Edgar Wallace, the future novelist and then also employed as a war correspondent in South Africa, would set the event to verse:

> There's risk on the ballasted roadway,
> There's death on the girded bridge,
> Red ruin from sleeper to sleeper,
> And wreck on the bouldered ridge.

The *Morning Post*'s readers were treated to a less poetic but more graphic first-hand account:

> The Boers held their fire until the train reached that part of the track nearest their position. Standing on a box in the rear armoured truck [the train was now moving backwards] I had an excellent view through my glasses. Suddenly three wheeled things appeared on the crest, and within a second a bright flash of light ... Then two much larger flashes ... The iron sides of the truck tanged with a patter of bullets. There was a crash from the front of the train ... The Boers had opened fire on us at 600 yards with two large field guns, a Maxim firing small shells in a stream, and from riflemen lying on the ridge ... I got down from my box into the cover of the armoured sides of the car ... the driver [Charles Wagner] put on full steam, as the enemy had intended. The train leapt forward, ran the gauntlet of the guns, which now filled the air with explosions, swung round the curve of the hill, ran down

a steep gradient, and dashed into a huge stone which awaited it on the line at a convenient spot.

To those who were in the rear truck there was a tremendous shock, a tremendous crash, and a sudden full stop. What happened to the trucks in front of the engine is more interesting. The first, which contained the materials and tools of the breakdown gang and the guard who was watching the line, was flung into the air and fell bottom upwards on the embankment. (I do not know what befell the guard, but it seems probable that he was killed.) The next, an armoured car crowded with Durban Light Infantry, was carried on twenty yards and thrown over on its side, scattering its occupants in a shower on the ground. The third wedged itself across the track, half on and half off the rails.

Haldane admitted to being dazed and for the moment indecisive, while Churchill, 'quick witted and cool was speedily on his feet'. Haldane's subsequent official report takes up the story: 'Mr Winston Churchill ... offered me his services and knowing how thoroughly I could rely on him, I gladly accepted them, and undertook to keep down the enemy's fire while he endeavoured to clear the line. Our gun came into action at 900 yards, but after four rounds was struck by a shell and knocked over.'

Churchill had now assumed control.

Together with the engine-driver Charles Wagner's grandson, who shares his name, I revisited the scene a century later. What he showed me confirmed how cleverly the Boer trap had been sprung. From that curve in the track the view all around is today much as it was then: open and bare. The rails have been repositioned in order to make the curve where the ambush took place less sharp, so the modern Johannesburg to Durban express can thunder through without hindrance. The original line of the railway, still visible as a dirt track on a low embankment, is dominated by the higher ground ahead, so that the Boer gunners would have had an easy target. The curve in the line is on a slight downward incline, so the train would already have been running at speed. It needs little imagination to visualise the driver putting on more steam as soon as the Boer guns opened fire. He probably never saw the boulders that had been placed on the track around the bend, as his engine was in the middle of the train. In any case, he would have been going too fast to stop in time, and derailment was inevitable.

As we stood there on the very spot where our grandfathers had come under such intense fire on 15 November 1899, we looked at the old sepia photographs taken after the event. It was not difficult to picture the scene: the iron trucks hurled at crazy angles while their khaki-clad occupants, many of whom were wounded, scampered for cover among the wreckage. Running along the line towards the engine, oblivious to the bullets ricocheting off the metal and the shrapnel bursting overhead, the young Winston Churchill. Wounded in the head, the engine-driver Charles Wagner had abandoned all thought of continuing at his post, and took shelter behind an armoured truck.

His grandson and I recalled the scene, which both our grandfathers had remembered in much the same way. 'No man is hit twice on the same day,' Churchill had told Wagner, who was the only man capable of driving the train and the troops to safety. Encouraged by this improbable assertion, and also by the promise of a reward for gallantry, Wagner wiped the blood from his face and climbed back into his cab.

As we walked away from the scene of the ambush, both of us moved by our grandfathers' shared experience, we spoke with pride of their actions. We also reflected that if just one of the many bullets and pieces of metal flying around had found their mark, this joint pilgrimage a century later could not have taken place.

Having quickly sized up the situation, Churchill called for twenty volunteers to clear a way for the engine by manhandling the wreckage of one of the trucks, which was blocking the line. Deterred by the constant fusillade of Boer rifle-fire and the frequent exploding shells, the majority remained under cover in and around the trucks, and only nine men, led by Captain James Wylie of the Durban Light Infantry, stepped forward. Wylie was to be badly wounded, but recovered to enjoy a distinguished career, finally retiring as a Brigadier. Thirty-six years after the action, he described Churchill as 'a very brave man but a damned fool'.

Churchill had no military rank or authority. He carried the day entirely as a result of the inspiring leadership which, forty years later, his country came to take for granted. The fact that he had to make do with only half the number of men he called for is hardly surprising. Dr Moorhead, an Englishman who was serving with Red Cross ambulances supporting the Boer forces, described the scene: 'All the time the Boers were pouring in a dreadful fire from practically perfect cover, and the artillery kept putting shells clean through the trucks.'

As might be expected, the picture Churchill painted was more vivid than the doctor's. It shows him revelling in the danger:

> I have had, in the last four years, the advantage, if it be an advantage, of many strange and varied experiences. But nothing was so thrilling as this: to wait and struggle among these clanging, rending iron boxes, with the repeated explosions of the shells and the artillery ... the grunting and puffing of the engine – poor, tortured thing, hammered by at least a dozen shells, any one of which by penetrating the boiler, might have made an end of it all.

There was, for him, nothing so exhilarating as a risk successfully run.

Had the Boer artillery been more accurate and better directed, it would surely have destroyed the stranded engine. The guns had a clear view over open sights of their target, yet only three shells inflicted any telling damage, starting a fire in the tender and severing a water pipe, but still not incapacitating it. Some fourteen years later General Botha, speaking as a guest of the Durban Light Infantry, recounted that he was so annoyed by the poor shooting that he pushed one gunner aside and fired the gun himself. His aim was no better, and he quickly ushered the man back into his rightful place. Nevertheless, the artillery fire was effective enough to keep all but the bravest handful of men cowering in the shelter of the armoured trucks. Shells burst above them, rending the air with flying shrapnel. Others glanced off the steel plating, spinning away across the veldt. Haldane's official report continued:

> The Boers maintained a hot fire with rifles, three 15 pdr Creusot guns and a Maxim shell gun ... For an hour efforts to clear the line were unsuccessful ... but Mr Churchill with indomitable perseverance continued his difficult task, and about 8.30 a.m. the engine forced its way past the obstructing truck, which, however, again fell forward some inches across the line.

Although the tender could now get past, the engine was six inches too wide. After several unsuccessful attempts to nudge the obstacle aside, going carefully lest the engine should derail itself, the risk was taken of driving at it at full tilt. In Churchill's words: 'There was a grinding crash; the engine staggered, checked, shore forward again, until with a clanging, tearing sound it broke past the point of interception, and nothing but the smooth line lay between us and home.'

Churchill had hoped that the engine would be able to tow the rear trucks and all the men to safety, but was dismayed to find that shellfire had smashed the couplings, leaving the trucks stranded some way behind. He ran back to Haldane and suggested the men push the trucks forward, but the enemy fire became too intense when the task of pushing prevented the troops from shooting back. Haldane decided to abandon the trucks and use the engine and its tender to evacuate the wounded and provide a shield behind which the remainder could escape on foot. Once they were across the Blaaw Kranz River the troops could hold out in the houses around Frere station, while the engine returned to Estcourt for assistance.

With Churchill directing operations, the wounded were loaded on to the engine and tender, which then began to move towards the trestle bridge half a mile away. Those who had been sheltering in the trucks ran alongside. Churchill, squashed in the crowded cab, was well placed to provide *Morning Post* readers with a vivid description:

As many wounded as possible were piled on to the engine, standing in the cab, lying on the tender, or clinging to the cowcatcher ... The shell firing Maxim continued its work, and its little shells, discharged with an ugly thud, thud, thud exploded with startling bangs on all sides. One, I remember, struck the foot-plate of the engine scarcely a yard from my head, lit up into a bright yellow flash, and left me wondering why I was still alive. Another hit the coals in the tender, hurling a black shower in the air. A third – this also I saw – struck the arm of a private in the Dublin Fusiliers. The whole arm was smashed to a horrid pulp – bones, muscle, blood, and uniform all mixed together. At the bottom hung the hand, unhurt, but swelled instantly to three times its ordinary size. The engine was soon crowded and began to steam homewards – a mournful, sorely battered locomotive – with the woodwork of the firebox in flames and the water spouting from its pierced tanks. The infantrymen straggled along beside it at the double.

The enemy fire increased. It was remarkable that the engine kept moving. A special edition of the *Natal Advertiser* that evening described its sorry state: 'The armoured engine has many bullet marks, and the dome-cover smashed ... The tender is pitted with bullet marks.'

The din of bursting shells and the whine of ricocheting bullets induced driver Wagner to increase speed, and the men running alongside the engine began to fall behind. Churchill's dispatch continued:

Seeing the engine escaping the Boers increased their fire ... The shells which pursued the retreating soldiers scattered them all along the track. Order and control vanished ... The engine, increasing its pace, drew out from the thin line of fugitives.

Churchill told Wagner to cross the river and wait in the relative safety on the other side while he went back to shepherd in the men who had been left behind. Wagner waited a while, but when it was clear that no stragglers would turn up he steamed back to Estcourt.

Robert Clegg, the stationmaster, met the engine when it returned. He was shocked to see the tender piled with wounded, but relieved to find his son, who had been one of the railwaymen on the train, and who would one day succeed him as stationmaster, unhurt aboard the engine.

I was led by Charles Wagner to the spot where our grandfathers had parted company, Wagner to coax his damaged engine to the other side of the river, Churchill to go back along the railway line to captivity, escape and international fame. The engine-driver had remembered Churchill's words as he jumped down from the cab: 'I can't leave those poor beggars to their fate.'

Even though I knew the ending to the story, my pulse still pounded with anticipation as I retraced the steps that my grandfather had taken nearly a hundred years before. Exhausted but exhilarated as a result of the morning's action, he must have felt very vulnerable as the train pulled away, leaving him, as he thought, alone.

The ground is open, with a slight rise between the site of the ambush and the Blaaw Kranz River. Through this slight rise the original line of the railway runs in a shallow cutting, now shaded with gum trees, through which, at a distance of about two hundred yards, can be seen the lattice ironwork of the bridge. With my back to the bridge I could picture Churchill running along the line searching for the straggling soldiers who, unknown to him, had already surrendered.

Fresh in my mind as I followed in his footsteps was my grandfather's account of the incident in *My Early Life*. His words brought the platelayers' hut at the end of the cutting and the two soldiers who appeared from behind it vividly to life: 'My mind retains its impression of these tall figures, full of energy, clad in dark flapping clothes, with slouch, storm-driven hats, poising on their levelled rifles hardly a hundred yards away.' In such circumstances the cutting must have seemed a death trap, and to anyone else surrender would have been inevitable. Yet Churchill turned and ran. He felt bullets sucking the air to his left and right, and scrambled up the bank.

I also scrambled, breathless, from the cutting to the place where he took cover in a small depression. I could see the river gorge, within sprinting distance. In my mind's eye I also saw the horseman who approached at a gallop and pulled up forty yards away, rifle in hand. I could imagine no option but surrender.

However, the fugitive still had other ideas. Although he was officially a civilian correspondent, Churchill habitually carried the Mauser pistol which had served him so well at the battle of Omdurman. He reached for it, intending to shoot his way to freedom, but found it was missing. He remembered that he had unbuckled his belt and placed it in the cab while he was working to free the engine after the ambush.

Unarmed as he was, even Churchill realised there could be no escape from the horseman who was now standing stock-still and squinting at him along his sights. Churchill held up his hands. It was only five days since he had written to the Adjutant-General criticising troops who had given up without a fight. No one could accuse him of being fainthearted, yet he was uneasy. Thirty years later, he remembered the moment of his surrender:

> 'When one is alone and unarmed,' said the great Napoleon, in words which flowed into my mind in the poignant minutes that followed, 'a surrender may be pardoned.' Still he might have missed; and the Blue Krantz ravine was very near … However, the deed was done. Thereupon my captor lowered his rifle and beckoned me to come across to him …

It was probably just as well that Churchill had left his pistol in the cab of the armoured train. (It was recovered by his valet Walden, and was eventually returned to him.) One man with a pistol against three rifles in open country could have had only one outcome: he would have been gunned down. On the other hand, had the Mauser still been in his possession, and had he chosen to surrender the moment the Boers came upon him, he could hardly have discarded and disowned it, for when he had purchased it from the London gunsmiths Holland & Holland he had instructed them to engrave it with his name. He would have had some difficulty in explaining why he, a civilian, was carrying a weapon.

As Churchill plodded through the wet grass beside his captors he remembered, with some concern, that in each of his breast pockets was a Mauser ammunition clip. Moreover, the only ammunition supplied for the Mauser was of the soft-nosed 'dumdum' variety, severely frowned on in military circles because it caused huge wounds. Why, the Boers might ask, would a civilian have such items in his pockets? He managed to take the clip from his right pocket and drop it to the ground unnoticed. The clip from the other pocket was in his hand when one of his guards asked, 'What have you got there?' Churchill dissembled, opening his hand and asking him what was this curious object he had just picked up. The Boer leaned over to take it, then, with a shrug, threw it away.

A drizzle of rain was falling when the three soldiers and their prisoner reached the Boer focal point, where the headquarters of General Piet Joubert, the commander of all the Boer forces in Natal, was in a tent pitched in a hollow in the hills. Hundreds of mounted Boers in long dark columns, holding black umbrellas over their heads, streamed into view. The other survivors from the armoured train – including Aylmer Haldane – were already assembled under guard. In all fifty-six unhurt or slightly wounded prisoners had been rounded up. The dead, and those seriously wounded who had not escaped on the engine, had been left at the scene. The wounded would be collected by the Boers later, and three of the dead buried on the spot. Their graves, the lettering picked out with spent cartridges from the action, stand as a memorial to this day.

Considering the ferocity of the ambush, it seems remarkable that only six British died: four during the action, and two of wounds. The explanation is that only nine men had responded to Churchill's call and stepped into the open to try to clear the track of wreckage; the remainder, taking cover among the trucks, were well protected by armour plate. Sixteen badly wounded escaped on the engine, while of those who were left behind ten were delivered by the Boers to the besieged garrison of Ladysmith, and three kept in their field ambulances. Among the prisoners there were seven slightly wounded, including Churchill, who had been hit in the hand. He

summed up the number of casualties: 'Not many, perhaps, considering the fire, but out of 120 enough at least.' The Boers had four
men lightly wounded during the ambush, and two more were killed
in a skirmish with a British patrol later in the day.

By now Churchill should have been back in Estcourt having
breakfast with his fellow correspondents. Instead, as he later
recounted to Atkins, he had been rounded up with the other prisoners 'like cattle. The greatest indignity of my life.'

For the moment it also seemed the greatest misfortune: a calamity
for someone so ambitious, so determined to make a name for himself. Churchill sat drenched and miserable under the dark, lowering
sky, munching a bar of chocolate he had found in his pocket. His
morale at its lowest ebb, he considered the other option he could
have taken. No one would have blamed him had he ridden back to
Estcourt on the engine. He would probably have been well received
at the garrison, considering all he had done to enable so many to
escape. Instead he had been taken prisoner to no purpose, after
returning to the scene to shepherd in men who had already surrendered. He had cut himself off from exciting and boundless adventure, and could no longer hope to explore the avenues of
advancement which this war had opened up.

Churchill declared to his guards that as a correspondent and a
non-combatant he should be released, and his credentials were
taken to General Joubert's tent. After a while, his civilian status
began to give him some cause for concern, particularly when he
was picked out from the other prisoners and told to stand to one
side. His clothes, designed for campaigning, were cut in a military
style, and in his state of low morale he began to worry that a civilian
in a sort of uniform, who had taken a prominent part in a military
action, might well find himself facing a firing squad. There were
many precedents for such summary justice.

In fact he need not have worried, for the discussion within the
tent centred not on whether he was a civilian who had taken up
arms, but simply on whether he was a civilian or a combatant. In
the tent with General Joubert was the thirty-year-old Jan Smuts,
then the Transvaal Attorney-General. He advised that Churchill's

participation in the action cast him in the role of a combatant rather than a civilian, and that he should therefore be held as a prisoner of war. He was told to rejoin his companions. In later years, Smuts and Churchill would collaborate as world statesmen, but at their first meeting outside Joubert's tent, Smuts saw only a prisoner who was 'very young, unshaven, dirty looking and very angry at my decision'.

Perhaps the name Churchill was better known than liked at that time in the Transvaal, Lord Randolph having criticised the Boer administration in articles for the *Daily Graphic* during his tour of Southern Africa nine years earlier. 'We don't catch the son of a lord every day,' said Churchill's Boer guards now.

The prisoners were lined up and told they would march under escort to the Boer railhead at Elandslaagte, some sixty miles away. There they would entrain for Pretoria, the capital city of the Transvaal, where British prisoners of war from earlier engagements were being held.

It began to pour with rain.

SIX

The Botha Legend

> 'An acquaintance formed in strange circumstances and upon an almost unbelievable introduction ripened into a friendship which I greatly valued.'
>
> WINSTON CHURCHILL, *My Early Life*

AS CHURCHILL'S FAME INCREASED THROUGHOUT his long life, so it became ever more prestigious to be identified with his capture on 15 November 1899. Ultimately, more than forty men were to assert that they had played some part in the event. As late as the 1970s obituaries in South African papers were recording the passing of men whose main claim to fame was to have apprehended Winston Churchill, and descendants are still coming forward to claim the honour for their distant relatives. Clearly there has been a good deal of exaggeration.

After his capture Churchill would have come into contact with many members of Louis Botha's commando, some of whom, having had temporary custody of their famous captive, could legitimately claim him as their prisoner. But guarding him was far from actually capturing him. Other claims, from those whose participation in the ambush had contributed only indirectly to his capture, are even more tenuous.

All the evidence points to Field Cornet Sarel Oosthuizen, known otherwise as 'the Red Bull of Krugersdorp', as the galloping horseman whose levelled rifle finally convinced Churchill that escape was impossible. There is a single piece of contemporary evidence, which in itself is compelling. It is a two-page telegram, dated 28 November 1899, which was sent to the Secretary of State of the Transvaal, Francis William Reitz, by Captain Daniel Theron, a legendary officer who was commanding the Boer scouts. Among other comments on Churchill's conduct during the action, it reports: 'He also refused to stand still when Field Cornet Oosthuizen warned him to give himself up. It was only when Oosthuizen took aim at him with his rife that he surrendered.' As Sarel Oosthuizen would die of wounds later in the war, the list of pretenders was able to grow, with no one to challenge their accounts until the historians weighed in.

The identity of the two foot-soldiers who appeared from behind the platelayers' hut cannot be established with the same certainty. Dolf De La Rey and his brother-in-law François Changuion are two names which crop up in a number of accounts, and on examination they emerge as the most likely contenders. Changuion's account of the event is recalled by his great-niece, Mrs Yvonne Knowles. According to him, Churchill asked, 'Who may my captors be?' as he and the two riflemen trudged beside the mounted Oosthuizen towards the Boer headquarters, which has a ring of authenticity.

Churchill, however, became convinced that his captor was none other than General Louis Botha, later to become the first Prime Minister of the united South Africa, himself. He was persuaded of this when the two men met at a private luncheon in 1902 while Botha was visiting London to seek assistance for his war-devastated country. Churchill recalled their conversation:

> We talked of the war and I briefly told the story of my capture. Botha listened in silence then he said, 'Don't you recognise me? I was that man. It was I who took you prisoner. I myself,' and his bright eyes twinkled with pleasure. Botha in white shirt and frock coat looked very different in all save size and darkness of complexion from the wild war-time figure I had seen that rough day in Natal. But about the extraordinary fact there can be no doubt. He had entered upon the invasion of Natal as a burgher; his own disapproval of the war had excluded

him from any high command at the outset. This was his first action. But as a simple private burgher serving in the ranks he had galloped ahead and in front of the whole Boer forces in the ardour of pursuit. Thus we met.

The facts hardly support this account. Botha was by no means a private burgher serving in the ranks, but was the leader of the commando which ambushed the armoured train. Within a week of that action he was to take charge of all Boer forces in Natal. Even allowing for Botha's energy and flair, it is unlikely that he would have abdicated command at a crucial moment to become the lone horseman to whom Churchill raised his hands. Had he personally effected the capture, or even interviewed the prisoner, he would surely have mentioned it in a letter which he wrote to his wife the following day which describes the action in some detail and ends with the instruction: 'Publish this.' It seems likely that Botha was not even aware at this stage that such an important prisoner had been taken.

How was it that Churchill could have got his facts so wrong? The answer probably lies in Botha's limited command of English. Churchill may simply have misunderstood his account of both his involvement in the early stages of the war and his position of overall command during the ambush. However, Churchill had been convinced by their conversation, and henceforth the two men, who had clearly taken to one another, fostered this agreeable tale. Sixty years later, when historians were still debating the matter, Churchill was in no mood to change his mind. When his official biographer, his son Randolph, produced historical evidence to the contrary, he replied: 'I was captured personally by Botha as stated in my book [*My Early Life*],' the word 'personally' being a handwritten insertion in an otherwise typed letter.

Some explanation is needed as to why Churchill's usually open mind remained closed for ever on this subject. For one thing, he had no reason to doubt his understanding of Botha's description of events. That conversation harking back to the battlefield forged a bond between the two men, and bonds forged in battle tend to last a lifetime. In this case the bond was struck three years after the battle, but, resulting from a shared experience of mortal danger still fresh in their minds, it was to prove enduring. Churchill and Botha were to become firm friends, and to collaborate on such momentous issues as the granting of self-government to the Trans-vaal and the Orange Free State in 1907, and they would sit together in the Imperial War Cabinet during the First World War. Churchill was to write: 'Few men that I have known have interested me more than Louis Botha.' He took a romantic view of Botha – a 'grand, rugged figure' – and saw in him 'the Father of his country, the wise and profound statesman, the farmer-warrior, the crafty hunter of the wilderness, the deep, sure man of solitude'. It is not surprising that Churchill rejected subsequent accounts which did not fit the version of his capture as he had interpreted it from the man who had apparently claimed to be the lone galloping horseman.

When Botha, as Prime Minister of the Transvaal, came to London for the 1907 Colonial Conference, he brought with him as his official hostess his daughter Helen. As a Minister at the Colonial Office, Churchill saw a good deal of Botha during this visit, and, evidently, even more of Helen. Although this was her first trip to Britain she spoke English perfectly, having been educated for seven years in Brussels under the care of Madame de Rounge, who was related to the Belgian royal family. At nineteen Helen was sophisticated, vivacious and pretty. She was already the toast of several European Courts, and during her stay in England she would visit Buckingham Palace on a number of occasions, catching the eye of King Edward VII.

When the Bothas arrived in London Churchill was free of roman-tic entanglements. His pursuit of Pamela Plowden had ended six years previously, and more recently he had unsuccessfully proposed to a rich heiress, Muriel Wilson. Tongues began to wag over the attention he was paying to Helen Botha. This seldom-mentioned gossip seemed worth investigating.

'The friendship between Winston Churchill and General Botha's daughter is a story that has been passed down through the family,' said Becky Smit, Helen's great-niece, in answer to my enquiry.

Helen Botha had said that Churchill was 'very entertaining'. But was there more to their relationship than just friendship?

At the time, an imminent engagement was rumoured. A kite-flying, reply-prepaid telegram to Churchill from the *Manchester Chronicle* asked for confirmation of 'something interesting'. From the South of France Muriel Wilson sent tongue-in-cheek congratulations, having herself lately experienced Churchill's ineptitude as a suitor due to his complete absorption in politics.

Interviewed sixty years later for a British Sunday newspaper, Helen Botha denied any romance: 'It was so unlikely I would fall for him. After all, I was a Transvaaler.' This was a somewhat disingenuous statement, as her father and Churchill got along famously. What is more to the point is that it would have been out of character for Churchill to contemplate marriage to a young Boer woman, no matter how vivacious and intelligent she might be. His huge ambitions demanded a wife who would be a political asset, and as a rapidly rising star, it was likely that he would find one soon enough.

By the time he met Helen Botha he had come a long way since his weary march, as a dishevelled prisoner of war seven years earlier, along the muddy tracks to Elandslaagte.

SEVEN

Into Captivity

'This misfortune, could I have foreseen the future, was to lay
the foundations of my later life.'

WINSTON CHURCHILL, *My Early Life*

WATER POURED FROM A LEADEN SKY as the motley band of
prisoners was assembled: two officers and fifty men in bedraggled
khaki; four sailors in jaunty straw hats embellished with HMS *Tartar* in gold lettering on their black ribbons; several railwaymen
in sodden overalls; and one hatless war correspondent in a wet
buttoned-up tunic, baggy trousers and long leather gaiters. '*Voor-
warts*,' came the order, and the procession moved off, surrounded
by Boers, their horses steaming in the rain. For Churchill, with the
fair complexion of a redhead, the rain was probably preferable to
the burning South African sun. After a few paces one of the Boers
took pity on the hatless civilian and threw him an Irish Fusilier's
forage cap, a trophy picked up after an earlier battle.

Churchill's immediate surroundings had only a temporary and
marginal effect on his morale. His emotions encompassed humiliation at the indignity of being taken prisoner and frustration at
being a captive, but above all concern that he might miss the rest
of the war and the opportunities it could offer. As he plodded along
the muddy track, in a hat the like of which he had not worn since
he had left Sandhurst, his mind was already racing ahead to the
one avenue of opportunity which, at least to him, was clearly sign-
posted. He knew that his part in the armoured train action would

feature with credit in the British press. His misadventure could thus be turned to advantage.

In his autobiography *A Soldier's Saga*, Aylmer Haldane portrays Churchill as looking ahead with confidence even in the first hours following his capture:

> Churchill must have been cheered by the thought, which he communicated to me, that what had taken place, though it had caused the temporary loss of his post as war correspondent, would help considerably in opening the door for him to enter the House of Commons. As we trudged wearily over the damp veldt he remarked to me that in allotting him what I might call the 'star turn' I had effaced myself, while his work of clearing the line had brought him into prominence ... He added that so far as I was concerned he would at first opportunity publish the facts in his newspaper.

Churchill's suggestion to Haldane that he had been allotted the starring role was no more than a polite way of glossing over the fact that he had reacted positively to the crisis, seizing the initiative while others were still in a state of shock. Haldane, perhaps recognising that his own performance had been eclipsed and not wishing to see that implied in print, responded with a stiff upper lip: 'While thanking him, I replied that being satisfied that I had done my duty and acted in what I considered the wisest way in the circumstances no explanation as to what had occurred was necessary.'

Churchill's fame was spreading even as he was being marched into captivity. That very evening the *Natal Advertiser* ran a special edition carrying a report of his 'courageous conduct' during the ambush. It had to rely on fragmentary accounts from those survivors who had made it back to Estcourt, for, as Reuter reported, 'the only war correspondent present was Mr Churchill', and he was at that moment incommunicado somewhere on the rain-soaked veldt. The report ended: 'Our friend Mr Churchill is a prisoner,' a tribute to the impact he had made in the short time he had been in Natal.

Two days later the paper carried a more lengthy account, based on the testimony of Captain Wylie, who had been wounded during the attack. He described Churchill's conduct 'in the most enthusiastic terms as that of as brave a man as could be found', and recounted how he continued to direct operations 'amid a hail of missiles'.

The same edition published a letter sent to the General Manager of the Natal Government Railways on behalf of the railway employees who had escaped on the engine: 'The railway men who accompanied the armoured train this morning ask me to convey to you their admiration of the coolness and pluck displayed by Mr Winston Churchill ... The whole of our men are loud in their praises of Mr Churchill ... I respectfully ask you to convey their admiration to a brave man.'

Testimonials to Churchill's gallantry came from a wide variety of sources, and from all levels. Captain Anthony Weldon wrote to Field Marshal Lord Wolseley, Commander-in-Chief of the British Army, to whom he was ADC: 'I had a talk with the engine driver of the train ... & also with a platelayer who had accompanied it ... they both told me nothing could exceed Churchill's pluck & coolness during the whole affair. He took off his coat & worked with the men getting the engine on to the lines again under a perfect hail of bullets & shells & after they had got safely away to Frere got down from the train & walked back alone ... to look for & help the wounded.'

A private in the Durban Light Infantry who, having been shot in both foot and throat had escaped on the engine, wrote to his sister: 'Churchill is a splendid fellow. He walked about in it all as coolly as if nothing was going on, & called for volunteers to give him a hand to get the truck out of the road.'

Even the enemy paid tribute to Churchill's courage. Dr Moorhead of the Red Cross, writing several months after the event, noted that the burghers 'gave glowing details about Winston Churchill's gallantry, which they must have heard from the soldiers'.

Back in Britain *The Times*, the *Daily Mail*, the *Manchester Guardian* and the *Daily Telegraph* all reported his courage in glowing terms. Inevitably a sour note crept into some of the more radical elements of the press, *Truth* seeking to disparage Churchill's actions by a rhetorical question: 'Mr Churchill is described as having rallied the force . . . Would officers in command on the battlefield permit a journalist to "rally" those who were under their orders?' The answer, as was implied by the unsolicited testimonials from many sources, showed that, unwittingly, the paper was living up to its name.

A matter-of-fact report came from Private Alexander Chisholm of the Durban Light Infantry, one of the very few to have escaped the ambush site on foot. His letter to his father was quoted in full in the *Buchan Observer* of 26 December 1899. 'I underwent a terrible experience last Wednesday, the 15th November . . . I expected to be done for at any second.' In a letter of some 650 words, 'Lieutenant' Churchill is the only person named, his rank presumed no doubt because he, rather than any of the officers present, took charge.

On hearing that Churchill was a prisoner, his valet Thomas Walden gathered his kit and deposited it at the Horseshoe Hotel in Pietermaritzburg. From there he wrote to Lady Randolph:

> I came down in the armoured train with the driver who is wounded in the head with a shell. He told me all about Mr Winston. He says there is not a braver gentleman in the Army. The driver was one of the first wounded, and he said to Mr Winston: 'I am finished.' So Mr Winston said to him: 'Buck up a bit, I will stick to you,' and he threw off his revolver and field-glasses and helped the driver pick up 20 wounded and put them in the tender of the engine. Every officer in Estcourt thinks Mr C. and the engine-driver will get the V.C.

Had Churchill been a conventional young officer and Wagner a soldier, there is little doubt that both of them would have received the Victoria Cross. But as civilians neither was eligible for it, or for any other military decoration, although the authorities could have recommended them for the Albert Medal, the civilian equivalent of the Victoria Cross. Not only would it have been well deserved, but its award to the driver would have provided a much-needed boost to the morale of those civilians who were providing indispensable wartime service to the Crown.

Churchill understood the place medals have in maintaining

morale. In the heat of action he had promised to see that Wagner would get a medal, and afterwards he could not ignore the authorities' failure to recognise the engine-driver's courage under fire. Writing to the editor of the *Spectator*, which had carried an article about the armoured train, he described Wagner's actions and concluded: 'He has received no recognition of any kind from the War Office, although one would have thought his services not less valuable and deserving than those of several young gentlemen who adorned the headquarters staff. Driver Wagner – he is driving an armoured engine still – is not likely to complain; but from time to time I get querulous letters from his comrades who think he has been gracelessly treated.'

Ten years later, on becoming Home Secretary, and in a position to advise the King on awards of the Albert Medal, Churchill was able to make good his promise. Charles Wagner was decorated with the Albert Medal First Class, while the train's second engineer, Alexander Stewart, received the Albert Medal Second Class.

Their grandchildren were among the first to respond to my broadcast appeal for descendants of anyone who had known Churchill during his time in South Africa to come forward.

After our nostalgic visit to the scene of the ambush, over lunch in Fort Durnford at Estcourt, I continued to discuss the action with Charles Wagner and his sister, Molly Buchanan.

'The family have always been proud that our grandfather had been under fire with Churchill,' said Molly.

'What did he say about it?' I asked.

'Not much. We knew he had been responsible for driving the engine away even though he was wounded, but apart from that he said very little about the actual battle. He just carried on driving engines.'

'Do you have any photographs?' I asked. I had seen an old, torn press cutting which carried a picture of Wagner standing with his second engineer, but the original photograph from which it had been printed had apparently vanished.

'The only photograph we had was of him with his engine,' said

Molly, 'and we gave that and his medal to the military museum in Durban.'

Wagner had obviously been a modest man, careless of the fame in which he might have basked, and all that was left in my pursuit of him was a visit to the military museum in Durban. There I found that even after two world wars, his exploit has not been overshadowed. The curator directed me instantly to Wagner's Albert Medal, which occupies pride of place among dozens of decorations from many campaigns. In an adjacent cabinet is a fading photograph of Driver Wagner, oil can in hand, standing confidently in front of 'Hairy Mary', a replacement engine for the one damaged during the ambush. Coupled to it are a few armoured trucks, and standing by are several soldiers.

Alexander Stewart, the second engineer's grandson, had driven 150 miles from Durban to Winterton (it was called Springfield in 1899) to tell his tale. We sat on the verandah of the farm where Churchill had camped after his escape. As we looked across the Tugela River to the bare summit of Spion Kop, baking in the midday sun, Stewart proudly showed me a photograph of his grandfather with the Albert Medal. Even more interesting to me was a studio photograph of Stewart and Wagner together, taken ten years earlier, a day or two after they had driven the wounded to safety. Wagner's head is bandaged. It was the missing press picture.

'Did your grandfather ever talk about mine?' I asked.

'Oh yes. His favourite story was the one when Churchill, passing through Pietermaritzburg some time after he had escaped his Boer captors, had gone to the railway yard and asked if the engineer was around.'

A message was relayed to Stewart that an important, but unnamed, man was asking for him. 'Tell him I'm in dirty overalls covered in oil and grease, and in no fit condition to meet anyone important,' he said.

When the reply reached Churchill, he exclaimed, 'Dirty overalls are nothing compared to what he and I went through together. I have to shake his hand, oil and all.' Then, to the delight of those present, Churchill strode through the railway yard to seek Stewart out.

There is no doubt that Churchill hoped that he himself would receive some official recognition of his action. In previous campaigns as a soldier he had sometimes been called a medal-hunter, but in reality he had been seeking action, and having found it, he prized the medals which commemorated his participation. There is nothing vainglorious about a young man aspiring to a decoration, particularly in the military field, and although in this case the young man was a civilian, his was a fine example of military action under fire.

Captain Haldane's report was virtually a citation for a decoration, and would normally have prompted official recognition of Churchill's bravery. At some risk to his own reputation – for in the heat of battle he, although the commander, had played the lesser role – Haldane described Churchill's part in the action, and concluded: 'I would point out that while engaged on the work of saving the engine, for which he was mainly responsible, he was frequently exposed to the full fire of the enemy. I cannot speak too highly of his gallant conduct.' Haldane's account would have been seen by the Commander-in-Chief in South Africa, General Buller, and because it concerned an important action he would have sent its substance, if not the whole report, to the War Office.

There were also the other testimonials to Churchill's courage, notably from members of the Durban Light Infantry and the Natal railwaymen. These had been sent to the Governor of Natal, Sir Walter Hely-Hutchinson, who forwarded them to the Colonial Office.

In May 1901, safely back in England and by then a Member of Parliament, Churchill raised the subject with his friend Joseph Chamberlain, the Colonial Secretary:

> It has occurred to me that if the papers sent by the Natal people to the Colonial Office were forwarded to the War Office, they would look very imposing taken in conjunction with this dispatch [Haldane's report], and I might get some sort of military mention or decoration.

In case this sounded too blatant a case of medal-hunting, he continued by advancing a political rationale:

> Of course in common with all the other members of Parlia-
> ment I care nothing for the glittering baubles of honour *for
> my own sake*: but I have like others – as you know – to 'think
> of my constituents' – and perhaps I ought to consider the
> feelings of my possible wife. This being so if you can trace
> these papers and feel inclined to send them to the War Office,
> I shall be much obliged. The case could then be considered
> with other cases.

Unfortunately for Churchill's hopes of a medal, his case was in the hands of the military hierarchy, the object of his frequent and telling barbs. No one in the War Office would champion his cause.

Unpopular he may have been among the higher reaches of the army, but his stock soared with the public. At a time when those in charge of the South African campaign seemed to be getting everything wrong, the young Churchill had turned in a bravura performance, and the British people, as they would do again a couple of wars hence, put the bad news behind them by applauding this hero.

The journey to Pretoria took the prisoners seventy two-hours – two days' marching and one by train. Within a few hours of his arrival there, Churchill had, as if to emphasise his non-combatant status of war correspondent, begun a series of dispatches to the *Morning Post*. It may seem strange that his captors allowed him so much licence, but – quite apart from the civilised conventions which then existed between captors and captured – the Boers may well have thought that public opinion abroad could be influenced in their favour by Churchill's informative, non-partisan accounts, which were cabled, uncensored, to London.

His dispatch of 24 November described how the column had halted on their way when they reached the Boer guns which had ravaged the armoured train a few hours before:

two strangely long barrels sitting very low on carriages of four wheels ... They looked offensively modern, and I wondered why our Army had not got field artillery with fixed ammunition and 8000 yards' range. The commander, Adjutant Roos – as he introduced himself – made a polite salute. He regretted the unfortunate circumstances of our meeting; he complimented the officers on their defence ... above all he wanted to know how the engine had been able to get away, and how the line could have been cleared of wreckage under his guns. In fact, he behaved like a good professional soldier should, and his manner impressed me.

In other circumstances Churchill would have needed no invitation to explain how he had cleared the line. He would have plunged into a discussion of the action, no doubt telling the commander how he could have better conducted the battle. However, the war correspondent was anxious to play down his participation in the action. He had already, by the skin of his teeth, escaped the mortal peril of being condemned as a combatant in civilian clothes. Having successfully confirmed his civilian status he was now bent on turning it to advantage, in order that he might be released. He need not have been so uncharacteristically modest, for by the time he arrived in Pretoria his captors were fully aware of the significant part he had played in the ambush.

The column rested near the guns while the Boers searched the wreckage of the train and its vicinity for dead and wounded. After an hour the march continued, and by evening Churchill was close to the little town to which he had advanced on foot during his first foray on the armoured train a week before: 'It was with a feeling of utter weariness I saw the tin roofs of Colenso rise in the distance. We were put into a corrugated iron shed.'

Presently the locked doors were opened, and the prisoners invited to dry themselves around several campfires. Food was provided, in the shape of strips of newly slaughtered ox to be toasted over the flames. Churchill characteristically took the opportunity to start a discussion with two brothers among the guards, 'Afrikaners by birth, Boers by choice'.

* * *

For me, the story continued in a conversation with Alan Raubenheimer, the grandson of one of the brothers, Benjamin Raubenheimer. We chatted much as our grandfathers had done a century before – except that our lunch, at Hermanus on Walker Bay west of Cape Town, was a good deal more appetising than the toasted ox served by the campfire at Colenso.

'Field Cornet Benjamin Raubenheimer was thirty, and had taken part in the opening battle of the war at Talana Hill,' said his grandson. 'He was a very patriotic Boer and enjoyed his discussion with Churchill. At the time the war was going well for the Boers, but Churchill was confident Britain would win.'

'Was it a friendly discussion?'

'I think they agreed to disagree. At any rate my grandfather offered Churchill his blanket.'

'Yes,' I said. 'My grandfather wrote about that. It was a blanket with a hole in it, worn like a cloak.'

'Ah, but what your grandfather didn't say was that he at first refused it. I think he was just being polite. The incident is recorded in our family history. My grandfather pressed the offer again, and it was gratefully accepted.'

'What,' I wondered, 'did your grandfather think of mine?'

'Oh, he later wrote it down. He remembered Churchill as a nice young man to talk to who never gave any trouble.'

A depressed Churchill spent a fitful night sharing Raubenheimer's blanket with Lieutenant Thomas Frankland of the Dublin Fusiliers – destined, fifteen years later, to die as a colonel on the beaches of Gallipoli. His spirits revived with daybreak, and he began to think of escape. He planned to burrow beneath the straw that covered the floor of the shed and hide until the column had marched off, but was thwarted when a guard ordered them all outside.

After a breakfast of cold toasted ox, left over from the previous evening, and rainwater from a large puddle, the prisoners continued on their way. They halted for a rest close to the Boer lines around Ladysmith, and Churchill's dispatch records some of the banter which passed between the Boer commandos and the captured

British troops. The Boers, he wrote, 'are all keen politicians and as curious as children'. It was clear that they had a loose but effective form of discipline. One old Boer questioned the wisdom of using an armoured train, saying that if the Field Cornet ordered him into one, he would reply, 'Field Cornet, go to hell.' Another declared: 'The English died for their country while the Afrikaners lived for theirs.' Churchill sensed that the Boers were not as confident as they made out, and, seeking to encourage their fears, told them that the real war had not even started. Indeed, it is doubtful if anyone taking part in that conversation on the veldt could have imagined the carnage which lay ahead.

The British observation balloon at Ladysmith was visible to the column of prisoners: 'High above the hills,' wrote Churchill, 'to the left of the path, hung a speck of gold-beater's skin. It was the Ladysmith balloon. There, scarcely two miles away, were safety and honour . . . Beleaguered Ladysmith, with its shells, its flies, its fever, and its filth seemed a glorious paradise to me.'

Ten hours' marching, which included fording the chest-deep Klip River, brought the column in mid-afternoon to that night's camp. There, although soaked to the skin, Churchill was sufficiently refreshed by tea and bully beef to feel equal to further argument in the Field Cornet's tent. It was his antidote to captivity. In the war of words – probing the thoughts of his captors, and planting the seeds of doubt among them – the prisoner retained the initiative. After an evening thus spent, the officers and men were directed to separate areas. Not unnaturally, Churchill accompanied the officers. His mind still firmly on escape, it was a choice he soon regretted.

For his London readers, the African veldt would have been as alien as the surface of the moon. Churchill's dispatches were the equivalent of today's television news reports from remote corners of the earth, and were equally effective.

> The dark shadow of Bulwana mountain flung back over the Dutch camp, and the rugged, rock-strewn hills rose about it on all sides. The great waggons were arranged to enclosure a square, in the midst of which stood clusters of variously shaped

tents and lines of munching oxen. Within the laager and around it little fires began to glow, and by their light the figures of the Boers could be seen busy cooking and eating their suppers, or smoking in moody, muttering groups. All was framed in the triangular doorway of the tent, in which two ragged, bearded men sat nursing their rifles and gazing at their captives in silence.

After Churchill's companions had fallen asleep, he peered through a tear in the tent, and discovered that four sentries were posted outside it in a manner which denied any attempt at escape. Had he gone with the men rather than the officers he might have had some chance of getting away, as they were less closely guarded. At midnight the sentries were changed, and Churchill again assessed the situation, looking through the tear at the nearest guard: 'He was quite a child – a boy of about fourteen – and needless to say appreciated the importance of his duties. He played this terrible game of soldiers with all his heart and soul; so at last I abandoned the idea of flight and fell asleep.'

At first light the prisoners were roused and told there was to be a five-hour march to the railway station at Elandslaagte. 'We stood up – for we had slept in our clothes and cared nothing for washing – and said we were ready.' The commandant of the laager brought breakfast of more tea and bully beef, apologising for the plainness of the food and explaining that it was all his men had themselves. He then sought his prisoners' assurance that they were satisfied with the treatment they had received. Churchill's dispatch reported: 'We gladly gave him this assurance, and with much respect bade goodbye to this dignified and honourable enemy.' Once again, the account of this civilised farewell makes odd reading a century later.

It was late morning when the column reached Elandslaagte. By now it had been joined by prisoners taken in other engagements. Their imminent arrival had attracted a crowd of colourfully dressed Indians, near-naked tribesmen and stout Boer women – the latter bearing rusks for the hungry prisoners. While he was drawing rations from the railhead a Boer soldier, Johannes Nortje, heard that the son of Lord Randolph Churchill was a prisoner, and asked for him to be pointed out. He remembered Churchill as 'a small young man, standing slightly aside, who was resolute in appearance and constantly scanning the horizon and all activity around him, unlike the other prisoners, who were downcast and dejected'.

The section of track through Elandslaagte fell under the jurisdiction of a railway official named Willem Punt. The story of what befell Churchill on his arrival at the station has been handed down through the family, and was told to me by his grandson, also Willem Punt.

'It began to rain, and when the prisoners were told to take shelter in the baggage room, Churchill was taken to one side and put under guard in the ticket office. But the fun started when they were all told to board the train. One or two officers who had just joined the party objected to travelling with a newspaper man.'

This seems extraordinary, given Churchill's military background and his recent exploits. It is possible that the officers feared the consequences of Churchill's determination to escape.

'My grandfather,' Willem Punt continued, 'told the officers that they would have to put up with the newspaper man. He was unaware of the newspaper man's identity but I'm sure that in any case he would have ignored the officers' objections.'

Among the people crowding curiously around the carriages, Churchill wrote in a dispatch on 30 November, was a young doctor who, seeing Churchill's bandaged hand, enquired if he was wounded. The doctor's great-niece, Angela Caccia-Lloyd, came forward and identified him in response to my broadcast: 'He was Thomas Visser. He was in charge of a number of ambulances. When he looked at Churchill's hand he found the wound had begun to fester, and he sent for proper dressings.' Had he known more about Visser, Churchill would have approved of him. He was a patriot who, within a year of treating Churchill at Elandslaagte, was sentenced to two years' imprisonment because of his anti-British activities. He would go on to become a prominent doctor, politician and benefactor in South Africa.

Placed in charge of the guards aboard the train was one Paul du Plessis. 'This was because his English was the best among the guards,' his son Daniel told me. 'Churchill offered my father £5 if he could produce a bottle of brandy, but unfortunately he couldn't find one.' It is debatable who was the more unfortunate – Churchill without the brandy, or du Plessis without the money. £5 was equivalent to £300 at today's prices, and there is no doubt the *Morning Post* would have footed the bill.

In his dispatch of 30 November Churchill introduced one of his guards to the readers of the *Morning Post*: 'His name was Spaarwater . . .' His granddaughter, Martha Bam, has carefully preserved a faded but still legible note written in pencil on a scrap of paper:

> The Bearer, H.G. Spaarwater has been very kind to me and British officers captured in the Estcourt armoured train. I shall be personally grateful to anyone who may be able to do him any service should he himself be taken prisoner
> Winston S. Churchill. Nov. 17 1899

Spaarwater, wrote Churchill in his dispatch, was a farmer: 'In times of peace he paid little or no taxes. The Field Cornet, he remarked, was a friend of his. But for such advantages he lay under the obligation to serve without pay in wartime, providing horse, forage and provisions . . . He was a polite, meek-mannered little man, very anxious in all the discussion to say nothing that could hurt the feelings of his prisoners, and I took a great liking to him.' The *Morning Post*'s readers were then treated to an account of a good-hearted political discussion between the two men before the dispatch again turned to thoughts of escape while the train was in a tunnel. 'The possibility had, however, presented itself to Spaarwater, for he shut both windows and just before we reached the entrance opened the breech of his Mauser to show me it was fully loaded.'

The story handed down through Spaarwater's family confirms much of Churchill's account. The only significant difference concerns this incident in the Volksrust tunnel. 'Here,' Spaarwater told his family, 'Churchill whispered that every man had his price, and that the guards would be richly rewarded if they looked the other way in order that their prisoners could escape. But I was not to be bought.'

The Bearer, H.y. Spaarwater, has been very kind to me and British officers captured in the Pricourt armoured town. I shall be personally grateful to anyone who may be able to do him any service, should he himself be taken prisoner

W inston S. Churchill.

Nov. 1st 1899

Pencilled note from Churchill for H.G. Spaarwater, who guarded him on the train journey from Elandslaagte to Pretoria. (*Martha Bam*)

Spaarwater never had the chance to use his captive's note of recommendation. He was killed in action a year later.

Another of the guards was nineteen-year-old Daniel Swanepoel of the Krugersdorp Commando, whose daughter, Johanna de Wet, I met at her home on the outskirts of Cape Town, where she had assembled her daughters and grandchildren so they could hear the story. She produced a photograph of the youthful Swanepoel proudly standing in uniform with his rifle and fixed bayonet. 'My father sat opposite Churchill throughout the twenty-four-hour journey, and at Germiston station brought him a cup of coffee,' she said. 'Father thought it was made with burnt potatoes rather than real coffee, but Churchill seemed to like it.'

From what Mrs de Wet's father had told her, Churchill appears to have dominated the compartment. His guards were uncertain of his status, and thought he must be 'some kind of big man, perhaps a general'. Swanepoel remembered seeing some of the prisoners saluting Churchill when they arrived at Pretoria, which convinced him of his importance.

'My father later became a prominent Johannesburg businessman with a large butchery,' Johanna de Wet told me. 'He said that meeting Churchill changed his life. You know, they corresponded regularly in later years. During the war my father sent him a bible signed by important people in Johannesburg.'

'Do you have anything from my grandfather?'

'Oh yes. Churchill sent my father a signed copy of his book [*My Early Life*], and even when he was Prime Minister during the war sent Christmas greetings written in his own hand and dated 25 December 1940.'

During the journey Churchill and Thomas Frankland, the young Lieutenant from the Dublin Fusiliers, met the man who had been responsible for placing the boulders on the track which derailed the armoured train. Churchill took the opportunity to leaven his otherwise serious dispatch with humour. The Boer, 'a dear old gentleman . . . hoped we bore no malice. We replied by no means, and that we would do the same for him with pleasure any day.'

Frankland told the old man he thought his exploit warranted a medal; but the Boers, Churchill recorded, had more practical rewards, and he had been granted 'fourteen days' furlough to go home to his farm and see his wife. His evident joy and delight were touching. I said, "Surely this is a very critical time to leave the front. You may miss an important battle."

' "Yes," he replied simply, "I hope so." '

At Volksrust, the prisoners' first stop in the Transvaal, the guards were changed: 'The honest burghers who had captured us had to return to the front.' Churchill's readers were informed that the journey continued under the eye of 'a rather dilapidated policeman of a gendarme type, who spat copiously on the floor of the carriage and informed us that we should be shot if we attempted to escape. Having no desire to speak to this fellow, we let down the sleeping shelves of our compartment and, as the train steamed out of Volksrust, turned to sleep.'

The twenty-four-hour train journey to Pretoria ended at midday on 18 November. On a bright, sunny day, the prisoners were met by a considerable crowd. Churchill's next despatch, dated 3 December, describes the scene: 'ugly women with bright parasols, loafers and ragamuffins, fat burghers too heavy to ride at the front, and a long line of untidy, white-helmeted policemen – "zarps" as they were called ["Zuid Afrika Republik" was embroidered on their shoulder-flashes] – who looked like broken down constabulary . . . Now for the first time since my capture I hated the enemy.' He contrasted the 'simple valiant burghers at the front' with the 'slimy sleek officials' in whose hands he now found himself: 'Here were the creatures who had fattened on the spoils.'

At first Churchill was put with the soldiers, who were to be marched off to an enclosed camp at Pretoria's racecourse. A photograph shows Churchill, still wearing the Irish Fusilier's forage cap, standing nonchalantly to the side of an assembly of soldiers in pith helmets. The men's morale was suffering from the events of the past three days, which led Churchill to tell them to brace up and show the onlookers that they cared for the cause for which they fought. When they responded positively to his leadership, he began to think how an uprising and escape, or even a rebellion, might be organised.

It was a thought which he was to develop in the days ahead, but meanwhile, having been reunited with the captured officers, he hastily scribbled a note which he handed to his captors when he arrived at the States Model School, which was being used to housed British officers who had been taken prisoner: 'Morning Post, London. Captured unarmed 15th Frere detained Pretoria urge release meanwhile instruct Robertson Club Durban act for me. Churchill.' 'Robertson, Durban Club', was what he actually meant.

EIGHT

The States Model School

'Prisoner of War! That is the least unfortunate kind of prisoner
to be, but it is nevertheless a melancholy state.'

WINSTON CHURCHILL, *My Early Life*

THE STATES MODEL SCHOOL LOOKS, today, much the same as
it did when Churchill was imprisoned there. Only the interior has
been modified to accommodate the library it now contains. A large,
single-storeyed brick building with a high, steep corrugated tin roof
and a wide verandah, it housed two hundred pupils and sixteen staff
when it opened in January 1897 as a boys' school and college of
higher education. In October 1899 it was requisitioned to provide
quarters for officer prisoners of war. Declared a national monument
in 1963, it now stands at the intersection of two busy dual car-
riageways. They were no more than broad, dusty thoroughfares for
pedestrians, riders, carriages and carts when Churchill trudged
along Skinner Street and turned left into Van der Walt Street
before halting in front of the school's arched entrance.

What was then a grass-covered playground to the rear is now
tarmacked over and occupied by low, whitewashed administrative
buildings. In Churchill's time it contained scattered tents, a cook-
house and latrines, and was separated from the main building by a
ten-foot-high wire fence. The whole area of the school and its
grounds, some seventy yards square, was enclosed by nothing more
than a chest-high ornamental iron fence at the front and sides, and
six-foot iron railings to the rear. The bustling, built-up Pretoria of

Winston Churchill, war correspondent, by Mortimer Menpes.

ABOVE The *Dunotar Castle*, on which Churchill sailed for South Africa on 14 October 1899.

LEFT General Sir Redvers Buller.

Estcourt in 1899.

Estcourt station, where Churchill pitched his tent.

Churchill in South Africa, by Mortimer Menpes.

ABOVE Churchill with Colonel
Julian Byng, commander of the
South African Light Horse.

RIGHT Captain Aylmer Haldane.

'Hairy Mary', the armoured train, with driver Wagner (*right*).

LEFT The Boer commander General Louis Botha, later reputed to have personally captured Churchill.

BELOW Daniel Swanepoel (*right*), who guarded Churchill on the train to Pretoria.

OPPOSITE
LEFT The armoured train approaching Blaaw Kranz bridge.

RIGHT Driver Wagner (*with bandaged head*) and Second Engineer Stewart, photographed shortly after the action.

Churchill *(right)* with other prisoners of war on arrival at Pretoria.

The States Model School at the time of Churchill's imprisonment.

the present-day, now crowding in on all sides, was in 1899 a residential area of scattered houses, bungalows, spacious gardens and willow trees. The ten sentries patrolling the railings and fence were the only outward evidence that the building housed some sixty officer prisoners of war and their dozen soldier-servants.

Inside the building, the twelve classrooms on either side of a long corridor had been turned into dormitories, while four large rooms, two at each end of the school, were used for dining and recreation. Churchill shared a dormitory with Haldane and four other officers. Later Haldane and two companions would make a trapdoor in the floorboards and a tunnel in which to hide; they emerged to escape when the building was vacated and the prisoners were moved to other accommodation. The trapdoor is preserved to this day, thus identifying Churchill's room at the front of the building, facing Van der Walt Street. When the weather became oppressively hot he often slept on the verandah, separated only by the iron railings from curious passers-by and freedom beyond.

The prisoners' rations were adequate, but alcohol was forbidden until a week after Churchill's arrival, when the authorities rescinded this prohibition and allowed the purchase of bottled beer. This, and food to alleviate the monotony of the rations, could be obtained from a local dealer, Mr Boshof. It soon became apparent that, for a price, he could provide almost anything short of weapons, and a postscript to Churchill's first letter to his mother, written the day he arrived in Pretoria, showed he was already alert to the possibilities: 'Cox's [Cox & King's, his bank] should be instructed to cash any cheques I may draw.'

One unusual concession was the issue of a civilian suit to each officer. As they were all of a similar cut, and were in a mustard colour, they would have instantly identified an escaped prisoner. No one seemed to suspect anything when Churchill bought a suit of dark tweed, but when he requested a slouch hat he was told he would have to make do with one of the many available pith helmets if he wanted protection from the sun while walking in the compound.

The prison regulations were decided by a four-man board of

management chaired by the Transvaal Secretary of State for War, Louis de Souza, whom Churchill described as 'a far seeing little man who had travelled to Europe, and had a very clear conception of the relative strengths of Britain and the Transvaal'. Churchill also took a liking to two of the other board members, Commandant Opperman, 'an honest and patriotic Boer', and Dr Gunning, 'an amiable little Hollander'. The fourth, though, was 'a foul and objectionable brute . . . better suited to insulting the prisoners in Pretoria than fighting the enemy at the front'. This was Field Cornet Malan, whose rank had been acquired because he was the grandson of President Kruger, and whose reputation was as low with many of the Boers as it was with the prisoners. 'He is no man but a brute,' is just one of the heartfelt entries about him in the diary written meticulously in English by de Souza's wife Marie. Malan's notoriety earned him exile to Ceylon when he was captured by the British in August 1901.

The prisoners of war were permitted unhindered communication with the outside world, and Churchill provided regular contributions to the *Morning Post*, and sent letters whenever he wished. Even Haldane's official report to the British Army on the armoured train ambush was dispatched from the prison.

A glimpse of the living conditions within the States Model School has been provided by one of Churchill's fellow prisoners, Adrian Hofmeyr. His book *The Story of My Captivity* contains a sketch of the prison space he had made his own. The caption describes it: 'My little corner in the Staats Model School – eight feet by six feet – in a room occupied by eight officers. Kaffir blankets make a good tablecloth and carpet, and an umbrella stand upside down a bookcase. The table I bought, and flowers my sister sent me.' Hofmeyr was a pastor of Dutch extraction, a colonial-born Afrikaner who had remained loyal to the Queen, and who had urged both sides to compromise rather than go to war. He was well liked by the British officers, his evening services being far more popular than those of the vicar of Pretoria's St Alban's Cathedral, the Reverend Godfray, whom Churchill thought 'rather a poor creature'.

That the prison regime was not at all arduous is further apparent from a journal kept by Lieutenant Frankland, but relaxed though it might seem, it did not suit Churchill. Years later, in *My Early Life*, he chose the heading 'In Durance Vile' for the chapter which dealt with his time in the States Model School. He did not intend to remain a prisoner of war for long. Initially he hoped that the Boers would soon let him go as a non-combatant, and his first letter to his mother emphasised his expectation of an early release: 'I do not imagine they will keep me. They have always treated Press Correspondents well and after Majuba Hill the Morning Post correspondent was released after a few days detention.' To Pamela Plowden he wrote: 'I expect to be released as I was taken quite unarmed and with my full credentials as a correspondent.' By writing in this vein he hoped, through the censor who would read his letters before dispatch, to downplay his role during the ambush and to invoke a precedent for the release of a correspondent.

If the Boers would not let him go, escape was the only acceptable alternative. On the same day that he wrote to Lady Randolph and Pamela, 18 November, he also began a disingenuous correspondence with Louis de Souza, in which, by concentrating the minds of the Boer authorities on the arguments for his release, he intended to divert them from any thought that he might attempt to escape.

Over the next three weeks he was to write a further three letters to de Souza, to one of which was appended a note from Haldane certifying that: 'Mr Winston Churchill, Correspondent of the *Morning Post* accompanied the armoured train on the 15th November as a non-combatant, unarmed and took no part in the defence of the train.' Unquestionably Churchill was a non-combatant. His action in clearing the line was not concerned with the defence of the train, but with the rescue of wounded men. What he did was not incompatible with the status of a non-combatant, although the Boers could be excused for thinking otherwise in view of the number of men who escaped on the engine. Churchill was, however, carrying a pistol. But as, on the veldt, a pistol could be no more than a means of self-defence, and as Churchill had discarded it as an encumbrance, Haldane felt justified in saying he was unarmed.

Once again, Churchill was fortunate that he had inadvertently left his pistol in the cab of the engine.

On his first afternoon in the States Model School Churchill attempted to send his first dispatch as a prisoner to the *Morning Post*. Written cryptically, in telegraphic style on pages torn from a child's exercise book, his original words were amended in places to make them more acceptable to the Boer authorities. He described the armoured train action and his discussions with his Boer guards during the march into captivity. He wrote that he admired the 'skilful pious soldiers' – then deleted the word 'soldiers' and substituted 'burghers'. He offered his readers his assessment of Boer attitudes, and urged that 'Boer prisoners should be shown all consideration.'

Commandant Opperman, who acted as censor, at first declined to dispatch the telegram. His reasons, given in writing, were that it demonstrated Churchill's 'persistent jingoistic attitudes' and might encourage Britain to send out more troops. However, within a few days he relented, and Churchill was given a free rein to write whatever he wished. Between 20 and 30 November he composed three dispatches, running to a total of ten thousand words and covering in great detail all the subjects which had caused his original telegram to be withheld.

Recalling the thoughts, provoked by his contact with the soldiers on his arrival in Pretoria, about how an uprising might be organised, Churchill urged Haldane to become involved in an audacious scheme to seize Pretoria. Its outline was formulated soon after their arrival, and for days the younger officers plotted the details. Of the guards, forty middle-aged Zarps, only ten were on duty at any one time. At night the remainder were in a marquee, most of them rolled up in their blankets. Those awaiting their turn as sentries relaxed, without their boots and belts. Rifles not in use were hung

opposite Draft dispatch written by Churchill in the States Model School on 22 November 1899 and discovered in the Orange Free State by Miss Netta Levine, who sent it to Churchill in 1912. It appears to be an earlier draft of his dispatch of 30 November, and was presumably left in the States Model School when he escaped. (*Brenthurst Library, Johannesburg*)

WITH HEADQUARTERS
IX.
In the Boer Camp.

Pretoria 22ⁿᵈ Nov. 1899

At five o'clock the next morning our captors bade us rise and continue the march, and by a quarter to six having drunk a little water and chewed such pieces of meat as had been saved from the previous night, we were on our way. The road led across the footbridge of the Tugela and then twisted into the hills behind Colenso. We trudged forward painfully - for all were stiff with yesterday's both and walking - for five hours. Occasionally parties of Boers met the column of prisoners galloping up to & and greeting us with much hand shaking and professions of delight. Sometimes we forded rivers, hopping from one stone to the other across the smaller, wading through the larger. Once we came upon an ambulance camp - a little hospital with a Red cross flag tucked away quietly nestling in the green hollow, and here they lent us a cup to drink water out of. It was nearly eleven o'clock before we halted at one of the pickets in the line of investment round Ladysmith. Nearly a hundred Boers gathered about us and in the shade of the trees were tents and other shelters. A sack of broken biscuits was given to the soldiers and the field cornet who had charge of the escort presented the officers with two small tins of bully beef. He apologised for the hardships the prisoners were put to, saying through an interpreter - for he was a true Dutchman - that until we reached the waggon trains there was scarcely any commissariat arrangement. We replied that it was war and it was well and thanked him for his courtesy and then - feeling like the whipped dog grateful for any bone - began to eat.

The Boers of the picket sat round us in a

around the tent poles in improvised racks. The lighting of the entire compound depended upon wires which passed through the officers' dormitories, and a simple disconnection would plunge everything into darkness. There seemed a good chance that sixty resolute officers could seize control of the States Model School.

The next step would be to overcome the guards at the enclosed camp on the racecourse, where two thousand British soldiers were guarded by 120 Zarps with two machine guns. Having freed the soldiers and seized the Zarps' weapons it would be a simple matter to overcome the town guard, which consisted of fewer than five hundred burghers, all of them deemed unfit for the front. President Kruger would then be a prisoner in his own capital.

In Haldane's own words, 'blessed with less imagination than Churchill the idea savoured of the fantastic', and he and the other senior officers summarily vetoed the plan. Years later, with no less imagination but with infinitely more experience, Churchill wrote: 'One is reminded of the comic opera. The villain impressively announces, "Twelve thousand armed muleteers are ready to sack the town." "Why don't they do it?" he is asked. "The police won't let them." Yes, there was the rub. Ten men awake and armed may be a small obstacle to a great scheme, but in this case, as in so many others, they were decisive.'

For the moment, while Churchill developed other plans, he continued to press his claims for release as an unarmed correspondent. There had already been a flurry of communications between various Boer authorities. On 19 November General Joubert, the senior Boer commander, urged the Transvaal State Secretary, F.W. Reitz, that 'the son of Lord Churchill ... must be guarded and watched as dangerous for our war; otherwise he can still do us a lot of harm. In one word, he must not be released during the war. It is through his active part that one section of the armoured train got away.' Captain Daniel Theron, the officer who identified Field Cornet Oosthuizen as Churchill's captor, wrote to Reitz, 'In my view Churchill is one of the most dangerous prisoners in our hands.'

In seeking his release Churchill went as far as offering 'to give any *parole* the Transvaal Government may require *viz* either to

File cover from Louis de Souza's office at the States Model School. The heading refers to a telegram from General Joubert giving his opinion that 'the son of Lord Churchill . . . must not be released during the war'.
(*National Archives Repository, Pretoria*)

continue to observe noncombatant character or to withdraw altogether from South Africa'. Within three days Joubert ordered that Churchill must 'if necessary be even more strictly guarded' than other prisoners, while Reitz had confirmed that 'The Government does not intend to release Mr Churchill.'

With time on his hands, Churchill marked his twenty-fifth birthday, 30 November, with two long letters. Over a thousand words went to Edward, Prince of Wales, and almost as many to Churchill's American friend Senator Bourke Cockran. To the Prince of Wales he wrote that the main object of his letter was to recommend the armoured train driver, Charles Wagner, for a gallantry award. However, it was a skilfully written letter with several motives in mind, and in describing the ambush Churchill emphasised the non-combatant aspects of his actions. This was for the benefit of the Boer censor, who, it was intended, would also be struck by the writer's regard for Boer 'courtesy, courage and humanity', and his praise for 'a great concession which we owe to Dr Gunning' of the prison board of management, who had allowed the officers to become members of the state library.

Churchill's high opinion of the Natal colonists, in particular of the volunteers who had taken up arms on behalf of the Crown, had been reinforced by the actions of the civilian railway employees on the train. In the hope of influencing opinion in London, a few words were slipped in to commend the 'splendid devotion' of these loyal citizens and to hope that they would not be forgotten 'when the time comes to heal the wounds of war and crown its heroes'.

Finally, the letter turned to Churchill's recent book on the Sudan campaign. Sensitive to the Prince of Wales's view that young officers should not engage in contentious discussion involving senior members of the army's hierarchy and military strategy, he wrote: 'I hope your Royal Highness was interested in my new book *The River War* and did not think any of my criticisms improper or unjust. When I wrote it I was not a soldier.'

The letter to Bourke Cockran was in a more philosophical vein. Churchill ranged across imperial power, freedom, economics and religion before touching on his unjust detention and ending with the despairing cry: 'I am 25 today – it is terrible to think how little time remains.'

Walking around the States Model School, I began to wonder how such a restless character as my grandfather occupied his time during the twenty-five days the Boers managed to hold him. Other prisoners played games and exercised in the makeshift gymnasium. These were diversions in which Churchill, for whom exercise and sport involved being on horseback, was little interested. He wrote letters and continued his dispatches to the *Morning Post*, but, given his facility and speed with a pen, there would still have been many hours to fill. As I delved into his life as a prisoner of war I met and heard from a number of people who enabled me to form a better picture of the incarcerated Churchill.

I knew from his own account that the troublesome prisoner was often visited by the Transvaal Secretary of State for War, Louis de Souza, whom Churchill described as 'a kind hearted Portuguese'. As I trawled through the de Souza papers, meticulously preserved by his grandson Jonathan de Souza, it became clear that an affinity developed between the two men. Marie de Souza's detailed diary comments on Churchill's dispatches and records her husband's visits to see him. On 21 November she wrote: 'I read some of the letters which Winston Churchill had written for the Morning Post. They are very good. I feel wild about his treatment.' And on 3 December: 'Louis took the officers some fruit!!!' Jonathan de Souza explained to me that the exclamation marks indicated that concealed in the basket beneath the ripe South African fruit was a bottle of whisky. At other times the bottle was concealed in the tail pocket of de Souza's coat.

Churchill passed some of the time reciting poetry with James Gage Hyde, a civilian prisoner who occupied the adjacent room. Interestingly, Hyde was the son of George Clarence Hyde, who during the Zulu War had treated the wounded after the battle of Rorke's Drift in 1879. This certainly would have appealed to the romantic nature of his fellow prisoner, who had heard about this episode in 1880, as a five-year-old. His nanny Mrs Everest's brother-in-law, a warder at Parkhurst jail, remembered the young Churchill as an eager participant in discussions about the graphic newspaper accounts of the war, which had captured the boy's imagination.

James Gage Hyde's daughter, Mrs Molly Pringle, told me that her father had owned a farm at the foot of a hill called Tchrengula (translated: 'hang out the clothes'), on which the Irish Fusiliers were entrenched to protect the flank of a larger British force. In the battle of Nicholson's Nek on 30 October 1899, Hyde had joined in with the Fusiliers and, having been taken prisoner in the rout which followed, he was taken to the States Model School. Here he met Churchill, who, he told his daughter, was 'a cocksure little devil'.

Churchill had demonstrated his prodigious memory at Harrow, where, as a new boy in the bottom form, he had beaten the entire school in a competition by reciting twelve hundred lines of Macaulay's *Lays of Ancient Rome* without a single mistake. In James Gage Hyde he found a companion who also had a love of poetry and a good memory. 'Together,' Molly Pringle's father had told her, 'we recited Longfellow, Shakespeare and Macaulay. Churchill knew a lot of Macaulay. We recited poetry not only for its own sake, but also to confuse the guards. We took great pleasure in their bewilderment. They could not understand what we were saying, and called us the "daft English".'

In talking of the prisoners' life within the school, Hyde had described a lax regime: 'Boer women came into the prison and exchanged fruit and vegetables for our tobacco rations.' Nevertheless, with armed guards all around, he thought it would be dangerous to attempt an escape. But, he said, 'As often as I warned Churchill of the dangers, he dismissed them. He had a sublime certainty that he would overcome whatever dangers he encountered. Although we were much of the same age, I felt, because of his impetuous nature, I should advise him in a fatherly manner, but my advice was always brushed off.'

Hanging on the walls of what had been Churchill's dormitory, now preserved under glass, are coloured campaign maps. The cartographer, encouraged by Churchill, had been Lieutenant Thomas

Frankland. Under Churchill's eager eye these maps were maintained in order that the inmates could follow the course of the war. How, I wondered, was the necessary information obtained? Haldane noted that Churchill 'received many visitors with whom animated discussions on the all-absorbing topic of the war were engaged in'. Churchill wrote that he 'received them sitting on my bed in the dormitory, and when they had lighted cigars, of which I always kept a stock, we had a regular "durbar" '. These visitors, who included the Transvaal Under-Secretary for Foreign Affairs Mr Grobelaar, the American Consul Mr Macrum and Reuters agent Mr Mackay, were no doubt the main sources of information; but it was two other legends which interested me most.

The first was of the Englishman who worked at the Pretoria post office, and used semaphore to signal from his house to the imprisoned officers in the school, which was just across the street. They would be alerted to look out by his granddaughter who, as if by accident, would bounce her ball over the railings, where an officer would retrieve it and return it to her. For fear of reprisals, the child's father was said, on his deathbed, to have asked that the family name should never be revealed. The second concerned a man, mentioned by Haldane, who regularly walked his dog past the school and passed information to the officers. Now, so long after the events, there could be no fear attached to identifying these men, and I appealed to any descendants to provide names to go with these stories.

The story which emerged contained elements of both legends. It was given to me by William Atteridge, who had heard it from his uncle Richard Xavier Atteridge. The latter had emigrated from Newcastle upon Tyne to South Africa, where had become a naturalised burgher, and had worked as a telegraphist in the Pretoria post office. On the outbreak of war he had been called up, but, unwilling to fight against his former countrymen, had fled to Natal. On his return after the war he learned that a friend of his in the post office, a Mr Patterson, had passed information to the British officers in the school when he walked his dog past the railings. If guards were within earshot, he had patted the dog's head in Morse code. For fear of his being branded a traitor by his colleagues, Patterson's family and Atteridge were for ever sworn to secrecy.

One evening, as Churchill stood taking the air on the Van der Walt Street side of the school, the whispered message from Patterson was that General Methuen, who was intent on relieving the beleaguered British garrison at Kimberley, had defeated the Boers at Belmont, sixty miles south of the besieged town On Frankland's maps the red and green patches which represented the opposing forces were adjusted to take account of the good news. To Churchill there now seemed but one obstacle, the River Modder, between Methuen and his objective. Churchill felt confident that the siege of Kimberley would soon be lifted, and took delight in forecasting this when Louis de Souza came visiting the following day.

'Who can tell?' shrugged de Souza. He put his finger on the map. 'There stands old Piet Cronje. We don't think Methuen will get past him.' Events would prove de Souza right. He was indicating the position of Magersfontein Hill, a significant tactical feature to which the amateur cartographers had paid insufficient attention.

When it was rumoured that there was to be an exchange of prisoners of war, Churchill attempted to make the most of the Transvaal government's unwillingness to recognise him as a press correspondent. He wrote at once to the British Military Secretary in South Africa, Colonel Stopford: 'Unless I am regarded for the purpose of exchange as a military officer, I am likely to fall between two stools. Pray do your best for me.' By the time Stopford received the letter he was able to reply: 'I am glad you do not need my help, wh I would have gladly given.' Churchill had by then escaped, and was back with the British Army.

The escape was originally planned by Captain Haldane, in conjunction with Regimental Sergeant-Major Brockie of the Imperial Light Horse. Brockie had joined Churchill and Haldane on their way to Pretoria, having been taken prisoner while on patrol, and had passed himself off as a lieutenant in order to get better quarters. Haldane thought him essential to any escape plan, as he spoke Afrikaans, Dutch and the local dialect.

On 1 December Haldane told Churchill about their escape plan, and eight days later, having given up any hope of early release, Churchill asked to join it. Haldane and Brockie were reluctant to accept him, as they thought that his presence would jeopardise their chances of getting clean away. By far the most prominent prisoner, Churchill would be missed within a few hours, while, because there was no regular roll-call, Haldane and Brockie's absence might go unnoticed for much longer. They also thought, with some justification, that Churchill was less agile than they were, and that any difficulty he might have in scaling the prison fence could attract a sentry's attention.

Under pressure, Haldane relented. He said he could not, in the face of Brockie's opposition, actually invite Churchill to join them. However, he could hardly refuse his request, considering Churchill's conduct during the ambush and his selflessness in not escaping with those he sent back on the engine. Having left the decision to Churchill, Haldane could not have been surprised when he chose to participate. Six months later, Haldane summed up the situation: 'He suggested coming with us. We consented, though the certainty he would be missed lessened the chances of success.' However, Haldane did not give Churchill any details of the planned escape route to Portuguese East Africa. He would be expected to conform to Haldane's orders.

The escape was to be made from a circular-shaped latrine situated against the iron fence at the back of the school. The lighting left this spot in relative darkness, and only one sentry was in a position from which he could see anyone climbing the fence. There was a good chance of escape without detection during dinner, as it seemed to be the custom that at that hour the sentry moved along the enclosure to chat with another guard.

On 7 December, shortly before the planned escape, two soldier-servants, Privates Cahill and Bridge, successfully climbed the school fence, but were caught on the outskirts of Pretoria. Their escape was not reported to the prison authorities, who remained unaware of the event. The fact that Cahill and Bridge had got away encouraged Haldane to believe that their scheme would work, but the possibility that the incident might lead to the prison regime being tightened up added urgency to the plans now afoot.

Even as he was about to escape, Churchill was still pleading his case with the Boer authorities for his release as a non-combatant. In a letter to de Souza which he asked should be forwarded to General Joubert, Churchill offered to give 'any parole that may be required not to serve against Republican forces or to give any information affecting the military situation'. The letter was intended to serve two purposes: should escape prove impossible, the plea for release might bear fruit; meanwhile, its tone would allay any suspicion that he was about to attempt to flee.

The letter would have arrived on Joubert's desk soon after he had telegraphed the authorities in Pretoria about the proposed exchange of prisoners which had prompted Churchill to write to Colonel Stopford. Joubert's telegram of 10 December had agreed to an exchange, but resolutely declined to include Churchill or any of the officers captured on the armoured train. Even as Churchill's letter was causing Joubert to have second thoughts, its writer was testing the prison's perimeter.

During the evening of 11 December Haldane and Churchill strolled separately to the latrine. Brockie, carrying maps and compass, was to follow. Churchill had left a cheeky letter to Louis de Souza on his pillow. To throw the authorities off the scent, he implied that the escape was made with the help of outside assistance.

> I do not consider that your Government was justified in holding me ... and I have consequently resolved to escape. The arrangements I have succeeded in making in conjunction with my friends outside are such as give me every confidence. But I wish in leaving you thus hastily & unceremoniously to once more place on record my appreciation of the kindness which has been shown me and the other prisoners by you, by the Commandant and by Dr. Gunning and my admiration of the chivalrous and humane character of the Republican forces. My views on the general question of the war remain unchanged, but I shall always retain a feeling of high respect for the several classes of the burghers I have met and, on reaching the British lines I will set forth a truthful & impartial account of my

experiences in Pretoria. In conclusion I desire to express my obligations to you, and to hope that when this most grievous and unhappy war shall have come to an end, a state of affairs may be created which shall preserve at once the national pride of the Boers and the security of the British and put a final stop to the rivalry & enmity of both races. Regretting that circumstances have not permitted me to bid you a personal farewell, Believe me

> Yours vy sincerely
>
> Winston S. Churchill

As a touch of humour, he had written the letters 'p.p.c.' (*pour prendre congé* – to take my leave) on the envelope. Unfortunately, the letter had to be retrieved, as that evening the sentry refused to budge from the very spot over which Churchill and Haldane intended to climb. They postponed their attempt for twenty-four hours.

The next day, 12 December, General Joubert telegraphed Reitz, the State Secretary, withdrawing his objections to Churchill's release. He had wearied of discussing the pros and cons of holding or setting free this troublesome prisoner, and had noted Churchill's promise that if released he would not serve against the Boers. Although he remained sceptical, he had taken at face value Churchill's hints that, having been well treated, his dispatches would scarcely be to the Boers' disadvantage. Joubert's lengthy telegram balanced Churchill's protestations that he was a non-combatant against his exploits, which had been fulsomely reported in the world press. It concluded: 'if I accept his word, then my objections to his release cease . . . I have no further objections to his being set free, without our accepting somebody in exchange. P.J. Joubert, Commandant. P.S. Will he tell the truth? He will also be a chip off the old block.' The postscript was a reference to Lord Randolph's criticism of the Boer administration when he had visited the Transvaal in 1891.

Joubert had dithered too long, and his telegram had yet to reach the authorities in Pretoria when Churchill once more placed his letter to de Souza on his pillow and together with Haldane made a second attempt to escape. Once again, though, they judged the circumstances too hazardous. The sentry remained in a position

State Schools Prison
Pretoria.

Dear Mr. deSouza,

I do not consider that your Government was justified in holding me, a press correspondent and a non combatant as a prisoner, and I have consequently resolved to escape. The arrangements I have succeeded in making in conjunction with my friends outside are such as give me every confidence. But I wish in leaving you thus hastily & unceremoniously to once more place on record my appreciation of the kindness which has been shown me and the other prisoners by you, by the commandant and by Dr. Gunning and my admiration of the chivalrous and humane character of the Republican forces. My views on the general question of the war remain unchanged, but I shall always retain a feeling of high respect for the several classes of the burghers I have met and, on reaching the British lines I will set forth a truthful & impartial account of my experiences in Pretoria. In conclusion I desire to express my obligations to you, and to hope that when this most grievous and unhappy war shall have come to an end, a state of affairs may be created which shall preserve at once the national pride of the Boers and the security of the British and put a final stop to the rivalry & enmity of both races. Regretting that circumstances have not permitted me to bid you a personal farewell, Believe me

Yours vy sincerely

Winston S. Churchill.

Dec. 11th 1899

from which it was likely he would see them climbing the fence, and if he opened fire he could hardly miss at such short range. They returned to the verandah, and Haldane explained the situation to Brockie, who replied, 'You're afraid.'

'See for yourself,' said Haldane, whereupon Brockie walked across the yard to the latrine. When, after some time, he had not returned, Churchill went in search of him. He found him at the latrine entrance, about to make his way back. When Brockie reached the waiting Haldane he angrily reported, 'That damned fool Churchill wanted to stop and talk in earshot of the sentry. I told him it was useless to try to escape then.'

Churchill could see another night being wasted. Determined to clinch the matter once and for all, he waited in the latrine until the sentry turned away, then scrambled over the fence, only for his waistcoat to become entangled with the ornamental metalwork. He glanced at the sentry, who was now cupping his hands to light a cigarette, tore his clothes free and lowered himself to the ground. There, among a few shrubs in the garden of an adjoining house, he awaited Haldane and Brockie. It was a quarter past seven.

Time passed. At a quarter to eight the moon rose. Churchill was still crouched in the deep shadows, anxious and impatient to know what the other two intended. A man came out of the house and stood within a few yards of him, then a companion joined him and lit a cigar, before they both moved off together. They stopped when a cat, being chased by a dog, let out a screech of alarm on colliding with the crouching Churchill. Having seen the cat emerge from the shrubs, with the dog still in pursuit, the men walked through the gate and on into the street.

There are inconsistencies in the details of the various accounts of what happened during the time Churchill was hiding in the shrubs. In his dispatch to the *Morning Post* he mentioned two British officers who came to the fence an hour after he had clambered over it and, amid a jabber of nonsense in Latin, mentioned his name.

OPPOSITE Letter written to Louis de Souza by Churchill prior to his escape.
(*Hugh de Souza*)

He risked a cough, and having established contact, learned that Haldane and Brockie could not escape. He explained that he could not get back over the fence, and would therefore go on alone. In *My Early Life* he gave much the same version.

He wrote a more detailed account in 1912 in connection with a libel action against *Blackwood's Magazine*, which had alleged that in escaping alone Churchill had abandoned his friends. This account, presumably written for the benefit of his lawyers, was never published. In it he wrote that he waited in the garden for more than an hour and a half for Haldane and Brockie to join him, and that fifteen minutes after he had got over the fence he had attracted the attention of a prisoner and asked that they should be told to follow as soon as possible. The two came to the fence, but as Haldane attempted to scale it he was challenged by a sentry, and returned to the main building. Churchill put this at about half an hour after he had climbed over. He continued to wait, and at length heard tapping on the other side of the fence. Going close to it, he spoke with Haldane, who said there could be no further attempt that night, and that Churchill should go on alone. Haldane's version, written in 1935, does not differ materially from this account. It merely adds that, having made a further unsuccessful attempt to scale the fence undetected, he offered to throw Churchill the maps and the compass, but that he declined for fear that the noise would alert the nearby sentry.

Putting all versions together and accepting the common elements, it is clear that after Churchill had scrambled over the fence Haldane and Brockie, unaware of his success, had gone to supper. They subsequently returned, and when they were prevented by a sentry from escaping, Haldane agreed that the only course was for Churchill to go on alone.

Churchill put on a slouch hat he had acquired from Adrian Hofmeyr and had adorned at the last moment with a puggaree of the Transvaal colours. He walked casually through the garden, passing within five yards of the sentry, and out into the street. There were plenty of people about at that hour, but none paid any attention to the man humming a tune as he walked down the centre of Skinner Street.

NINE

Controversy

'My conscience is perfectly clear on the whole episode; I acted with perfect comradeship and honour the whole way through.'
WINSTON CHURCHILL, quoted in Randolph S. Churchill,
Winston S. Churchill, VOLUME I

THE DAILY ENTRIES IN Adrian Hofmeyr's diary describe the boring nature of life for the prisoners in the States Model School. But in the entry for 13 December 1899, the tenor changes abruptly: 'Great excitement. Churchill escaped last night.' Hofmeyr's *The Story of My Captivity* describes the consternation caused by Churchill's disappearance: 'Yes it was a great to-do: it stopped the whole machinery of state. It paralysed the officials. It seemed to me that even the war was forgotten.'

Marie de Souza's diary also reflected the mood in Pretoria: 'Wednesday 13th. An exciting day! Mr Churchill escaped last night & it was only discovered at 10.30am! He must have bribed the guards who are policemen! There are 18 around the building . . . I am afraid of the consequences which may fall on the other prisoners.'

After Churchill had gone, Haldane and others had made up his bed so that it appeared to be occupied. So effective was the deception that early on the morning of the thirteenth a soldier-servant, failing with a discreet cough to wake the sleeper, left the usual early-morning cup of coffee on a chair beside the bed.

* * *

I discussed Churchill's escape with Herman van Cittert, the son of Johannes van Cittert, who had been a seventeen-year-old guard at the States Model School. The young Boer had thought Churchill 'a cheeky man who was very upset at finding himself a prisoner. He was a stroppy sort of fellow who was always causing a fuss.' Of the actual escape, Johannes van Cittert had said, 'As I recall it, he went to the lavatory and didn't come back.' He went on to describe the confusion that ensued the following morning: 'The discovery that Churchill was missing might have been long delayed had Henri Adelaar, the barber, not called. He was to shave Churchill and collect fifteen cents owed for a shave and haircut the previous day. Escorted by a policeman, he received no answer to his knock on Churchill's door. He then dashed about the building, asking if anyone had seen his customer. The other prisoners were not very helpful, directing the barber to the most unlikely places. Eventually the policeman realised the prisoner was missing.'

The barber had lost his money, and the gaolers had lost their most important prisoner. Consternation now turned to panic. The odious Field Cornet Malan stormed about the building telling the trembling guards that General Joubert would hang them if they could not produce Churchill. A thorough search of the school and its grounds produced nothing more than the missing prisoner's letter to de Souza. At 9.30 Commandant Opperman ordered a roll-call, which finally confirmed that Churchill had indeed flown.

For the moment the Boers could only guess at the manner of his escape. Among the rumours was one that he had been disguised as a woman, and at first the authorities, like Marie de Souza, suspected either complicity or slackness among the sentries. Opperman's handwritten report to de Souza concluded: 'In my view the only way he could have escaped was by bribing one or more of the guards, because the guards were so placed that it would have been impossible for him to escape without their knowledge.'

One sentry, Stephan Schotel, who had been on duty at the time of the escape, was to harbour a resentment of Churchill all his life. His only consolation, he later told his wife, was the humiliating way in which he believed Churchill had got away – by horse cart, hidden in one of the containers used for emptying the latrines. Was Schotel, I wonder, the guard who, turning away to light his cigarette, gave Churchill the few seconds he needed to scramble over the fence? Standing so close to the latrine, he would not have believed that a prisoner could have eluded him. His version of events persists in his family to this day.

In fact, Opperman's report was passing the buck: in a properly run prison, the escape by Privates Cahill and Bridge five days before Churchill's would have alerted him to the loopholes in his regime. Churchill, though, could afford to take a lenient view of the sloppy discipline. On reaching safety he telegraphed de Souza: 'Escape not due to any fault of your guards.'

The misleading reference in Churchill's letter to 'the arrangements I have succeeded in making in conjunction with my friends outside' had its intended effect. The Boers, assuming there were accomplices at large in Pretoria, wasted considerable time and effort searching the houses of possible suspects. The Pretoria magistrate's search warrant revealed their belief that Churchill was hidden in 'a certain house in this town inhabited by certain parties, to be pointed out by Detective Donovan'. Donovan must have worked by trial and error rather than on any actual information, for a great many houses were searched – including that of Dr Gunning, the Deputy Commandant at the States Model School, who came under suspicion because he had an English wife.

The Reverend Godfray gave up his Sunday services at the school, worried lest he be suspected of complicity in the escape. (Later, when Pretoria was occupied by the British, Godfray would claim to have assisted Churchill's flight. Haldane poured scorn on this claim, as Godfray was not much regarded by the British officers, and was invariably accompanied by the commandant throughout his visits. Churchill also denied it in a letter dated 30 November 1900 to Godfray's niece, Miss Haccquoil, who had written to him about her uncle's story.)

The government's annoyance at the escape of their important prisoner just as they were about to let him go was reflected in its

The handwritten 'wanted' poster.

erratic response. A number of English living in Pretoria, including a nurse from the hospital adjacent to the States Model School, were evicted from the Transvaal, and several policemen suspected of complicity were sent to the front. One girl who had smiled at the prisoners on the other side of the railings was fined £25, while another was accused of distracting the guards by dropping a ring. Marie de Souza's diary records: 'Saturday 16th. Churchill's flight has caused all this unpleasantness – houses searched and girls arrested for writing love letters. It is cruel!'

The initial description issued by the authorities on 13 December described Churchill as: 'About 5ft 8in or 9in, blond with light thin moustache, walks with slight stoop, cannot speak any Dutch, during long conversation he occasionally makes a rattling noise in his throat.' On the eighteenth a handwritten poster offering £25 for his recapture 'dead or alive' was posted at Government House, Pretoria. It was accompanied by a photograph 'taken most probably about 18 months ago', and a more complete, if unflattering, description:

> Englishman, 25 years of age, about 5 feet 8 inches in height, medium build, stooping gait, fair complexion, reddish brown hair, almost invisible moustache, speaks through his nose, cannot give full expression to the letter 's', and does not know a word of Dutch. Wore a suit of brown clothes, but not uniform – an ordinary suit of clothes.

The poster was issued by an official named Lodk de Haas, a volunteer from Europe in the Hollander Corps who was the secretary in the Commission of Peace and Order, which was responsibility for security in Pretoria. He later confided in a South African diplomat he met in Belgium, Ambassador du Buisson, that he had been sufficiently concerned by Churchill's escape to put up the reward money personally. In 1908 Churchill and de Haas were to correspond personally about the poster. Churchill, while thanking de Haas for his good wishes on the occasion of his marriage, added: 'I think you might have gone as high as £50 without an overestimate of the value of the prize – if living.'

Some doubt has been cast on the authenticity of the handwritten poster. This seems to have arisen as a result of the appearance of bogus printed posters which purported to be original reward notices and which included a translation into English – in a typeface which was not designed until 1928. There can, however, be no doubt that the poster issued by de Haas was handwritten, in Dutch. In a letter dated 13 December 1944 to Mrs Kathleen Hill, Churchill's personal private secretary, de Haas wrote: 'I enclose a photo of the

proclamation written and signed by me during the Boer War offering £25 for the escaped Prisoner of War Churchill, dead or alive.'
Soon after this de Haas visited No 10 Downing Street, following
which, on 27 December 1944, he again wrote to Mrs Hill, drawing
attention to an error in the English translation on the false poster,
a copy of which had been reproduced in *My Early Life*: 'The correct
English rendering is not "on behalf of the Special Constable to
anyone" but "to the Special Constable who . . ." In other words
my offer was made to the police and not to the general public.'

Rumours soon began to circulate of Churchill's recapture, and a
number of suspects were actually apprehended, including a young
British soldier with a resemblance to Churchill who was captured
in the Eastern Transvaal and paraded before the authorities in
Pretoria.

As Marie de Souza had feared, measures were now taken by the
prison authorities to prevent further escapes. A twice-daily roll-call
was instituted; no visits were allowed to patients being treated in
Pretoria's hospital; prisoners were confined within the main school
building after 8.30 p.m.; and sleeping on the verandah was pro-
hibited. Additional measures, such as the prohibition of beer and
newspapers, were simply punitive, and were implemented with
delight by Field Cornet Malan, in response to public opinion in
Pretoria.

Within twenty-four hours of Churchill clambering over the iron
railings, a formal inquiry was convened under Advocate Schagen
van Leewen and H.W. Zeiler, a judicial commissioner. It achieved
no more than to show that discipline in the prison was extremely
lax. One of the guards, Corporal Scheepers, reported that a restless
Churchill would walk around the compound until three or four in
the morning. It was established that of the nine guards who should
have been on duty in and around the building when the escape
took place, only eight were in fact present. The sentry who might
have seen Churchill climbing the fence was missing. When the
guard changed at 8 p.m. the post was again occupied, but the sentry,
Jan Montgomery, noticed nothing unusual when Churchill passed

within five yards of him as he walked into Skinner Street. The only startling revelation made by the inquiry was the earlier escape of the two private soldiers, which the guards had thought inadvisable to report to their superiors.

The blustering Malan levelled the charge of breaking parole at Churchill, leading Adrian Hofmeyr to comment: 'A man gives his parole, and yet he is guarded by men armed to the teeth . . . some of these officials will do anything for a fig-leaf.' Shamefully, on 16 December, with motives it is hard to fathom, the *Daily Nation*, a Durban paper, sought to blacken Churchill's character: 'Mr Winston Churchill's escape is not regarded in military circles as either a brilliant or an honourable exploit. He was captured as a combatant, and, of course, placed under the same parole as the officers taken prisoner. He has, however, chosen to disregard an honourable undertaking, and it would not be surprising if the Pretoria authorities adopted more strenuous measures to prevent such conduct.' The piece was erroneous in all respects.

The allegation that Churchill broke his parole would prove impossible to scotch, in spite of various legal actions he would bring over the years to contest it. In some ways it is not surprising, for his trail of immense achievements, political and otherwise, would inevitably leave in its wake those who would jump at any chance to disparage him. The story was still being repeated as late as 1964, when, while taking part in a ninetieth-birthday television tribute to Churchill, the former Labour Home Secretary Herbert Morrison said: 'I think I remember his name in the Boer War where he was taken prisoner and then was put on parole and then broke his parole.' Lord Morrison, as he then was, subsequently apologised. It is probable that he did not appreciate the full implications of his words, having himself been a conscientious objector when of military age, and thus unaware of military traditions. Even while I was researching this book, an eminent British newspaper editor asked me how I would deal with 'the matter of Churchill breaking his parole and leaving his friends in the lurch'.

The question of parole is conclusively dealt with by reference to the Transvaal Archives Depot. As the correspondence between the

State Secretary of the Transvaal, F.W. Reitz, and General Joubert makes clear, the authorities were determined to guard Churchill at least as closely as the other prisoners. Then, when he had escaped, Joubert, furious that the man over whose release he had been dithering had made off of his own accord, did his best to malign the fugitive by implying he had broken his parole, suggesting to Reitz: 'I wonder whether it would not be a good thing to make public the correspondence about the release of Churchill to show the world what a scoundrel he is.' Reitz, knowing that Churchill had never in fact been offered parole, declined to publish any documents, as he knew that an attempt to defame Churchill by releasing the correspondence would be likely to backfire.

That Churchill had abandoned his friends was another myth connected with his escape which would provide fertile ground for those who sought to disparage him. The first shots came in 1900 from Lord Rosslyn, who had arrived in South Africa as a war correspondent at the beginning of that year, joined Thorneycroft's Mounted Infantry, was taken prisoner, escaped and then recaptured. In his book *Twice Captured* he wrote of Churchill: 'He was not a persona grata with his fellow prisoners, and, as far as I can ascertain did not play quite fairly with the others who concocted the plot but according to them followed the principles of *sauve qui peut* [every man for himself] rather than shoulder to shoulder.'

Churchill wrote to Haldane, who had himself escaped from the States Model School in March 1900, enclosing a copy of the offending page of Rosslyn's book, together with his recollection of what had actually occurred. Haldane's reply has been lost, but in 1935, amplifying his unpublished diary, wrote that Churchill's account 'threw quite an unexpected light on the matter, and I replied that I laid no blame on him for departing when he did'.

Churchill had no need to pursue the issue further, as William Blackwood & Sons, the publishers of *Twice Captured*, halted the distribution of the book, and agreed to delete the offending passage from future editions. Thus, the 'unexpected light' remained, for the moment, unexplored.

The matter was not dealt with entirely to Churchill's satisfaction,

Telegram from General Joubert to F.W. Reitz, the Transvaal State Secretary, suggesting: 'I wonder whether it would not be a good thing to make public the correspondence about the release of Churchill to show the world what a scoundrel he is.'
(*National Archives Repository, Pretoria*)

as copies of the book were already in circulation. However, he at least had the satisfaction of publicly humiliating Rosslyn when he spoke as guest of honour at the annual dinner of the Pall Mall Club on 25 October 1900. In addition to defaming Churchill, Rosslyn had cast serious aspersions on certain British regiments and commanders, and it was this which Churchill took as his cue as part of a wider-ranging speech. He began lightly: '"Twice Captured". That is a curious title; it is not a very difficult thing to be captured. [Laughter] A man might just as well call his book "Twice Bankrupt". [Laughter]' He ended this part of his speech: 'I think it intolerable that a person who, by his own fault or folly, has fallen in the mud, should endeavour to hide his own ignominy by splashing mud over other people.'

The story that Churchill had deserted his friends was again aired in 1907, in an attempt to discredit him when he was to speak in support of a Liberal candidate at a by-election. The allegation was made to Major Sandham Griffith, an acquaintance of Haldane's. Griffith thought this an unfair tactic, and even though he supported the Liberal's opponent, he wrote to Haldane asking him to send a telegram to the effect: '[I] contradict absolutely [the] statement that I ever said Churchill deserted me in Pretoria.' In his letter Griffith explained that 'this statement about cowardly desertion' came from a friend, who had been told it by 'a lady who said she heard it from you'. Haldane did as he was asked, with the result, as reported to him by Griffith, that the lady denied ever making the allegation. Haldane copied the exchange of letters to Churchill, saying: 'The enclosed correspondence may amuse you . . . I kept no copy of my reply to Griffith but it was in terms of [the] telegram he suggested I should send him.' Whatever his private feelings may have been, Haldane, to date, had supported Churchill whenever the allegations about his conduct during the escape were aired publicly.

His stance began to change in 1912 when Blackwood & Sons, in *Blackwood's Magazine*, again suggested that Churchill had not played fair with his fellow prisoners, and Churchill brought an action for libel against them. The hearing was scheduled for 20 May that year. According to his diary, Haldane, by 1912 a brigadier, was summoned to a meeting on 25 April by Churchill, then First Lord of the Admiralty, who wanted him to testify in his favour. The resulting discussion revealed that they had interpreted events differently. While Haldane had already declined Blackwood's request to give evidence against Churchill, he now also declined to testify in his favour in the detailed manner he wanted.

According to Haldane's note of their meeting, when he was asked to state that Churchill had behaved 'quite fairly and properly', he replied that, 'believing him to be a man of honour, I would be prepared to go into the witness box and depose that, having heard his statement which, however, differed from my own view, I would accept his word in the matter and assume he had escaped with no idea he was not behaving fairly to Brockie and myself.' Whereupon, in Haldane's words, Churchill 'assumed a browbeating air and said that if I would not give him support he would state in Court that Brockie and I had funked going'.

It is perfectly possible to imagine Churchill, seated in his imposing office, haranguing his visitor, who, being a long way below him in the military pecking order, wished to avoid a quarrel with someone who could do his career real harm. However, Haldane stuck to his guns. He took the view, he said, that Churchill should not have gone alone, and would not have words which suggested otherwise put into his mouth. If Churchill would send him his proposed statement, Haldane would inform him what he would be prepared to say.

In the event, Blackwood's chose not to defend the case. Haldane wrote to Churchill's friend and lawyer, F.E. Smith, three days before the date set for the hearing: 'I see by the papers, however, that the case is fixed for Monday next when it is impossible for me to be in London. As it is undefended I do not suppose my absence will make any difference to Churchill or you.'

From that moment Haldane seems to have developed an increasingly jaundiced view of Churchill's actions, and to have become considerably embittered against him. The publication in 1930 of Churchill's autobiography *My Early Life*, which gave his own heroic version of his escapades in South Africa, inevitably left the impression that on the occasions when Haldane and he acted in concert on the armoured train and in the prison escape, the soldier was eclipsed by the younger war correspondent. The fact that so were all the others who came within Churchill's orbit would have been little consolation to the man who retired in 1925, after a distinguished military career, as General Sir Aylmer Haldane.

In a letter in April 1931 to Lord Knutsford, a Conservative politician, Haldane wrote that *My Early Life* maintained 'what I honestly think is a fiction so far as his escape enters into it'. This judgement was tempered with an honest appreciation of Churchill's qualities, which he had observed at close quarters, and the letter continued: 'Though I have not much faith in him, I admire his undoubted courage, physical and moral, and we can't afford in these days of sloppy statesmen to ignore that quality.' Nevertheless, the bitterness was palpable.

Knutsford had previously written in a very different vein to Churchill. His letter was dated 26 October 1930, shortly after the publication of *My Early Life*: 'I have a lot of work to do but could not leave your book for a moment. I bought it, & have had 2 days real enjoyment. THANK YOU.' On the subject of the escape, he wrote: 'You will certainly have a 2nd edition of this book. May I without offence suggest you emphasising the point that you escaped with the cordial agreement of your fellow prisoners . . . you might add a footnote on the point that it was agreed that each should escape in turn, & that to go back (you do say this) would have been impossible.' Thanking Knutsford for his letter, Churchill added: 'I should have no difficulty in proving the good faith in which I acted, but the argument is more suited for a libel action than for an agreeable book.'

Those inmates of the States Model School whom Haldane claimed in his diary would have corroborated his version of events had long since died. Lieutenant Frederick Le Mesurier, who joined Haldane in his escape from the school in March 1900, and Thomas Frankland both fell in the First World War, at Ypres and Gallipoli respectively. Brockie was killed in a mining accident soon after the Anglo–Boer War. As far as is known, Le Mesurier had made no comment on the escape. Frankland's views are also not known, but it is clear that he harboured no resentment against Churchill, as on the occasion of the latter's marriage in 1908, he presented him with Herbert Maxwell's two-volume *Life of Wellington*, beautifully bound in red morocco and emblazoned in gold with the Churchill coat of arms and the family motto: *Fiel pero desdichado* – Faithful but unfortunate.

Having read in Haldane's diary how Brockie railed against Churchill after the escape, I thought I would approach Brockie's family for an explanation. It seems that any resentment on Brockie's behalf did not extend to his widow, Annie. I spoke to her granddaughter, Mrs Vera Gallony.

'I have in my possession,' she said, 'a letter from your grandfather addressed to my grandmother. I've kept it all these years. I knew some day it would be of use to someone.'

Annie Brockie, having fallen on hard times following her husband's death, had sought assistance from Churchill. He replied on 21 September 1902: 'Dear Mrs Brockie, I am not a rich man and have to earn by writing all I spend. I send you a cheque for £10 which I hope may be of some assistance to you, and I regret it is not within my power to do more. Yours very truly, Winston S. Churchill.'

In 1935, when amplifying his diary, Haldane wrote: 'I must allow myself a few words regarding articles by Churchill in the *Strand Magazine* . . . and the book he has since published [*My Early Life*].' He makes two points of criticism. The first is that had Churchill 'on the night of 12th December carried out the arrangements which had been thought out with great care, and were for the general advantage of himself and his companions, he would have found that most of the difficulties he [later] encountered had been foreseen and, as far as possible, accounted for'. This, as we shall see, is a ridiculous claim. The second point is: 'Had Churchill only possessed the moral courage to admit that, in the excitement of the moment, he saw the chance to escape and could not resist the temptation to take advantage of it, not realising that it would compromise the escape of his companions, all would have been well.'

The facts are that Churchill showed the way, where his companions hung back. Their escape was compromised by their hesitation. Churchill waited for them, risking his own recapture, until Haldane admitted defeat. Although the three were supposed to flee together, there was obviously never any question of them scaling the fence simultaneously. Someone had to go first, and wait for the others to follow. As Churchill was thought to be the least agile of the three – it was noted that he took no physical exercise – he was to have been given a leg-up by Haldane, who would then follow him. Brockie would go last, having waited in the main building until the first two were over the fence. Had the attempt by Churchill and Haldane been successful, they would have had to wait for Brockie. He might well have been balked, as he and Haldane were after Churchill had got over. No one would then have accused the two of abandoning the third.

When Haldane and Churchill returned to the verandah from the latrine on the night of the twelfth after their second abortive attempt, Brockie taunted them with being afraid. However, having had a look himself, he came back defeated, passing Churchill on the way. Brockie had always been contemptuous of Churchill, and declined to discuss the situation with him as their paths crossed in opposite directions. Yet almost immediately Churchill had succeeded where Brockie had failed. It was a matter of taking a chance when the going seemed good. Churchill was not hijacking Haldane's plan but simply pushing on where the others were hesitating, thinking, reasonably enough, that they would follow and seize similar chances. Given the circumstances, what other action would Brockie have expected Churchill to take? Surely not to return to the main building and report that the coast had been momentarily clear a few minutes before.

Once he was over the fence, Churchill waited a long time. Although it is not possible to confirm the full ninety minutes he mentions in his own testimony, it is certain that he waited for at least an hour. This can be calculated from a combination of Hofmeyr's account and the movements of the sentries as reported by the Transvaal authorities' inquiry. While Churchill was waiting, in extreme peril of being discovered, Haldane and Brockie went off to have their supper, intending to try again later. Hofmeyr places Churchill's escape at 7.15 p.m., when, as we know from the inquiry, a strategically situated sentry was absent from his post. By the time Haldane and Brockie returned the guard had been changed, and the sentry was back in position. The inquiry states that he had been there since 8 p.m. Haldane's next abortive attempt to escape, which took place some time after this, and his subsequent whispered conversation with Churchill, would take the latter's time in the garden to at least an hour. In that time Haldane and Brockie had missed their chance. It seems extraordinary that they allowed supper to come before their escape attempt. Had they shown more determination, been more curious about Churchill's movements and followed him, it is very likely they also would have succeeded.

Brockie's summary judgement that escape was impossible, and his contemptuous dismissal of Churchill, may well have been responsible for the failure to follow up the latter's success. Brockie's 'sneering allusions after the event to "Your trusted friend – a nice kind of gentleman!"' reported in Haldane's diary, were no doubt fuelled by the realisation that he had been proved wrong. Brockie's attitude was hardly pertinent, as Haldane implied, to the question of whether or not Churchill had abandoned them.

It is difficult not to sympathise with Haldane, himself an outstanding and much-decorated officer, who, had he but known it, was in harness with a colossus of the twentieth century. The man whose watchword – 'Never, never give in' – would reverberate around the world had infinitely more determination than his accomplices, and was not prepared to delay the escape any longer. He was not abandoning them, but simply showing the way.

There seems little doubt that Haldane's bitterness, possibly stemming from Churchill's overbearing manner in 1912 and fuelled by *My Early Life*, caused him to revise, in 1935, the history of their personal relationship. Their correspondence in the early 1900s had been both amicable and mutually supportive, with no trace of resentment or any hint of the 'unexpected light' thrown by Churchill's account of his escape. Haldane, for example, went out of his way to send Churchill copies of two Boer telegrams dating from November and December 1899 concerning his imprisonment and escape. He also suggested how Churchill should explain his possession of them, as he had come by them officially and had no authority to pass them on. For his part, Churchill lobbied his influential friends in order to clear Haldane from General Buller's reproaches over the loss of the armoured train, and wrote to Haldane: 'I think you would be most unwise to entertain the idea of leaving the service. People who are your friends are coming into power . . .' By the end of his life Haldane's resentment had waned, and his warmer memories of their campaigns together prevailed. When his memoirs, *A Soldier's Saga*, were published in 1948, two years before his death, he presented Churchill with a copy inscribed: 'With the profound admiration of an old ally.'

However, such is Churchill's place in history that his escape so long ago still arouses interest and controversy. When Haldane's letter to Knutsford of 1931, in which he stated that Churchill 'slipped off without myself or the third man', came to light in 1997, having been buried in the library of a Los Angeles collector of Churchill memorabilia, it was immediately seized as ammunition by one or two historians seeking to diminish Churchill's reputation. Here was a new angle for them.

In a *Sunday Times* article of 1 June 1997, headed 'Boer War Letter Reveals Churchill the Bounder', John Charmley, author of *Churchill: End of Glory*, commented: 'If you believe Haldane, and the letter has an authentic ring about it, young Winston broke the gentleman's code of honour.' However, the evidence, as we have seen from several sources, shows conclusively that Churchill had not 'slipped off'. John Ramsden, Professor of Modern History at Queen Mary and Westfield College in London, was quoted as saying: 'There have been suspicions about Churchill's mythmaking – Sir Hubert Gough, a Boer War commander, said he did not recognise one event as described by Churchill – and this letter confirms contemporary fears about the man's reliability.' Of all people, a historian should not be surprised if events that take place in battle imprint themselves differently on different participants, particularly when the individuals are relatively junior, and are in the thick of the action. He could also reflect that, for a variety of reasons, a senior general in the First World War might make slighting remarks about a First Lord of the Admiralty who was never reluctant to interfere with War Office business. In any event, the conjunction of a letter written in bitterness and remarks based on the recollection of events in action many years before is hardly convincing evidence of unreliability. A third historian, Andrew Roberts, commented more realistically: 'He was a young man in a hurry who always broke the rules. It was a secret behind his greatness.'

In general this may well have been the case, although Churchill broke no rules when he escaped from the States Model School. However, had he not, as a non-combatant, stretched them during the armoured train ambush, the engine and the badly wounded men would not have escaped. More significantly, had the newspaper reporter not returned to the fray when, with honour, he could have escaped on the engine and filed his copy, he would never have been taken prisoner. His was an example which any soldier would have been proud to follow.

TEN

Wanted Dead or Alive

'I was in the heart of the enemy's country. I knew no one to
whom I could apply for succour. Worst still I could not speak
a word of Dutch or Kaffir.'

WINSTON CHURCHILL,
dispatch to the *Morning Post*, 22 December 1899

WHEN THE NEWS OF CHURCHILL'S escape arrived over the
wires in London on 14 December, Oliver Borthwick, the editor of
the *Morning Post*, lost no time in relaying the glad tidings to Lady
Randolph: 'Just received the following from Reuter, "Churchill
escaped". The country being free from Boers & knowing his practical turn of mind I have no doubt that he knows what he is about
and will turn up with an extra chapter of his book finished in a few
days time at some British encampment.'

Borthwick's prediction was closer to the truth than he realised,
for even as he was writing the letter, Churchill had turned up at a
British encampment of sorts, a coalmine run by an Englishman.
But the reassuring letter in no way reflected Churchill's situation.
The hue and cry his escape had caused across the veldt had given
him a difficult and dangerous forty-eight hours, and his hideaway
in the coalmine could be no more than a temporary sanctuary on
the hazardous road to freedom.

Two days earlier, having emerged from the bushes beside the
prison railings, Churchill had walked down Skinner Street to the
Apies River, to this day a dry streambed except after heavy rain,

when it can suddenly burst into flood, where he sat on the parapet of a bridge to consider his plans. A story which was to be widely spread in South Africa had him boasting of wading the 'mighty Apies'. It is unlikely that the river would have been in flood in December, and in any case, there was the bridge on which he had sat. Never guilty of undue modesty, Churchill would surely have remembered and written about crossing a river in flood. Years later he attributed the story to a reporter's imagination, but by then an electricity sub-station on the Apies had been named 'Winston', and the legend established.

In a brown suit and Adrian Hofmeyr's hat, Churchill was indistinguishable from the burghers taking the night air, and for the moment in no danger. That would come when, as a lone figure, he set out to cover the three hundred miles to Komatipoort, on the border with Portuguese East Africa (now Mozambique). He assumed that by dawn his escape would be discovered. The Boers would cover all exits from Pretoria, and throw their net across the Transvaal. It was imperative that he move on as soon as possible, but the compass and map which would have provided directions, and his intended means of sustenance, meat lozenges and opium tablets, were back with Haldane and Brockie in the States Model School. Still, he had £75 in his pocket, which might buy his way out of trouble, four slabs of chocolate to keep him going, and the constellation Orion shining brightly above for guidance. He would find the railway and follow it eastwards. He struck the line half a mile further on, at a point where, winding through the hills, it ran north to south. Hazarding a guess at the right direction, he began to walk along it:

> The night was delicious. A cool breeze fanned my face, and a wild feeling of exhilaration took hold of me. At any rate, I was free, if only for an hour. That was something. The fascination of adventure grew. Unless the stars in their courses fought for me, I could not escape. Where, then, was the need for caution? I marched briskly along the line. Here and there the lights of a picket fire gleamed. Every bridge had its watchers. But I passed them all, making very short detours at the dangerous

places and really taking scarcely any precautions. Perhaps that was the reason I succeeded.

After two hours he saw the signal lights of a wayside halt which, judging from the distance he is likely to have covered, must have been the small settlement of Koodoespoort. Skirting around the platform, he hid in a ditch some two hundred yards beyond it, intending to wait for a train and jump aboard before it had gathered too much speed after stopping at the station. After an hour he finally heard the whistle and rumble of an approaching train, and saw the yellow headlights as it slowed to a halt at the station. Five minutes later, a further blast of the whistle and a sudden hissing of steam signalled its departure. As soon as the engine had passed him, Churchill sprang from the ditch, clutching at the nearest handhold. However, the train was travelling faster than he had anticipated, and it was only after several attempts that he managed to hold on, and heave himself onto the couplings of the fifth truck. Clambering into the wagon, he found it full of empty coal-bags, and realised he had jumped a goods train returning to a colliery. Still unsure if the train was going his way, he burrowed among the bags and settled down to sleep. At least it was carrying him away from the enemy's capital at a steady twenty miles an hour.

'How long I slept I do not know, but I awoke suddenly with all feelings of exhilaration gone, and only the consciousness of oppressive difficulties heavy on me.' Churchill decided to leave the train well before dawn, in order to find water and a hiding place while it was still dark. He would lie up by day and jump another train the following night. If he could repeat the procedure two or three times he would arrive in Portuguese East Africa while still sustained by his slabs of chocolate, and without having to run the risk of foraging for food.

He crawled from among the coal-bags, lowered himself to the couplings, and jumped. 'The train was running at a fair speed ... My feet struck the ground in two gigantic strides, and the next instant I was sprawling in the ditch considerably shaken but unhurt. The train, my faithful ally of the night, hurried on its journey.'

Churchill found himself among high grass, wet with dew, in a wide valley. He discovered a pool, from which he drank long to quench his thirst and stave off its return during the sweltering day ahead. Climbing from the valley to find a hiding place in the surrounding hills, he saw with relief that the railway line ran towards the expanding sliver of light on the eastern horizon. He had taken the right train.

He selected a hiding place among trees on a hill which commanded a view of the whole valley. Three miles to the west he could see the tin roofs of a small village, which must have been Balmoral, while at the foot of the hill was a native kraal, with its inhabitants dotted about the surrounding patches of cultivation or tending their flocks of goats.

As the day dragged on and the heat became oppressive, Churchill longed to drink from the pool barely half a mile distant, but was deterred by the occasional figures of white men riding across the valley, and one Boer who came shooting birds close by. He remained within the cover, his sole companion 'a gigantic vulture, who manifested an extravagant interest in my condition, and made hideous and ominous gurglings from time to time'. Churchill ate a slab of chocolate, which satisfied his hunger but increased his thirst.

> The elation and excitement of the previous night had burnt away . . . I was so nervous and perplexed about the future that I could not rest . . . I realised with awful force that no exercise of my own feeble wit and strength could save me from my enemies, and that without the assistance of that High Power which interferes in the eternal sequence of causes and effects more often than we are prone to admit, I could never succeed.

Churchill was not, nor would ever become, a religious man in the conventional sense, but he 'prayed long and earnestly for guidance'. Then, on the principle that the 'High Power' helps those who help themselves, he watched the railway line and planned his onward journey.

As there appeared to be no shortage of rail traffic by day, he saw no reason to suppose that there would not also be trains by night.

After all, he had arrived in his present position by night train. He planned to scramble aboard at a point where a gradient would slow the train to a walking pace, and where a curve in the line meant he would be unseen by the occupants of both the engine and the guard's van. It was with increasing impatience that he awaited nightfall.

> The long day reached its close at last. The western clouds flushed into fire; the shadows of the hills stretched across the valley; a ponderous Boer wagon with its long team crawled slowly along the track towards the township, the Kaffirs collected their herds and drew them round their kraal; the daylight died, and soon it was quite dark. Then, and not until then, I set forth.

He made haste for the railway line. Scrambling among boulders and through high grass, pausing only to drink from a stream, he found a point on the track which would suit his plan, and settled down behind a small bush to await the next train. The hours passed in silence. When it seemed that the railway must have shut down for the night he set off on foot, determined to cover at least ten more miles of his journey before daybreak.

In this part of the Transvaal, which was far from the fighting, there would have seemed to be no reason why every bridge should be guarded by armed men. But they were, probably as a result of the authorities' determination to apprehend the escaped prisoner. At intervals there were stations, with the usual tin-roofed houses round about. The bright moon, which otherwise would have eased his path, now became a hindrance, and Churchill was forced to make wide detours around these potential traps. His twenty-five-day enforced idleness in prison had left him unfit for the arduous process of wading the many streams, and he was drenched and tired when he came upon Brugspruit station, no more than a platform on the open veldt between Balmoral and Witbank, with three long goods trains laid up in the sidings. If one of these trains was destined to depart eastwards the following morning, it might help the weary fugitive on his way.

First, it was essential to determine their destinations, and so avoid the ignominy of being unloaded with the contents at some station short of the frontier. Churchill had crept between the trains to examine the wagon labels when he was disturbed by the shouts of native labourers and what seemed to be a European voice giving orders. He quickly turned tail, slipped into the long grass and doggedly tramped on.

Eventually, as he came over the crest of a hill, Churchill saw the bright lights of Witbank station far ahead. Closer, to his left, at what he thought was no more than a couple of miles away, gleamed several fires, which he imagined were from a kraal. Having heard that the Bantu people hated the Boers, and were better disposed towards the British, he considered approaching them. He spoke not one word of their language, but he recalled that sign language had seen him through when he had been lost in the Sudan the year before. Some of his British banknotes might also induce them to help him. Leaving the railway, he walked towards the fires, then, exhausted and suddenly beset by indecision, partially retraced his steps.

After a while he stopped and sat down, quite unable to decide what he should do. Then, as suddenly as they had appeared and for no logical reason, his doubts were dispelled: 'I just felt quite clear I would go to the Kaffir kraal. I had sometimes in former years held a "Planchette" pencil and written while others had touched my wrist or hand. I acted in exactly the same unconscious or subconscious manner now.' Psychics have sometimes claimed Churchill for one of their own, and in later life he would say that he would die on the anniversary of his father's death. As though determined to fulfil this prophesy, he lingered for ten days between life and death, finally giving up the unequal struggle early in the morning of 24 January 1965, seventy years to the day after Lord Randolph's death. Psychic or not, it is certain that he had a strong sense of destiny.

After an hour spent trudging towards the fires they seemed as far away as ever, and Churchill concluded he had considerably underestimated the distance. However, his extreme exhaustion and the broken ground, rather than distance, were responsible for his slow progress: a look at the scene today confirms his first estimate of about two miles. Eventually, after he had waded one more stream and climbed a slope, he saw the outline of buildings silhouetted against the light of fires. A tower and a large winding wheel told him he had arrived at a coalmine. What he had taken to be the fires of a kraal were in fact the furnaces of the engines.

Churchill had been on the run for thirty hours. Haldane and Le Mesurier, who would escape with Brockie the following March, and who would follow the same general route, took six days to cover the same distance, losing Brockie on the way and being reunited with him only when they reached Lourenço Marques. The comparison makes nonsense of Haldane's claim that had Churchill carried out the arrangements carefully thought out by Haldane and Brockie, he would have been able to foresee and surmount most of the difficulties he experienced.

Churchill now approached what he later described as a small two-storey house. In fact it was a bungalow which, having a verandah and being built on a slope, may well have appeared to have an extra floor as he approached it from below. He had no idea of the reception he would receive. It was common knowledge that a number of Englishmen had been allowed to remain in the country to keep the mines working, but there were also other nationalities in the region who were unsympathetic to the British cause, although with these a bargain might be possible. If he revealed his identity, Churchill thought he could assure £1,000 to anyone who could smuggle him across the border. Meanwhile, his £75 in English notes might ease his immediate future. 'Still the odds were heavy against me, and it was with faltering and reluctant steps that I walked out of the shimmering gloom of the veldt into the light of the furnace fires, advanced towards the silent house, and struck with my fist upon the door.' It was 1.30 in the morning of 14 December.

A light came on, a window opened and a voice called out, '*Wie is daar?*' The enquiry in Dutch caused Churchill's heart to sink, but he replied in English that he had had an accident, and needed help. After a short interval the door was unbolted and abruptly opened. In the dark passageway stood a tall man with a pale face and a drooping dark moustache. His clothes had been pulled on hastily. In his right hand was a revolver. 'What do you want?' he asked in English.

Churchill now had to improvise rapidly. He was, he said, a burgher, Dr Bentick by name, and had been on his way to join his commando at Komatipoort when he had fallen off the train while skylarking and dislocated his shoulder. This unlikely story must have sounded even more unbelievable when related in English rather than Dutch.

The tall man hesitated, then invited Churchill to enter, ushering him into a dining room cum office. He struck a match, lit an oil lamp and looked his bedraggled guest up and down before saying, 'I think I'd like to know more about this railway accident of yours.'

Churchill, who had sunk into a chair at the head of the table, said he had better tell the truth.

'I think you had,' replied the tall man.

When all had been told, Churchill's host locked the door and introduced himself as John Howard, manager of the Transvaal and Delagoa Bay Colliery at Witbank. As the two men shook hands, Churchill felt 'like a drowning man pulled out of the water and informed he had won the Derby'. Howard had locked the door not, as Churchill had momentarily feared, to prevent his escape, but to safeguard them from prying eyes. Now Howard explained that great care was needed, as there were spies everywhere. Only the day before, a field cornet had arrived at the mine with a description of Churchill, and instructions that Howard should arrest him on sight. This was the only house for miles around at which Churchill would not have been immediately handed over to the Boers. Howard, an Englishman, had become a naturalised burgher some years previously, but had been allowed to remain in charge of the mine rather than being called out to fight. There were several other British men working at the mine, and although they were under parole to observe strict neutrality, they would help to hide Churchill while a plan was concocted to get him to safety in Lourenço Marques, Portuguese East Africa.

Churchill realised that, as a naturalised burgher, his host was committing treason, and would be liable to be shot if he was found out. He therefore felt duty-bound to say he would move on, and asked only for provisions, a pistol and a pony. Howard would not hear of it. 'We will fix up something,' he said. Then, turning to a more immediate problem, he added suddenly, 'But you are famishing.' He bustled off to the kitchen, first telling his guest to help himself to the whisky and soda on the sideboard.

By the time Churchill had done full justice to the meal provided, Howard had conferred with his secretary, John Adams, and enlisted the help of his British colleagues and the mine doctor, Dr Gillespie. The fugitive would be hidden down the mine until some means could be arranged to get him across the border. 'One difficulty,' said Howard, 'is the *skoff*. The cook will want to know what happened to the leg of mutton you've just eaten, and the Dutch girl sees every mouthful I eat. We'll work it out. Now you must get down the pit at once.'

Dawn was breaking as Churchill stealthily followed Howard across a yard to the winding wheel of the number one shaft. Beside the lift cage he was introduced to the engineer, Daniel Dewsnap, a native of Oldham, the constituency in which Churchill had been defeated in a Parliamentary by-election only five months previously. Dewsnap grasped Churchill's hand and whispered, 'They'll all vote for you next time.' With that the cage door was closed, and the three shot down into the mine.

Two men with lanterns were waiting at the bottom of the shaft: Joe McKenna and Joe McHenry, respectively the mine captain and a miner. The party set off through the labyrinth of workings until they reached a well-ventilated chamber, in which a new and so far unused stable had been built. McKenna and McHenry had brought a mattress and blankets, with which they sought to make Churchill as comfortable as possible. Howard explained that even if the Boers searched the mine, they would not find him. There was a place in one of the tunnels where water touched the roof for a foot or two. McHenry would dive through it with Churchill into the workings cut off by the water, where no one would ever think of looking.

Howard handed over candles, a bottle of whisky and some cigars. 'Don't move from here,' was his parting instruction. 'There will be Kaffirs about after daylight, but we'll make sure none of them wanders this way.'

'My four friends trooped off with their lanterns, and I was left alone. Viewed from the velvety darkness of the pit, life seemed bathed in a rosy glow.' Churchill had again lifted his eyes to the future. His long-term ambitions were back in clear focus. 'I saw myself once more rejoining the Army with a real exploit to my credit. In this comfortable mood, and speeded by intense fatigue, I soon slept the sleep of the weary – but of the triumphant.'

When he awoke many hours later he reached for a candle. Unable to find one, he remained in the darkness, relaxing on his mattress. Presently the glimmer of a lantern signalled someone approaching. It was Howard, carrying a cooked chicken, books and more candles. 'The rats have made off with your candle,' he said in explanation of its disappearance. These rats, white with pink eyes, were Churchill's constant companions during his time underground: 'The patter of little feet and a perceptible sense of stir and scurry were continuous.'

At Vereeniging, thirty miles south of Johannesburg, I met Daniel Dewsnap's grandson Errol Dewsnap and, in Cape Town, his grand-daughter Mary Bromley. They both remember their grandfather telling them the story of Churchill and the mine. What had clearly made the most impression on them as children was Churchill's description of his companions underground. 'Your grandfather,' they told me, 'said the rats were as big as cats.'

In spite of his bedraggled condition, Churchill made a great impression on Daniel Dewsnap. 'I never saw such a fellow. He was exhausted, but a drop of whisky revived him. Nothing frightened him. He wanted to get back into the war,' he told his grandson. He wrote in the same vein to Tom Harrop, his brother-in-law in Oldham, adding, 'The people of Oldham don't know what a jewel they lost when they threw him out.' He ended his letter: 'Vote for Churchill.'

My pilgrimage to Witbank was a disappointment. Of the mine

there is now no trace. Gum trees and long grass wave in the breeze where the winding wheel last turned forty-five years ago. The buildings, including Howard's house, and the railway sidings have recently been demolished. All that remains of this historic site is a concrete slab over the mine shaft down which my grandfather had 'shot into the bowels of the earth'.

I visited the former mine owner Julius Berlein's grandson, Anthony Berlein, in his lodge on the edge of the Kruger National Park. Over breakfast it was brought home to me just how lucky Churchill had been to turn up at the Transvaal and Delagoa Bay Colliery. Not only did he find himself among friends, but Julius Berlein, although a German, was staunchly pro-British. Had he been pro-Boer, like most other Continental Europeans, the welcome Churchill received at his mine might have been less than effusive.

There are strict rules in mines to prevent explosions caused by the ignition of gas. In the days before electric torches, Davy lamps shielded the naked flame with gauze. But, with typical insouciance, Churchill continued lighting cigars underground. Their smell, drifting through the workings, aroused the curiosity of a Coloured mineworker who traced it to the stable, where he came face to face with its temporary occupant. The man fled, shouting that he had seen a *tokolshe* – a small, hairy dwarf in black folklore. It was convenient for Howard to foster the story of the spook in the stable, which deterred further investigation by inquisitive workers. The inconvenience came later when, for a long time after the 'ghost' had gone, none of the men would work in that part of the mine.

Confinement underground did not suit Churchill. Feeling unwell on 15 December, he was brought to the surface for a stroll by night on the veldt, attended by Dr Gillespie, and was subsequently accommodated behind some packing cases in a spare room at the mine office. Food was now being provided by two young women, Ada Blunden and Ellen David, the housekeeper and cook who ran the workers' hostel at the mine. Once again Churchill was almost compromised when, thinking a knock at the door was one of the prearranged secret signals, he opened it to the office boy, who was merely banging about with his broom. On this occasion the boy was sworn to secrecy with the promise of a new suit of clothes.

Howard now brought a new player into the game: Charles Burnham, a local English storekeeper and shipping agent. At a meeting with Howard, Adams and Dewsnap, Burnham suggested smuggling Churchill across the border and all the way to Lourenço Marques in a consignment of wool which was due to go by rail on 19 December. He had six truckloads ready, and by spreading the consignment over seven he could make a hiding place for the fugitive among the bales. His mother would provide food for the journey.

The afternoon before he was due to leave, Churchill was reading Robert Louis Stevenson's *Kidnapped*. He could readily identify with the emotions and fears of David Balfour and Alan Breck, who had escaped into the glens, although he believed his situation was worse than theirs: 'The hazards of the bullet or the shell are one thing. Having the police after you is another . . . I dreaded in every fibre the ordeal which awaited me at Komatipoort and which I must impotently and passively endure if I was to make good my escape from the enemy.'

In this unhappy mood Churchill was startled by the noise of rifle shots close by. He remained in his hiding place behind the packing cases, anxiously awaiting the outcome of what could only be a gun battle between Howard and the Boers. Voices and laughter dispelled his anxiety, and when these had died away Howard came in to explain. There had indeed been a gun battle. The Boer Field Cornet had arrived with the news that Churchill had been captured at Waterval Boven, and to keep him from prying, Howard had challenged him to a shooting match, with a row of bottles as targets. Having won £2, the Boer went away delighted.

At two o'clock in the morning Howard led Churchill to the colliery siding, where the trucks stood waiting. Howard pointed to the end of one truck, and Churchill clambered in, finding a narrow tunnel between the bales of wool that led to a space with sufficient room for him to lie down or sit up. Looking around, he saw he had been provided with a revolver, two roast chickens, some slices of meat, bread, a melon and three bottles of cold tea.

Dewsnap and other British miners were loitering in the neighbourhood, ready to distract anyone who might discover what was afoot. Their presence, rather than diverting attention, raised the suspicions of a Boer detective, Ghert Trichardt, who was well known to the miners. 'Now, Dan, I know what your game is,' he said to Dewsnap, approaching the truck. 'You might as well give him up.'

'Now, Ghert,' replied Dewsnap, 'we have been friends for a long time, but you are not going to stop this business.' With that the detective was ushered away, not knowing quite what was going on. Months later, Dewsnap would tell him the full story.

After several hours, well after daylight had filtered into his hiding place, Churchill felt the bumping and heard the clanging of the wagons as they were coupled to the colliery engine which would pull them to the main line at Witbank station. There was a final jolt, 'And again, after a further pause, we started rumbling off on our journey into the unknown.'

Having seen Churchill on his way, Howard set out for Pretoria, finding himself on the same train as the prisoner whose capture had been announced by the visiting Field Cornet the day before. He was a young British soldier who bore some resemblance to the description of Churchill issued with the 'Wanted Dead or Alive' posters. The Boers had yet to discover their error, and the guard, much to Howard's amusement, proudly announced that his prisoner was Mr Churchill. Years later Howard wrote: 'I well remember the look of the official's face who met the train at Pretoria Station expecting to receive his illustrious prisoner. I would have given much to have had a hearty laugh.'

It would be some time before Howard could be publicly credited with his part in Churchill's escape, but nevertheless he was under suspicion. A Boer commandant and five burghers arrived at the mine in early 1900 with the intention of taking him to Pretoria for interrogation. He saw only two courses of action open to him: to bribe them, or, because it was a matter of his life or theirs, to

ABOVE Sergeant Major Brockie.

BELOW The Revd Adrian Hofmeyr.

ABOVE Louis de Souza, Transvaal Secretary of State for War, and his wife Marie.

LEFT John Howard's house at the Transvaal and Delagoa Bay Colliery.

FAR LEFT John Howard, mine manager.

BELOW The mine shaft down which Churchill was hidden.

Daniel Dewsnap, mine engineer.

BELOW The watch presented to Dewsnap by Churchill for having assisted in his escape.

Churchill (*to right of bending man in straw hat*) about to disembark from the *Induna* in Durban.

Churchill on the jetty in Durban.

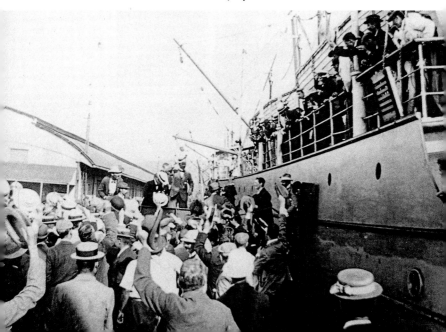

Churchill making the first of his two speeches in Durban.

Churchill in Durban – with the cowboy hat he purchased in Lourenço Marques.

Winston L. S. Churchill.
War Correspondent.

OGDEN'S CIGARETTES

EACH PACKET OF
OGDEN'S TAB CIGARETTES
Contains a Photo of one of the
LEADING GENERALS
AT THE WAR.

Winston L. S. Churchill, war correspondent of *Morning Post* in South Africa. Taken prisoner near Colenso, Nov. 14th; afterwards escaped from Pretoria.

BRITISH MADE BY BRITISH LABOUR.

Cigarette card issued after Churchill's escape.

LEFT Churchill commissioned as a Lieutenant in the South African Light Horse.

BELOW Churchill visits the wreck of the armoured train.

ABOVE LEFT Major-General the Earl of Dundonald, who commanded a locally raised cavalry brigade.

ABOVE Anna Beyers, who served Churchill in her uncle's farm shop, and who told the story of him chasing a chicken.

LEFT Lieutenant-General Sir Charles Warren.

shoot them. He ushered them into his dining room for whisky and refreshments, inviting them to lean their rifles in the corner next to the door, then left the room, ostensibly to change for the journey. He returned with his hands in his pockets, and a loaded pistol in each hand. Standing by the rifles, he offered the Boers £50 on the spot and a further £200 when the war was over if they would go away. They accepted his offer and returned to Pretoria, to report that Howard had disappeared.

By this time Howard had also helped Haldane and Le Mesurier, who escaped four months after Churchill, to safety. It seems an extraordinary coincidence that, with no word having passed between them, they should have found refuge and help at the same coalmine. But the mine was near the railway which both provided the fugitives with a directional guide towards the nearest neutral territory and offered the possibility of a ride. It was entirely to be expected that they would take the same route. Like Churchill before them, Haldane and Le Mesurier were in dire straits as they approached the area of Witbank. Churchill, having eaten only a little chocolate and walked a long way through difficult country, had been hungry and physically exhausted after thirty hours on the run. Heading towards what he hoped might be a friendly bantu kraal, he had found himself at Howard's house. Haldane and Le Mesurier, out of food after six days, approached the Bantu for help and were directed to the British miners in the vicinity. Haldane later wrote of his amazement at discovering that Churchill had been there before them. From Witbank onwards their escape was arranged in much the same manner as Churchill's.

It had soon became apparent to Charles Burnham that he himself would have to travel with the wool if he was to be successful in smuggling Churchill across the border. None of the goods trains ran all the way to Lourenço Marques, and unless he was present to smooth their journey, the wagons might stand interminably in sidings awaiting their turn for onward movement. Claiming that a sharp fall in wool prices was imminent, and that there was thus a need to avoid any delay, Burnham obtained a travelling permit from the Field Cornet, paid the railwaymen at Witbank to hitch his

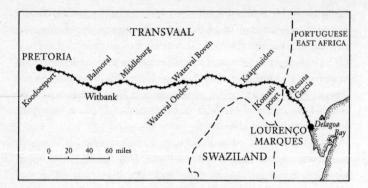

Churchill's Route to Freedom

wagons to the next train that came through, and rode with them in the guard's van. At Middleburg a further bribe speeded his consignment as far as Waterval Onder, where the wagons spent the night in a siding.

Having plied the guard with whisky, Burnham had no trouble in effecting an introduction to the guard of the next train, although it was intimated that another bottle would help for the next leg. To purchase this and to have dinner, Burnham went to the local hotel, where the proprietor assured him that Churchill had passed that way two days before, dressed as a Roman Catholic priest. Heartened by the circulation of this false rumour, which he hoped would put any hunters off the scent, Burnham returned to the station, where the relief guard coupled his wagons to a passenger train bound for Lourenço Marques.

The train reached Komatipoort with only one alarm when, at Kaapmuiden, Burnham had to entice an armed Boer away from Churchill's wagon with the offer of a cup of coffee at the station stall. At Komatipoort, where the train waited for the night, the customs officer agreed that in order to avoid delay the consignment could cross the border without being searched. However, the following morning the stationmaster on the Portuguese side at Resana Garcia steadfastly refused to allow the goods wagons to accompany the passenger train, although he promised to send them on by the very next goods train, which would arrive in Lourenço Marques late that afternoon.

The passenger hidden in the wool, unaware of anything that had happened en route, had been looking forward to 'the excitement of rejoining the Army' and 'the triumph of a successful escape'. He had also been 'haunted perpetually by anxieties about the search at the frontier'. It was thus with some apprehension that he had faced the night stop in Komatipoort, but once the train was through Resana Garcia and away from the border area, 'I pushed my head out of the tarpaulin and sang and shouted and crowed at the top of my voice. Indeed, I was so carried away by thankfulness and delight that I fired my revolver two or three times in the air as a *feu de joie*. None of these follies led to any evil results.'

Arriving in Lourenço Marques at 4 p.m., Churchill, black from the coal dust in the bottom of the wagon, slipped down between the couplings and, 'mingling unnoticed with the Kaffirs and loafers in the yard – which my slovenly and unkempt appearance well fitted me to do – strolled my way towards the gates and found myself in the streets of Lourenço Marques'.

Burnham, who had been briefly arrested for loitering while waiting near the wool trucks, set off for the British Consulate. Churchill followed some yards behind. At the Consulate the secretary thought the dishevelled caller was a fireman from one of the ships in the harbour, and told him to come back during office hours. The subsequent altercation brought the Consul first to an upstairs window and then to the door. 'From that moment every resource of hospitality and welcome was at my disposal.' That evening, Churchill's penchant for hats, well known in his later life, manifested itself in Lourenço Marques, where, in Burnham's words, 'We drove to a store where he bought a complete rig-out and a cowboy hat.' To Howard they telegraphed: 'Goods arrived safely.'

Churchill then sent an amusing telegram to the editor of the Pretoria newspaper the *Standard and Diggers News* to say he would be happy to give them details of his escape when he was next in Pretoria, which he estimated – optimistically, as it turned out –

would be in March. The editor published the telegram from the escaped prisoner in the same edition which carried an advertisement calling for volunteers to guard prisoners of war.

A small coaster, the *Induna*, was sailing that evening for Durban, and lest Boer agents should attempt to kidnap Churchill, 'nearly a dozen gentlemen escorted me to the ship armed with revolvers'. Where others would have taken the opportunity to relax for the first time in many days, Churchill now completed a dispatch of almost five thousand words to the *Morning Post*: 'It is from the cabin of this little vessel ... that I write the concluding lines of this letter.' This was the 'extra chapter' which, in his letter to Lady Randolph, Oliver Borthwick had prophesied only a week before.

ELEVEN

A Soldier Again

'Youth seeks Adventure. Journalism requires Advertisement.
Certainly I had found both. I became for the time quite famous.'

WINSTON CHURCHILL, *My Early Life*

WINSTON CHURCHILL WAS NOW A household name. The hero
of the armoured train had cocked a snook at the Boers by climbing
over their prison wall, evading his pursuers and returning to the
fray. He was soon to be elevated to the senior ranks of the army by
Ogden's cigarettes – boasting themselves 'British Made by British
Labour' – which would feature him in their cigarette-card series
'Leading Generals at the War'.

Churchill arrived off Durban on board the *Induna* during the
afternoon of Saturday 23 December 1899. Some twenty troopships
and supply vessels were at anchor in the harbour, and three more,
crammed with troops, were circling outside it awaiting pilots.
Ashore, considerable excitement had been aroused by the headline
in that morning's *Natal Mercury*: 'WINSTON CHURCHILL'S
ESCAPE – ARRIVES HERE TODAY'. Durban's pre-war population
of eighteen thousand had been swelled to thirty thousand by
Uitlander refugees, for whom Churchill's triumph was a welcome
antidote to what became known as the 'Black Week' of the Boer
War. While he had been escaping and making his way across the
veldt, the British Army had suffered three staggering defeats, at
Magersfontein, Stormberg and Colenso. The casualties incurred –

two thousand wounded and nearly a thousand killed – had been on a scale hitherto unimagined, and had shaken British confidence in the certainty of victory.

On 9 December Lieutenant-General Lord Methuen, who had been given the task of relieving the beleaguered British garrison at Kimberley, had ordered an assault on Magersfontein Hill – the very hill which the amateur cartographers in the States Model School had overlooked, and on which Louis de Souza had placed his finger when Churchill had forecast the relief of Kimberley once the British had crossed the River Modder. Now it barred the way of Methuen's advancing forces, and would need to be taken before the siege could be raised.

The Highland Brigade under Major-General Andrew Wauchope was ordered to make a night march of three miles, to be followed by a dawn assault in drill-book formation against an enemy whose position was but sketchily known. Over three thousand British troops in a closely formed column walked towards a trap set by men who better understood the changing nature of warfare. As the day began to break, a ripple of fire from the hill tore through their massed ranks. The Highland Brigade went to ground. Pegged down, without water and under a blazing sun, they exchanged fire with the largely unseen enemy for nine hours. By the afternoon morale began to slump, and a trickle of men rearwards turned to a flood. Over nine hundred British dead and wounded were collected from the battlefield the following day. Among the dead was General Wauchope, whose body was found within two hundred yards of the Boer trenches. Personal bravery was no substitute for outdated tactics.

One Black Watch survivor, 'A Perthite who was there', evoked the feeling in the ranks after the disaster.

> Why weren't we told of the trenches?
> Why weren't we told of the wire?
> Why were we marched up in column?
> May Tommy Atkins enquire.
> Why were scouts not sent forward?
> Why were no scouts on our flank?

Why attack in quarter column?
Who made the mistake? Give his rank.
Do they know his name in old England?
Do they know his incompetence yet?
Tommy has learnt to his sorrow,
And Tommy can never forget.

There had been a similar débâcle at Stormberg, where on 10 December an attempt had been made to recapture a strategic railway junction. Lieutenant-General Sir William Gatacre's force, having been misled by a guide during a night march to the objective, was badly mauled by the enemy. Seven hundred men were missing or captured.

Within a week of these two disasters Buller himself had suffered a serious repulse in an attempt to cross the Tugela River and relieve Ladysmith. The main attack, which was to cross the Tugela at Colenso, was to be preceded by a crossing some three miles upstream by the Irish Brigade under Major-General Fitzroy Hart. Like Gatacre, Hart was misinformed by a guide. As a result his brigade found itself in a loop of the Tugela, being shot at from both sides from a distance of only a few hundred yards.

Meanwhile, at Colenso itself, twelve British field guns had come into action well in advance of the infantry which had been detailed to screen them. They were met by an overwhelming volume of rifle fire. Their commander, Colonel Long (the Estcourt garrison commander who had ordered out the armoured train), and his second in command were severely wounded. The gunners stuck to their guns, but were eventually forced into cover.

With Hart in trouble and the guns abandoned, Buller called off the operation. His main concerns were now to extricate Hart's men and to recover the guns. The survivors of the Irish Brigade eventually staggered back, while three officers and half a dozen gunners volunteered to retrieve the guns. The odds against them were overwhelming, and after two of the twelve had been recovered, Buller forbade any further attempts.

The casualties, no more than 5 per cent of the force involved, had not, proportionally, been as severe as those at Magersfontein or Stormberg. Only about 150 had been killed, and half of the 750 wounded were fit again after a few weeks. Buller himself had been badly bruised in the ribs by shell fragments, but admitted only to being a little winded. The army returned to their base at Frere, the small town near which Churchill had been captured. The battle had been a serious reverse rather than a disaster, and the troops' morale remained unimpaired. But Ladysmith was still under siege.

As a result of the three setbacks – Magersfontein, Stormberg and Colenso – the War Office appointed a new Commander-in-Chief in India, Field Marshal Lord Roberts, and relegated Buller to command the forces in Natal.

It was well known that Roberts and Buller were members of the opposing 'rings', Indian and African respectively, of the British military hierarchy. Roberts, who first made his name in Afghanistan, had the support of the War Minister, Lord Lansdowne, who had been Viceroy when Roberts was Commander-in-Chief in India. Buller belonged to the those whose association was with the African service. Their uneasy relationship could not have been helped by the telegram Roberts received a week before he sailed for South Africa: 'Your gallant son died today. Condolences. Buller.' Lieutenant Freddy Roberts, a galloper on Buller's staff, had died attempting to save the abandoned guns at Colenso.

For the moment, the people crammed along the Durban quayside were able to forget Black Week as the *Induna*, with their hero on board, slipped between the larger ships and steamed into a harbour decorated with flags. As the little ship approached the jetty, reported the *Natal Mercury*, Churchill was 'detected on the captain's bridge, his round boyish face shielded by a large brimmed hat. The instant he was recognised a ROUSING CHEER went up from the crowd which had gathered and as Mr Churchill bowed his acknowledgements he became the cynosure of all eyes, and all voices joined in one loud acclaim of welcome.'

With no vacant space at the quayside, the ship was forced to triple berth. No sooner had she tied up than an admiral, a general and the Mayor of Durban came aboard to greet Churchill. They were followed by a welcoming crowd who swarmed over the two intervening ships, carried him shoulder-high, and, in the words of the *Natal Mercury*, 'heedless of the dirt of coaling operations . . . would not be content until he had favoured them with a speech'. Once on shore, outside the African Boating Company's offices, Churchill gave his first, impromptu, public wartime speech. If it was not as measured and polished as his later oratory, the tone is unmistakably Churchillian.

> . . . We are in the midst of a fierce struggle with vast military power, which has grown up in the heart of this country, which is resolved at all costs to gratify its reckless ambition by beating the British out of South Africa. [Cries of 'Never!' and a voice: 'Never while we have such fine fellows as you!'] When I see around me such a crowd as this, such determination and such enthusiasm, I am satisfied that, no matter what the difficulties, no matter what the dangers and what the force they may bring against us, we shall be successful in the end. [Cheers and a voice: 'God bless you, my boy!'] . . . You will see in this country the beginning of a new era, when peace and prosperity shall reign, so that the Cape may be in fact as well as in name a Cape of Good Hope. [Tremendous cheers]

The crowd now commandeered the speaker and hauled him, seated in a rickshaw, through the streets to the steps of the town hall, where a cart had been drawn up as a platform from which he was again expected to speak. Hatless, hands on hips and with a Union Jack hoist beside him, he made his second battle-cry of the day, though not until the crown had sung 'Rule Britannia':

> I need not say how grateful I am for the great kindness you have done in your welcome to me. When I see this great demonstration I regard it not only as a personal kindness to me, and as a demonstration of hospitality to a stranger [Cries: 'You're not a stranger!'], but as a token of the unflinching and unswerving determination of this colony to throw itself into the prosecution of the war. [Cheers] . . . With the determination of a great Empire surrounded by colonies of unprecedented loyalty we shall carry our policy to a successful conclusion, and under the old Union Jack there will be an era

of peace, purity, liberty, equality and good government in
South Africa. [Cheers] I thank you once again for your great
kindness. I am sure I feel within myself a personal measure of
that gratitude which every Englishman who loves his country
must feel towards the loyal and devoted colonists of Natal.
[Tremendous cheers]

Churchill's words were reported by the press as reverently as if
they were statements of official intent uttered by the newly arrived
Commander-in-Chief himself. They were still commanding many
closely-printed column inches a week later, the *Natal Witness*
reporting on 30 December: 'He said we had not yet arrived at the
half way house in the great struggle but would carry the campaign
to a successful conclusion and under the Union Jack peace, liberty,
purity, equality, good government would be established in South
Africa.' This was a political vision towards which Churchill and
General Botha would work together during the next decade.

Churchill was rescued from the crowd by the town Commandant,
Captain Percy Scott. In the relative quiet of Scott's office he gave
the assembled reporters an account of his escape, carefully tailored
so as not to compromise John Howard and the others who had
sheltered him at the mine.

When he left, he found that he had still not finally escaped the
enthusiasm of Durban. The *Natal Witness* reported: 'From the
Town Hall to the Railway Station Mr Churchill's journey was a
triumphant procession, an ardent Britisher waving a Union Jack in
front of Mr Churchill's rickshaw ... ordinary passengers, of which
there was an exceptionally large number, had considerable difficulty
in getting to their seats ... Mr Churchill was accommodated in a
reserved compartment and seemed considerably relieved to escape
from the good natured attentions of the crowd.' When, after much
delay, the train steamed out, the crowd gave 'a final cheer for the
gallant gentleman who waved his final adieus from the carriage'.

In Pietermaritzburg Churchill was the guest of Sir Walter Hely-
Hutchinson, the Governor of Natal. The following day he met
the Prime Minister of the colony, Colonel Hime, and visited the
overflowing military hospitals. Conflicting emotions appear in his

dispatch of that day. He would always be appalled at the suffering and misery caused by war, and he made sure his *Morning Post* readers were aware of it: 'all this pruning and patching up of broken men to win them a few more years of crippled life caught one's throat like the penetrating smell of iodoform.' But he would also always be attracted by the danger and excitement of battle: 'Nor was I sorry to hasten away by the night mail towards the camps . . . morning had broken when the train reached Frere . . . So after much trouble and adventure I came home safely again to the wars.'

There is some confusion over the details of his return to the front. According to contemporary newspaper reports, he landed in Durban on 23 December, arrived at Pietermaritzburg the same evening and set out on the seventy-five-mile journey to Frere the following day. His dispatch to the *Morning Post* reads as if he arrived in Frere after daybreak on Christmas Day, yet it is dated the twenty-fourth. It seems likely that this is correct, as even allowing for his delay in departing from Pietermaritzburg, the night mail would have reached Frere before midnight, and in *My Early Life* he describes celebrating Christmas Eve there.

A doubt also arises over another minor matter: where he took up his new abode. In his dispatch he writes that he got down from the train on arrival at Frere and walked along the line looking for his tent, finding it pitched on the side of the very same cutting where he had fled from the two Boer riflemen less than six weeks previously. In *My Early Life* he was to write that he took up his quarters in the platelayers' hut from behind which the two Boers had appeared.*

What is beyond doubt is that Churchill spent Christmas 1899 within a few yards of the spot where he had surrendered to Field Cornet Oosthuizen on 15 November. In *My Early Life* he mentions only a dinner on Christmas Eve. The readers of the *Morning Post*, however, were treated to a detailed description of the festivities:

---

* A comparison between Churchill's memoirs and his dispatches reveals other small discrepancies. It seems safer – except where his dispatches dissemble deliberately, for example in his omission of some details of his escape – to rely on the contemporaneous accounts rather than on *My Early Life*, which was published more than thirty years later.

> Glory to God in the highest and on earth peace and goodwill
> towards men . . . the hostile camps remained tranquil through-
> out the day . . . both armies attended divine service . . . the
> British held athletic sports, an impromptu military tournament
> and a gymkhana . . . there were Christmas dinners . . . and
> various smoking concerts afterwards.

He lost no time in putting his literary affairs in order. On Boxing
Day he wrote to the editor of the *North American Review*, William
McRiderley, complaining about their parsimony in paying what he
regarded as an inadequate sum for an article of his that they had
published. Pointing out that he usually commanded ten guineas
per thousand words, he admonished them in future to state their
terms in advance, adding: 'I will do it if I think it good enough.'
McRiderley's reaction is scribbled in the corner of Churchill's
letter: 'Cheeky little cuss, ain't he?'

In his triumphal return Churchill did not forget those at the
Transvaal and Delagoa Bay Colliery who had helped him on his
way to freedom. For the moment he had no means of expressing
his gratitude. He could not even acknowledge their crucial contribution, but in order to protect them from Boer retribution had to
pretend that he had arrived in Lourenço Marques unaided.

However, back in England a year later, and with the risk of
revenge passed, he wrote to John Howard at the mine: 'I am sending
to South Africa by next week's mail 8 gold watches, which are all
of them engraved with suitable inscriptions . . . I hope you will do
me the honour to accept these small keepsakes of our remarkable
adventure, and believe that they also represent my sincere gratitude
for the help and assistance you all afforded me.' He also recommended to the Secretary of State for War that those who had
helped him should receive a medal for their actions, but given the
War Office's ineptness in arranging suitable awards to loyal civilians,
it was not surprising they ignored Churchill's recommendation.

My search for the watches was a fascinating venture in itself. In
view of Churchill's meticulous attention to detail, I found it surprising that there should have been so much confusion about them.

In a note from Churchill to a secretary, he gives eight names to be engraved: Dr James Gillespie, J.R. Adams, J.D. Dewsnap, Joe McKenna, Joe McHenry, Chas A. Burnham, Ellen David and Ada Blunden; together with the inscription: 'From Winston S. Churchill in recognition of timely help afforded him in his escape from Pretoria during the South African War. Dec. 13 1899'. If, as Churchill obviously intended, there was also to be a watch for Howard, nine should have been ordered.

The watches were consigned care of the Standard Bank in Cape Town. The manager there notified Howard of their arrival, writing that he would 'pack the five watches' for onward transmission. In the event, seven watches were apparently collected by the mine secretary, John Adams, for in a written statement made in 1970 by Howard's son Lewis, 'When my dad opened the parcel there were only seven watches to be seen, and none of them bore the inscription which should have gone with my dad's watch.'

Churchill instructed that a watch be ordered for Howard and enquiries made about the watch missing from the eight which he had ordered to be sent. We do not know which watch was missing from those ordered, or if a ninth was ever sent to John Howard. According to Lewis Howard, his father never received one. Further enquiry is not possible, as Howard has no living descendants, his grandson having been killed during the Second World War while flying with the South African Air Force.

At the time of writing the fate of six watches is known. Of these, I have handled three: Daniel Dewsnap's, which is with his grandson Errol at Vereeniging; Charles Burnham's, which is in the Killie Campbell Museum in Durban; and Joe McHenry's, which is on display at Chartwell, Churchill's country house in Kent, now owned by the National Trust. Joe McKenna's watch is with his grandson Mr Jay Hagger in Guernsey, while Dr Gillespie's passed into the hands of his nephew, Major-General Robert Urquhart, in Scotland. John Adams's watch was destroyed in a fire.

The bank manager in Cape Town could not have been correct when he wrote of five watches, as six were certainly received at the mine. Lewis Howard must also have been mistaken in giving the figure as seven. The final mystery concerns the two women's watches, for Ellen David and Ada Blunden, neither of which has surfaced. Perhaps, like John Howard's, they were never sent.

It was instructive to look through the letters which were later sent to Churchill by his accomplices at the mine. In 1907 John Howard wrote to thank him for an introduction to Lord Selborne, the British High Commissioner in Cape Town. In 1908 Charles Burnham wrote seeking an introduction in East Africa, where he and his two brothers were about to farm. He was also able to tell Churchill of the hazards he had overcome when bribing various officials during their journey from Witbank to Lourenço Marques, which he had not had time to mention before they had parted in 1899. Joe McKenna's son Joseph wrote in the same year, seeking help 'in the name of my father', who had put him through college in England and France with a view to him taking up medicine or the law, but the family finances had run out.

The amicable correspondence between Howard, Burnham and McKenna and Churchill was not reflected in that with Adams, the mine secretary. In 1921, having fallen out with Howard, Adams sought in a letter to a South African journalist, Dadge Stansfield, to diminish Howard's role in Churchill's escape, and also contradicted parts of Churchill's own account. Adams seems to have been his own worst enemy, as Churchill had written without success to various people on his behalf. The final piece of correspondence, which as far as is known elicited no reply, was a letter from Adams to Churchill in 1922 requesting £100 'as a loan until I make good, which won't he long as I have a splendid diamond proposition the details of which I could let you know later and also put you in the ground floor'.

The news of Churchill's arrival in Durban prompted an avalanche of telegrams and letters over the next few weeks congratulating him on his escape. Two of them announced that the writers' newly-born sons had been named Winston. Another suggested that 'after the heroic deeds . . . and sacrifices . . . made for Queen and country', Churchill should be 'known in history as Winston the Dauntless'.

Other letters came from relatives of prisoners of war, anxiously enquiring about their welfare. Churchill responded by writing reassuring articles in the *Natal Mercury* and *Natal Witness* describing the conditions under which captured officers and men were held.

Fame is double-edged, and cuts both ways. Not all of the communications Churchill received were complimentary. The retired generals and colonels whom he later called 'The Buck and Dodder Club' took exception to the unpalatable truths in his dispatch of 24 December, his first communication to his readers after he had received information about the progress of the war which had not been available to him in prison. He had commented favourably on the Boer strategy, while criticising the British: 'Tactically Ladysmith may be strongly defensible, politically it has become invested with much importance, but for strategic purposes it is absolutely worthless. It is worse. It is a regular trap.' He had also cabled the *Morning Post*, his patriotism on his sleeve as he suggested the formation of an irregular mounted unit to mirror those already raised in South Africa: 'Are the gentlemen of England all fox hunting? Why not an English Light Horse?' The *Morning Leader*, in a sarcastic vein, wrote that they were unable to confirm that Mr Winston Churchill had been appointed 'to command the troops in South Africa with General Sir Redvers Buller VC as his Chief of Staff'.

Fortunately, Buller took the same strategic view as Churchill. A month before the war started he had warned the Secretary of State for War, Lord Lansdowne, that troops should not be deployed north of the Tugela River. Now he wrote to Lady Londonderry, one of the foremost hostesses of her day: 'Winston Churchill turned up here yesterday escaped from Pretoria. He really is a fine fellow and I must say I admire him greatly. I wish he was leading irregular troops instead of writing for a rotten paper. We are very short of good men, as he appears to be, out here.'

Buller lost no time in sending for Churchill, whose opinion he sought on conditions in the Transvaal, and who offered what information he had been able to gather from peering through the chinks in his railway wagon. The General then said, 'You have done very well. Is there anything we can do for you?'

'A commission, please, in one of the irregular corps now being improvised.'

This delighted Buller. An irregular force of volunteer mounted infantry, raised at home and in South Africa, was Buller's answer to the tactical problems of the veldt, which the regular army was ill fitted to solve. He had already recognised, in his letter to Lady Londonderry, the contribution Churchill could make. There was, however, a difficulty to overcome, and Buller paused to consider this before he gave Churchill an answer. 'What about your paper?' he asked.

Although officers were no longer allowed to double as correspondents as a result of his own activities on the North-West Frontier and in the Sudan, Churchill could not afford to break his lucrative deal with the *Morning Post*. 'I am under a definite contract and cannot possibly relinquish this engagement,' he disingenuously replied.

There was a further pause while the General rose from his chair and circled the room, casting a quizzical eye on the potential recruit while considering how to circumvent the regulation. At length he said, 'All right. You can have a commission in Bungo's regiment. You'll have to do as much as you can for both jobs, but you'll get no pay for ours.' 'Bungo' was Colonel Julian Byng, subsequently Field Marshal Lord Byng of Vimy and Governor-General of Canada, who was then commanding the South African Light Horse, alias 'Bingo's Own', or the 'Cockyolibirds', because of the coloured plumes they wore in their slouch hats. Thus, having been the cause of the regulations forbidding officers from writing for the press, Churchill became the only man ever known to have broken them without reprimand.

Colonel Byng's regiment, which Churchill joined on 2 January 1900, was part of Lord Dundonald's cavalry brigade, recruited from hardbitten soldiers of fortune, farmers, colonists and 'gentlemen rankers' from Britain, the like of which Churchill had appealed to in his cable to the *Morning Post*. These first-class irregulars were led by a group of outstanding officers who nearly all rose to high rank in the First World War: three became army commanders and some half a dozen commanded divisions. One of the latter was Reginald Barnes, who had served with Churchill in the 4th Hussars, had gone with him to Cuba, and, having recovered from grievous wounds sustained soon after arriving in South Africa, was now a squadron leader in the Imperial Light Horse.

We should be wary of taking literally Churchill's words: 'I stitched my badges of rank to my khaki coat.' That was a task he would undoubtedly have delegated to his valet Trooper Walden, who had joined the South African Light Horse when Churchill was captured, and who would now be the perfect soldier-servant. We can, however, imagine Churchill, with his flair for headgear, sticking 'the long plume of feathers from the tail of the sakabulu bird' into his hat. Of the assertion that he 'lived from day to day in perfect happiness' we need have no doubt.

Churchill was immediately at home in this company, which messed together around the same campfires and slept under the same wagons throughout the campaign in Natal, becoming the best of friends. Colonel Byng, whom Churchill had met at Aldershot when newly commissioned, made him the Assistant Adjutant, and allowed him to roam where he liked when the regiment was not in action. Thus the *Morning Post* did not go short of copy.

It has sometimes been suggested that Churchill, never usually known for pulling his punches, muted his public criticism of Buller out of gratitude for the commission in the South African Light Horse. It is true that his private letters offer a more objective judgement than his dispatches, but those letters also explain why. To Pamela Plowden he wrote on 10 January 1900: 'Alas dearest we are again in retreat. Buller started out full of determination to do or die but his courage soon ebbed . . . I cannot begin to criticise – for I should never stop . . . but there is no well known General who is as big a man as he is and *faute de mieux* we must back him for all he is worth – which at this moment is very little.' No doubt Churchill had already suspected what he would conclude thirty years later: that a Victoria Cross earned as a young officer did not necessarily fit a man to command an army after a quarter of a century of easy living. But, as he explained to Pamela at the time, no one should publicly 'attack the best men the state can find'. For his London readers he would conceal the tongue in his cheek when, for example he wrote, 'Sir Redvers Buller and his staff rode up . . . and then we knew all was well.'

But in early January 1900 all was not well. The Boers, holding the heights along the north bank of the Tugela River, were still barring the way to Ladysmith, where the morale of the besieged garrison was wearing dangerously thin. The Boer artillery, two Long Toms firing at long range, were not especially effective, but their daily bombardment dominated life in the town. Living conditions and poor diet resulted in ten deaths a day from disease alone. The commander, General Sir George White, did little to maintain the 'Ladysmith' spirit. His appointment as General Officer Commanding Natal had been questioned by Joseph Chamberlain, the Colonial Secretary, who thought him too old and ineffectual, but the War Office had chosen him nevertheless. White's ineptitude had led to the siege, and now the more enterprising regimental officers chafed at his lack of leadership, which the civilians denounced in a poster prominently displayed around the town.

Faced with this uninspired defence, the Boers decided to settle the garrison's fate once and for all. It was a dark night with no moon when, in the small hours of 6 January, they attacked Ladysmith at several points simultaneously. The numerical inferiority of the Boers – the majority of the four thousand ordered forward flinched from the actual attack – was compensated for by the superior firepower of their Mauser rifles. On the British side the inability of many officers to understand the tactical implications of the magazine rifles' rapid fire, and their propensity to attempt to redeem any situation by personal gallantry, led to suicidal counter-attacks. Well after daybreak the struggle was still raging, the combatants often separated by no more than a few yards.

Sounds of the battle woke Churchill in his tent at Chieveley, eighteen miles to the south: 'Boom. Thud, thud. Boom. Boom. Thud – Thud thud – thud thud thud thud – Boom. A long suc-

Camp before Colenso. Jan 8th 1900

Boom. Thud, thud. Boom. Boom. Thud — Thud Thud — Thud Thud Thud Thud — Boom. A long succession of queer moaning vibrations began to broke the stillness of the sleeping camp. I became suddenly awake. It was two o'clock on the morning of the 6th of January. The full significance of the sounds came with consciousness. We had all heard them before — heavy cannonading at Ladysmith. They were at it again. How much longer would the heroic garrison be persecuted? [I turned to sleep rest gently with a savage once more. But the distant guns forbade sleep. The reports grew momentarily more frequent until at last they merged into one general roar. This was new. Never before had we heard such bombarding. Louder and louder swelled the cannonade and presently the deep note of the heavy artillery could scarcely be distinguished above the incessant discharges of field pieces. So I lay and listened. What was happening eighteen miles away over the hills? Another bayonet attack by the garrison! or perhaps a general sortie: or perhaps — but this seemed scarcely conceivable, the Boers had hardened their hearts and were delivering the long expected long threatened assault.

Churchill's dispatch to the *Morning Post* of 8 January 1900.
(*Brenthurst Library, Johannesburg*)

cession of queer moaning vibrations broke the stillness of the sleeping camp.' So his London readers were graphically introduced to the battle by his dispatch two days later.

Communication between Ladysmith and General Buller's head-quarters at Frere, five miles south of Chieveley, was by heliograph and searchlight. At the very moment in the late afternoon that the Boers were abandoning their assault, a violent thunderstorm rendered the heliograph useless, while flickering Morse code messages after dark were confused by a Boer searchlight. Thus it was not until the following day that Churchill learned the outcome of the battle. As usual, his dispatch was upbeat: 'by night the Boers were repulsed at every point . . . Their first experience of assaulting. Encore!' He did not know that the final counter-attack by the Devonshire Regiment had cost them all their remaining officers but one.

It had been a near-run thing. Next time, given better cooperation between the various Boer elements, the outcome might easily go the other way. A greater urgency now attended Buller's operations to relieve Ladysmith. Metaphors came easily to Churchill: 'The warning bell has rung. Take your seats, ladies and gentlemen. The curtain is about to rise.' So London was appraised of the strategic situation. '"High time, too," say the impatient audience, and with this I must agree.'

TWELVE

A General on Spion Kop

'Ah, horrible war, amazing medley of the glorious and the
squalid, the pitiful and the sublime, if modern men of light and
leading saw your face closer, simple folk would see it hardly
ever.'

WINSTON CHURCHILL,
dispatch to the *Morning Post*, 22 January 1900

CHURCHILL'S EXPERIENCES OVER THE NEXT few weeks would
probably influence his attitude to war more even than his time in
the trenches fifteen years later. From his first taste of battle in Cuba
on his twenty-first birthday to his days as wartime Prime Minister,
he was always drawn towards the sound of gunfire, exhilarated by
personal danger and relishing excitement. But it was during the
advance on Ladysmith that, for the first time, he weighed the tragic
aspects of war along with the heroic.

Acknowledging that the Tugela River was too well defended at
Colenso to force a crossing there, Buller abandoned his plan for a
direct advance on Ladysmith along the railway. Having assembled
nineteen thousand infantry, three thousand cavalry and sixty guns,
he now intended to turn the Boer right flank by crossing the Tugela
some twenty-five miles upstream from Colenso. On 11 January the
South African Light Horse seized a crossing at Potgieter's Drift
and the ford a further five miles upstream at Trichardt's Drift.

At Potgieter's a bend in the river enabled an unopposed crossing,
but blocking the way two miles to the north the Boer defences
presented a formidable obstacle, hinged as they were on Spion Kop

– 'Spy Hill'. It had been aptly named by the Boers during the Great Trek, as it commanded the country for miles around. On the other hand, the enemy covering Trichardt's Drift were estimated by Buller's intelligence to number only about six hundred. Buller therefore decided that his main attack, with two thirds of his force, would be west of Spion Kop, at Trichardt's Drift. He himself would attack at Potgieter's when the Boers had been outflanked at Trichardt's; the two prongs of the attack would then unite and advance on Ladysmith.

Trichardt's Drift and the course of the river are today submerged beneath the Spion Kop reservoir, but not much else has changed. When one stands beneath the awesome feature of the Kop, Buller's plan seems perfectly sound. Unfortunately for him, no plan can be expected to succeed unless it is competently executed.

The outflanking movement was entrusted to Lieutenant-General Sir Charles Warren. It was a curious choice. Warren was fifty-nine, and old for his years. He had commanded an expedition in Bechuanaland in 1884, and had then been seconded from the army to be Chief Commissioner of the Metropolitan Police. Recalled to an active command, he had only recently arrived in South Africa, and was quite untried in the newly evolving tactics of the war. Buller defended his choice of Warren several years later by explaining that he considered Warren had a comparatively easy task at Trichardt's, and that he reserved for himself the more difficult operation at Potgieter's.

In his dispatch of 13 January 1900 Churchill had noted the enormous baggage train of Buller's forces: 'I have never before seen even officers accommodated with tents on service ... but here today, within striking distance of a mobile enemy whom we wish to circumvent, every private soldier has canvas shelter ... all rapidity of movement is out of the question.' The fact that Buller's popularity with his troops survived so many reversals was, no doubt, due in part to his concern for their welfare. However, the longer it took Buller's men to reach their positions, the more complete would be the Boer defences, and the greater the cost of overcoming them. The *Morning Post* readers were left in no doubt of their young correspondent's views when he continued: 'It is a poor economy to let a soldier live well for three days at the price of killing him on the fourth.'

Churchill's criticism was more than justified. It was not until daybreak on 18 January, a whole week after the South African Light Horse, that Warren had most of his troops across the river. His leisurely and ponderous moves were easily covered by the more agile Boers, who were given ample time to extend their defences westwards along the heights of Tabanyama, which commanded the northern bank of the river. They were thus never in danger of being outflanked.

Lord Dundonald's cavalry brigade had no baggage train and, living largely off the land, was able to ride at will over wide areas of Natal. How widely they ranged can be seen from the spread of the beautiful pink cosmos flower, which, a native plant of Argentina, was imported into South Africa with the cavalry's horse fodder. Just as one can see the places where soldiers fell by the cairns on the battlefields, so one can mark their route by the pink swathes of cosmos. As I stopped to pick these lovely flowers I wondered if the seeds that had produced that very bunch had germinated in the belly of my grandfather's horse as he had ridden over that same ground.

I learned that no one was more adept at living off the country than Lieutenant Churchill of the Cockyolibirds. The young officer, with the long plume of feathers from the tail of a sakabulu bird in his hat, became well known among the farms and villages of Natal.

My favourite story of his foraging is the tale of the chicken at Springfield, now called Winterton. I went there with Churchill's description, in his dispatch of 13 January 1900, fresh in my mind: 'three houses, half a dozen farms with their tin roofs and tree clumps seen in the neighbourhood'. I soon found the stone foundations of what, a century ago, was a tin-roofed store with a backyard fenced off from the open country beyond. It was easy to imagine how the shop would have looked back then, its wooden counter and shelving stacked with the everyday needs of the local inhabitants.

I did not need to use my imagination to picture the scene on the day that the cavalry rode through shortly before the battle of Spion Kop, as Mrs Lette Bennet recounted the story exactly as she had heard it from her mother: 'My mother, Anna Beyers, was in my grandfather's farm shop at Springfield and remembered the day she served Winston Churchill. He trotted up the dusty lane and tethered his horse outside the shop. He bought candlesticks and sardines. My mother told me how she could never forget the way he lisped when he asked her for the sardines.' Mrs Bennet continued, chuckling: 'My mother then would tell the part she liked best. Mr Churchill then looked around and spotted the chickens in the yard. He asked if he could buy one, to which my mother replied, "Yes, if you can catch it."'

A young man who had been through so much was not going to be defeated by a chicken, and a few minutes later he rode off with his purchases – 'candlesticks, sardines and a chicken'. Future customers were treated to a hilarious account of Churchill chasing the chicken around the yard, thus spreading the story, which is told to this day.

A few yards from the ruined shop is the grave of Driver Linton, Royal Artillery. The first casualty in Warren's operations, he was crushed by the wheel of an ox wagon while crossing Tritchard's Drift, and drowned on 17 January 1900. Fifteen years later Andries Beyers, Anna Beyers' father and the owner of the farm, was buried beside him.

On 20 and 21 January Warren finally attacked the Boer defences. His infantry made some progress up the gullies leading to the crest of Tabanyama, but although they were well supported by artillery, which fired almost six thousand shells, they were halted in exposed positions well short of their main objective, and began to suffer considerable casualties. When Churchill arrived at the position of the Dublin Fusiliers, he found they had lost about half their number. As usual, his dispatch included some telling touches. He recounts a conversation with the Fusiliers' commanding officer: 'Very few of us left now,' said the Colonel. 'About 450 out of nine hundred.' He came across a young soldier whose trouser leg was soaked in blood. He was stoically munching a biscuit. When Churchill asked if he was wounded he replied, 'No sir; it's only blood from an officer's head,' and carried on eating.

Dundonald's cavalry, which had the task of protecting Warren's left flank, moved further westwards, where they successfully defeated a small force of two hundred Boers in the area of Acton Homes. For the young Churchill, this small, short but sharp engagement 'aroused the most painful emotions'. He had campaigned on three continents, and was no stranger to the gruesome aftermath of battle. He had seen thousands killed at Omdurman, and scores elsewhere. But never had he been so affected by the sight of a battle's victims.

Churchill's dispatch of 22 January captures exactly the British mood during the battle and in its aftermath: 'The desire to kill was gone. The desire to comfort replaced it.' He describes one bright-eyed and excited young officer crying 'Bag the lot!' as he galloped under fire towards the Boer position. Within a few minutes his exhilaration had given way to sadness, and he was saying of one of the fallen enemy: 'There's a poor boy dying up there – only a boy, and so cold – who's got a blanket?'

The *Morning Post*'s readers, safe and comfortable at their breakfast tables eight thousand miles away, were reminded that grief has little to do with the scale of events. The man dying of wounds or the woman left a widow experience the same pain and grief whether the cause is a brief skirmish or Armageddon itself.

Churchill's dispatch told of the Boer Field Cornet Mentz, grey-haired and more than sixty, who continued to load and fire his Mauser until he bled to death from a wound which could have been staunched had he surrendered. He was found holding a letter from his wife. 'The stony face was grimly calm, but it bore the stamp of unalterable resolve; the look of a man who had thought it all out, and was quite certain his cause was just.' Beside him was the body of a boy of seventeen, shot through the heart. Further on were two British riflemen, 'and I suppose they had mothers or wives far away at the end of deep-sea cables'.

Major Childe, 'a serene old gentleman', was among the British casualties. Years before, he had served in the Blues, since when he had been active and well liked in English racing circles. 'Old and grey as he was, the call to arms had drawn him from home, and wife, and comfort.' His gravestone, which stands close to where he fell in an action during which he earned 'the admiration of thousands of the infantry', carries the epitaph which he had chosen in advance, 'Is it well with the child? It is well!'

Beyond the scene of the engagement at Acton Homes lay open country and an easy route to Ladysmith. The cavalry, and in particular the experienced colonials among them, thought that a wider flanking movement through Acton Homes would be a better approach to Ladysmith than the one on which General Warren was presently bogged down. A Marlborough or a Napoleon would no doubt have agreed, but to Buller, whose forces moved so ponderously, it was hardly a feasible option.

By 23 January his patience was exhausted. Warren's men were badly positioned and continually exposed to enemy fire, with nothing to show for it. Buller ordered him to attack or have his force withdrawn. Warren decided his objective would be Spion Kop, the nub of the whole Boer position. Its commanding situation and precipitous slopes made it the hardest nut of all to crack, but if the Boer defences could be broken there, his route to Ladysmith would be open.

Churchill did not enter the fray on Spion Kop until late in the battle, but to appreciate his actions when he did join in, it is necessary to understand what went before. At 8.30 p.m. on 24 January Warren's assaulting troops gathered below his headquarters on Three Tree Hill, some six miles from the summit of Spion Kop. (It was, incidentally, the fifth anniversary of Churchill's father's death. 24 January would also be, as he prophesied, the date on which he died sixty-five years later.) In command was Major-General Woodgate, with two thousand men of his own Lancashire Brigade and two hundred from Colonel Thorneycroft's mounted infantry. Thorneycroft, a huge, imposing man, led the way at the head of his men. He had been one of ten special service officers sent to South Africa before the war to provide local intelligence, and on its outbreak he had raised and paid for from his own pocket a mounted infantry regiment of colonials and Uitlanders. Behind them Woodgate followed at the head of his two thousand men. An amazing omission from the equipment they carried was sufficient picks and shovels to dig defences once the objective was captured. Only one of each was taken for every hundred men in the force.

After about nine hours of hard going, Thorneycroft approached the summit of Spion Kop and deployed his men across the hillside to await the arrival of Woodgate, who, having lagged a good way behind, did not catch up until day was beginning to break. Under cover of the dense mist which now surrounded them, Thorneycroft's men stormed the crest and captured it at the cost of no more than ten men wounded. The prearranged signal of three cheers from his troops was heard by the waiting staff below, relayed to Warren on Three Tree Hill and signalled to Buller. The way to Ladysmith was open. It was evidently a British triumph and a Boer disaster.

But in battle things are seldom as good as they seem, and almost never as bad. For those who had created the good news, the mist which was covering their movements was also misleading them. The trenches they marked out for their defence did not cover the Boer approaches. Equally disastrously, Woodgate ignored Conical Hill and Aloe Knoll, two vital features from which rifle fire could sweep the summit of Spion Kop. Half a mile to the north and a quarter of a mile to the east respectively, their importance is obvious to anyone visiting this eerie battleground, and Woodgate, though hampered by the mist and an indifferent map, should have ensured that they were occupied. They would automatically have been included in his defensive perimeter had it been pushed out by the proper deployment of all the men at his disposal. As it was, he confined his defence to a small area of hilltop to be held from behind whatever protection twenty picks and shovels could scrape out.

General Botha took the bad news in his stride. He believed the situation could still be saved, providing the British were prevented

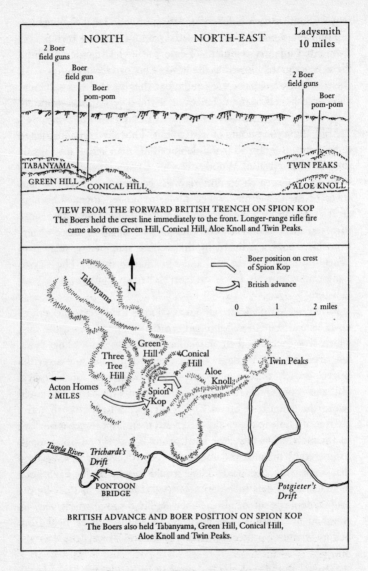

VIEW FROM THE FORWARD BRITISH TRENCH ON SPION KOP
The Boers held the crest line immediately to the front. Longer-range rifle fire
came also from Green Hill, Conical Hill, Aloe Knoll and Twin Peaks.

BRITISH ADVANCE AND BOER POSITION ON SPION KOP
The Boers also held Tabanyama, Green Hill, Conical Hill,
Aloe Knoll and Twin Peaks.

The Battle of Spion Kop

from bringing their artillery up Spion Kop. His own artillery covered the summit from several directions, while effective rifle fire could be maintained from Conical Hill and Aloe Knoll.

Botha's counter-attack was launched soon after daybreak. Several hundred men from the Carolina and Pretoria Commandos, supported by Mauser fire from Conical Hill, started up the northern slope of the Kop. On reaching the crest line they were met by a volley of fire from behind the boulders thrown up around the crescent-shaped trench less than two hundred yards ahead. There they went to ground, dead or alive. Some eased back and worked their way up to Aloe Knoll, from where they could fire into the British trench.

The British artillery was not suitably deployed to respond to the Boer guns which now poured shells into the British position. Woodgate was mortally wounded by a shell fragment, and his Brigade Major was killed. Among the other casualties were many of the officers to whom the men looked for leadership, so the defence soon lacked cohesion, and was often based on groups of intermingled survivors from different regiments acting independently. The senior officer left, Colonel Crofton, sent a panicky message to Warren that without reinforcements all would be lost. Only Thorneycroft attempted to take control of the situation. He rushed hither and thither inspiring, ordering, and on one occasion intervening between Boers and some British troops who were attempting to surrender.

The Boers, however, did not know the full extent of the plight of the British. The burning sun, a lack of water, the sight of the Kop littered with corpses which were now attracting swarms of flies, all began to sap their morale, so that by midday many of those who had so bravely advanced had begun to creep away down the hill. Nevertheless, supported as they were by artillery, enough determined burghers remained to hold their position.

Through a powerful telescope, Buller had been watching the struggle from his headquarters four miles away on Mount Alice, south of the Tugela. His personal staff officer attached to Woodgate's brigade, Colonel Charles à Court, had returned from the summit and reported the parlous state of the defences there. Buller realised, as Warren did not, that Spion Kop would be lost if a strong and determined commander did not immediately take control of the scene. At his suggestion Warren appointed Thorneycroft to supersede Crofton. The message was passed by heliograph to the summit, but because the runner there was shot dead as he reached Thorneycroft, it was some time before the man who had been the only effective commander on the scene for some hours heard of his official appointment.

Also watching the battle through a telescope was Churchill's companion from his days in Estcourt, John Atkins of the *Manchester Guardian*. War correspondents, while not usually privy to the larger designs, sometimes have a better grasp of the immediate situation than the generals. Atkins certainly had a better understanding than Warren: 'that acre of massacre,' he wrote, 'that complete shambles, at the top of a rich green gully with cool granite walls ... To me it seemed that our men were all in a small square patch; there were brown men and browner trenches, the whole like an over-ripe barley-field. I saw three shells strike a certain trench within a minute, each struck it full in the face, and the brown dust rose and drifted away with the white smoke.'

Major-General Lyttelton, Warren's second Brigade Commander, had so far played no part in the battle. As part of Buller's two-pronged plan, he had been waiting to assault at Potgieter's Drift after Warren's operations at Tritchardt's Drift had outflanked the Boers. At around midday, on his own initiative and with no reference to Warren, he sent the 60th Rifles to capture a feature called Twin Peaks some two miles to the east of Spion Kop. Troops holding this position could make life difficult for the Boers on Aloe Knoll, thereby relieving pressure on the summit. Even as the 60th were climbing the steep slopes, confusion almost resulted in their immediate withdrawal. One of Lyttelton's staff officers on the summit had signalled that the Boers were holding Twin Peaks and that the 60th's attempt could hardly succeed. Fortunately for the broader picture, but unfortunately for himself and for many others, the commanding officer, Colonel Riddle, who was to be killed during

the assault, ignored the repeated order to withdraw, and by late
that afternoon the peaks were in British hands. The cost was high:
a hundred casualties. Eventually, as dusk fell, the message to withdraw was acknowledged, and the 60th abandoned Twin Peaks. They
had, though, achieved their purpose, and the Boers who had been
holding the position fled, taking with them some of the artillery
and leaving a gaping hole in the Boer defences.

Following Crofton's alarming note from the battleground,
Warren sent Major-General Coke with three battalions as
reinforcements. One of these battalions, the Middlesex, provided
welcome relief at a crucial time. But Coke himself, who had been
ordered to assume overall command on Spion Kop, never reached
the scene, and appears not to have influenced the battle at all.

Meanwhile, on the summit, Thorneycroft had been on the go
for well over twenty-four hours, and under hellish fire for the best
part of a day. During the afternoon large shells from the Boer
artillery were falling on the hilltop at the rate of seven a minute,
while pompoms raked the ground with smaller explosive shells.
Apart from his promotion to command, Thorneycroft had heard
nothing from Warren, and was unaware that Coke's reinforcements
were on the way. He was also unaware of the preparations, albeit
dilatory, being made to manhandle artillery to the summit, and to
send up water, ammunition and stretcher-bearers. At 2.30 in the
afternoon he sent a note telling Warren that he required more
infantry and for the enemy guns to be attacked if Spion Kop was
to be held though the night. He added that many of his men had
been killed or wounded, and that the need for water was urgent.

The message passed through Coke, who though he was well
short of the summit and had no first-hand information of his own,
added the astonishing reassurance: 'We appear to be holding our
own.' As a result, Warren received conflicting and confusing information. Everything appeared to be in chaos.

This was the moment at which General Warren could have personally influenced events for the better by going forward, finding
out what was happening, and ensuring that Thorneycroft was aware
of the importance of hanging on. He could have explained that the

measures already in hand would enable the British forces to exploit the capture of Spion Kop, whereas any faltering at this stage could throw away everything which had been gained earlier that day. His appearance on the scene would have raised morale at a crucial moment. The foot of Spion Kop was no more than half an hour's ride from Warren's headquarters at Three Tree Hill. Had he ordered his horse to be saddled, the day could have been saved.

Although Warren was disinclined to exert much influence, there was, in the words of Thomas Pakenham, 'one self-appointed messenger who might have turned the balance in favour of the British . . . It was young Winston Churchill instinctively taking over the role of general.' That day Churchill's regiment were left out of the battle, and by four in the afternoon he could no longer contain his frustration.

He had been watching events unfold from Mount Alice, which, as can be seen from photographs taken in 1900, was then a bare hill affording an unhindered view of the surrounding country. Now, because of overgrazing and the elimination of game, the hill is covered by a mass of tangled bush and aloe trees. Pushing through the thorns, I arrived at the top. Here a memorial and the grave of Colonel Riddle mark the spot from where Buller and his staff had attempted to influence the battle. Even though it is now covered in bush, the hill still affords a magnificent view of Spion Kop, six miles away across the Tugela River, and I pictured my grandfather observing the shambles on that dreadful day.

The summit of Spion Kop dominates the surrounding features. Troops in firm possession of it would have made the containing Boer positions untenable. But, badly positioned, their chain of command confused, and inadequately supported by artillery, the British troops had been anything but firm. It needed little imagination to comprehend their plight, under fire from Twin Peaks and Aloe Knoll to their right, Conical Hill in front of them, and Green Hill and Tabanyama on their left.

The importance of Twin Peaks was obvious, and it was easy to understand why Lyttelton had ordered its capture. His faith in the

60th must have been absolute, as I would not have believed that any-one could have climbed those precipitous slopes under fire had Colonel Riddle and his men not succeeded in that seemingly imposs-ible task. The order for their withdrawal seemed incomprehensible now, though clearly it had not during the confusion of the battle.

I could imagine Buller's frustration as he watched impotently from Mount Alice. I could see an impatient Churchill swinging himself into the saddle and cantering down the slope towards the sound of gunfire to discover for himself what was happening.

Accompanied by a fellow officer, Captain Brooke, Churchill arrived at the ambulance village, between Warren's headquarters at Three Tree Hill and the summit of Spion Kop. Here they tethered their horses and continued on foot.

Up to this point Churchill, in describing the battle, had fewer advantages than he normally enjoyed over other correspondents. As a combatant as well as a correspondent he was usually well placed to describe events and comment authoritatively on them. But on this occasion, the first part of his dispatch on the battle was written from distant observation and information gleaned at second hand. From the moment he reached the ambulance village, his dispatch changes in tone: 'perhaps the reader will allow me to break into a more personal account of what followed'.

The idiom of Churchill's dispatches is Victorian, yet even a cen-tury after the events he describes, when television has deadened the senses, his description of battle conjures genuine excitement. Short, staccato sentences are set against melodious passages, reflecting the contrast between sharp engagements and the strategic ebb and flow of the wider campaign. Aged only twenty-five, he must rank among the great war correspondents. At the turn of the century the vast majority of his readers would have had only a glamorised image of war, and they must have been as shocked by his dispatches as Americans were to be over sixty years later when television brought Vietnam into their living rooms. But in 1900 the British people were deeply patriotic. Bad news simply increased their resolve.

As Churchill and Captain Brooke climbed Spion Kop they passed streams of men coming downhill:

> Men were staggering along alone, or supported by comrades, or crawling on hands and knees, or carried on stretchers. Corpses lay here and there . . . I passed about two hundred . . . There was, moreover, a small but steady leakage of unwounded men. Some of these cursed and swore. Others utterly exhausted fell on the hillside in stupor. Others seemed drunk although they had had no liquor . . . stray bullets struck all over the ground, while the Maxim shell guns scourged the flanks of the hill and the sheltering infantry at regular intervals of a minute.

I scrambled with my young son up the track which his great-grandfather had climbed a century before. Under a lowering sky we surveyed the scene of the carnage through which Churchill had crawled under shot and shell. Spion Kop is the most evocative of battlefields. The main British trench, which photographs taken the day after the battle show piled with dead, is marked by a long, curved mound with a low wall of white stones. It is the mass grave of the men who fell defending it. Monuments to regiments and individuals are silhouetted against the sky.

The summit of the hill is really a plateau, and I could see why the mist had caused mistakes in laying out the British position, thus leaving vital ground unoccupied. Twin Peaks and Aloe Knoll menaced the site from the left. Conical Hill was uncomfortably close in front. Green Hill and Tabanyama, though further away, added to the threat. On the crest line, only a few yards ahead, had been the forward Boer positions. The ground is hard and rocky; even with adequate tools it would have been difficult to dig satisfactory trenches. The shallow scrapes and piled rocks would have provided little protection from the Boer field guns and maxims.

And yet the British troops hung on. 24 January must have been their longest day. With hindsight it is clear that they should have prevailed. That was the conclusion my grandfather had reached by the time he decided to return and report to General Warren.

*   *   *

Churchill arrived in Warren's headquarters to find a debate in progress. The artillery were saying that they could not get their guns to the summit. The naval gunners, whom Buller had put at Warren's disposal, said they would try. Churchill's account of the dispute in *My Early Life* is at odds with that of Captain Levita, an officer on Warren's staff, who records Warren's irritation at what he considered Churchill's unwarranted intrusion. Churchill began to harangue the General, and Levita overheard him saying the words 'Majuba Hill' and 'the great British public' before Warren shouted, 'Who is this man? Take him away. Put him in arrest.' Eventually Warren was prevailed upon to listen to the bearer of bad news, and to allow Churchill to return to the summit with a message.

Churchill's account, by contrast, simply records that he was listened to 'with great patience and attention', after which he returned to the summit bearing the news, authenticated by a written message from Levita, that reinforcements, water, ammunition, food, sandbags and the guns were on their way.

His second, solitary journey to the summit was even more hair-raising than the first:

> The darkness was intense. The track was stony and uneven.
> It was hopelessly congested with ambulances, stragglers and
> wounded men . . . an intermittent crackle of musketry . . . Only
> one solid battalion remained – the Dorsets . . . Stragglers and
> weaklings there were in plenty. But the mass of the soldiers
> were determined men . . . Regimental officers everywhere cool
> and cheery, each with a little group of men around him . . .
> But the darkness and broken ground paralysed everyone.

Churchill found Thorneycroft, handed over the message and explained the plans for guns and reinforcements. When he asked for Thorneycroft's views he discovered that the decision to abandon the summit had already been taken. There had been some argument, of which Churchill was probably unaware, as he did not mention it in any of his accounts of the withdrawal. Two commanding officers had agreed to the withdrawal, but Colonel Hill of the Middlesex Regiment had refused. He considered himself senior to

Thorneycroft, and did not believe that the latter had been placed in command. Coke, who had not been told by Warren of Thorneycroft's elevation, supported Hill. But the will of the strongest man prevailed, as it had throughout the long and difficult day, and Thorneycroft's decision was accepted.

In a final attempt to persuade Thorneycroft to hang on, Churchill suggested that he return to Warren once more. Thorneycroft, physically and mentally exhausted, replied that it would be better to have six battalions safely off the hill than to have them mopped up in the morning. So the trek down the hill began.

Thorneycroft was not to know that the Boers had also accepted defeat. During the day many of them had slunk away, leaving a handful, tormented by the sun and the pitiful cries of the wounded, to hold off the British. Sometime before midnight the remaining Boers withdrew. A seventeen-year-old boy, Deneys Reitz, was one of the last to leave. Later, in his classic account of the Boer War, *Commando*, he wrote that they withdrew, 'fully believing that in the morning the British would be streaming through the gap to the relief of Ladysmith'.

So, in the darkness Spion Kop was abandoned by both sides to the dead and wounded. Leaving in opposite directions were two young men, then opponents but later both to command British regiments in Flanders in the First World War: Deneys Reitz and Winston Churchill.

As Churchill and Thorneycroft left the hill they came upon the Dorsets, the reserve battalion which had come up with Coke, still not deployed. Thorneycroft hesitated at the sight of these fresh troops, but for all he knew the Boers had reoccupied the summit, so he continued his descent. They next met the reinforcements coming up, with a written message from Warren telling Thorneycroft to entrench himself by morning. Thorneycroft brandished his walking stick – he was suffering from a twisted ankle – and ordered the reinforcements to turn back.

It took some time for Churchill to find his way in the darkness to Warren's headquarters. Years later he recounted: 'The General was asleep. I put my hand on his shoulder and woke him up.

"Colonel Thorneycroft is here, sir." He took it all very calmly. He was a charming old gentleman. I was genuinely sorry for him. I was also sorry for the army.'

The following morning, two burghers found the summit deserted. Botha's prediction that the situation could be retrieved had been proved correct, and now the Boers reoccupied the position in strength. Reitz records that in the shallow British trenches 'the soldiers lay dead in swathes, and in places they were piled three deep . . . There must have been six hundred dead men on this strip of earth.' Botha sent a flag of truce inviting the British to gather their wounded and bury their dead, tasks in which his men assisted. A Boer doctor, surveying the carnage, paid a tribute to British discipline when he commented, 'We Boers would not, could not suffer like this.'

Among the dead was a young man, a contemporary of Churchill at Harrow, who had hailed him the evening before as he crossed the pontoon over the Tugela. His shattered field glasses bore the name M'Corquodale: 'The name and the face flew together in my mind. It was the last joined subaltern of Thorneycroft's Mounted Infantry – joined in the evening, shot at dawn.'

On 25 and 26 January the whole of Buller's army withdrew across the Tugela. He had lost 1,733 men killed, wounded or captured. Absolutely nothing had been gained, except that, from Buller downwards, the army had perhaps learned something about modern war.

With hindsight, the Battle of Spion Kop had a huge potential to alter the shape of the twentieth century. There on the battlefield, within a mile of one another, were three men destined for greatness: Louis Botha, the Boer General; a young Indian lawyer, Mohandas Karamchand Gandhi, who was organising the Natal stretcher-bearers; and Winston Churchill, the intrepid British adventurer. What a difference one or two or three stray bullets would have made to the history of three continents and the world beyond!

Writing to Pamela Plowden afterwards, Churchill described his 'five very dangerous days – continually under shell & rifle fire and once the feather in my hat was cut through by a bullet'. To him, nothing was more satisfying than a risk successfully run. Pamela had urged him to come home, to which he replied: 'My place is here: here I stay – perhaps for ever.' Small wonder she married another man. At this stage in his life Churchill would have made a very unsatisfactory husband.

To his *Morning Post* readers Churchill wrote that the British people could regard the battle with equal pride and sadness: 'It redounds to the honour of the soldiers, though not greatly to that of the generals.' He tempered this criticism by reminding his public that the generals were, 'after all, brave, capable, noble English gentlemen, trying their best'. Certainly, during their long service, most of them had proved their valour, but at Spion Kop their capabilities were in serious doubt. However, because there were no substitutes to hand, Churchill was not about to undermine them completely in the public eye.

Churchill had failed in his self-appointed mission to turn the tide of battle, but in war soldiers can be more fairly judged by their efforts than by the outcome, which turns on so many unknowns. And, after all, Churchill was only an irregular Lieutenant. Had any of the generals, from Buller downwards, shown even a fraction of his resolution, the British would have triumphed at Spion Kop.

THIRTEEN

Into Ladysmith

'I knew all the generals and other swells, had access to everyone,
and was everywhere well received.'

WINSTON CHURCHILL, *My Early Life*

YEARS LATER, EVEN AFTER HE had held high political office –
Home Secretary, First Lord of the Admiralty and Chancellor
among others – Churchill would regard the two months he spent
fighting for the relief of Ladysmith as among the happiest memories
of his life. Even his dispatch of 4 February 1900, the first after the
fiasco of Spion Kop, reflects this, extolling the pleasures of the
soldier's life and comparing it with that of those in a 'civilised city
who . . . gained luxury at the expense of joy'. The young correspondent had enough experience of life in the round to know that there
were many city-dwellers for whom the merest form of luxury was
unknown – but they would not be readers of the *Morning Post*.
Those, he judged, needed a cheerful message after the recent disaster, and not a harbinger of further sacrifice.

Churchill loved the open air, and he commended to his readers
the delights of galloping across the veldt in bright, sunlit days, and
sleeping under a wagon, shoulder to shoulder for warmth and shelter from the cool night showers. He conjured up the atmosphere
of camp life, describing the surrounding hills taking shape in the
gathering light while the kettle boiled over the fire. Another day
begun, 'free from all cares'. His readers were then lightly returned
to the business in hand: 'All cares – for who can be worried about

the little matters of humdrum life when he may be dead before the night?'

Meanwhile, the garrison in Ladysmith was in dire straits, and the relieving army had returned to its tented lines south of the Tugela. There, in sight of the rusting remains of Churchill's armoured train, Buller addressed his troops, welcomed the reinforcements which more than made up for his recent losses, and planned the next attempt to reach Ladysmith.

Taken together, Churchill's dispatches reflect dismay at Buller's plodding leadership; but when they are read singly, as they were written, the faults are excused. The only criticism Churchill permitted himself on 4 February was to wonder why Buller had entrusted recent operations to subordinates, and waited so long before gathering the reins firmly to himself. 'Probably', he suggested disingenuously, because of 'some pedantic principle of military etiquette'.

That Churchill's muted criticism was in the interests of public morale, and was not intended to ingratiate himself with the military hierarchy, is demonstrated by the last quarter of this dispatch. He had just attended a church parade at which five thousand men formed up in a hollow square, with Buller and the chaplain in the centre. Here were men who had recently faced death, and who would do so again very shortly. In spite of the sunshine, life seemed precarious. This was an occasion at which the preacher should have given comfort and strength. Scathingly, Churchill describes how, in the face of a raucous chaplain, the soldiers 'froze into apathy, and after a while the formal perfunctory service reached its formal conclusion': 'The bridegroom Opportunity had come. But the Church had her lamp untrimmed.'

Continuing his criticism, Churchill reported a fellow officer musing on the fact that the medical profession had sent its best men to tend men's physical wounds, while their souls were left to the care of 'a village practitioner'. Churchill reflected on previous campaigns where he had also found the established Church wanting. He remembered 'the venerable figure and noble character of Father Brindle in the River War, and wondered whether Rome was again seizing the opportunity which Canterbury disdained – the opportunity of telling the glad tidings to men who were about to die'.

When the new Commander-in-Chief, Lord Roberts, read this dispatch, he considered it a slight on army chaplains. His feathers were further ruffled when, as a result of it, clergymen from all over Britain began to volunteer for service in South Africa. Churchill's few telling words had done some good, but he was now in Roberts's bad books. This would soon prove to his disadvantage.

At the end of January Churchill snatched a few days' leave in order to meet his mother and his younger brother Jack in Durban. Lady Randolph had been the moving force behind a committee of American women in London who, as a gesture of Anglo-American solidarity in opposition to the American government's sympathy for the Boers, had raised £45,000 to provide a hospital ship. Named the *Maine*, it had sailed in December 1899, with Lady Randolph on board to manage its nursing services.

On 28 January Churchill wrote to Pamela Plowden: 'My Mother and Jack arrive today at Durban in the Maine: Oh why did you not come out as secretary.' The long letter continues with snippets of news and comment, and includes the oft-repeated sentiment, 'I have a good belief that I am to be of some use and therefore to be spared,' and the statement: 'I am fairly satisfied with what has happened to me here. That is sufficient if you agree.' It ends: 'Why did you not come out on the Maine so I should be going to meet you now. Perhaps you are wise. Ever your loving and devoted Winston S. Churchill.'

What an adventure Pamela could have had, and what a wonderful escape it would have been from the constrictions of Victorian society – quite apart from the opportunity to see the man who was courting her, albeit in a rather half-hearted fashion. If she was more committed to Winston than he was to her, how galling it must have been to be asked why she had not accompanied his mother when he had never suggested it, and then for him to make matters worse by adding, 'Perhaps you are wise.'

It seems strange that Lady Randolph, herself unfettered by any maidenly inhibitions, and never one to conform, did not invite

Pamela to fulfil some suitable role on the *Maine* and thereby promote the marriage which she clearly desired for her son.

Hard on Lady Randolph's heels had been her younger son, for whom Churchill had obtained a commission in the South African Light Horse. Jack, who had sailed on a faster ship, joined her on the *Maine* when it sailed on to Durban. She and her two sons enjoyed a precious twenty-four hours together in the foothills of the Drakensberg Mountains, staying at Government House in Pietermaritzburg, before Winston took Jack off to war.

Lady Randolph had transported eight army reserve nursing sisters from Cape Town to Durban. Their entourage reflected the philosophy of General Buller's baggage train – each had brought her own lady's maid. 'I did not envy the hospitals which were to benefit from their services,' commented Lady Randolph.

On 5 February Buller made another attempt to relieve Ladysmith. On that day Churchill, mindful of the possible effect on morale at home of the army's recent reverses, wrote to his cousin Hugh Frewen: 'You must not allow your mother and friends to be despondent about this war . . . We are going to make a general attack . . . and I hope and pray you may soon have good news of victory.'

But the good news was still elusive. After three days spent attempting to cross the Tugela a few miles east of Spion Kop, Buller was again forced to acknowledge defeat. Once more the weary troops withdrew to the south bank, after three consecutive costly failures: Colenso, Spion Kop, and now what became known as Vaal Krantz, after the ridge which had been the infantry's objective.

In the years ahead there would be many critics of Buller. Foremost among them was Leo Amery, who had shared Churchill's tent at Estcourt and who would edit *The Times History of the War in South Africa*. It was a weighty work, running to seven volumes, in which Amery portrays Buller as symbolising all that was undoubtedly wrong with the British military hierarchy of 1900. Amery suggested that any well-planned attack would have succeeded in opening the way to Ladysmith where Buller had failed. This was an extraordinary oversimplification by a young reporter with no military expertise who had not been present, even as an observer, at the battles of which he wrote.

Churchill, on the other hand, had been in the thick of every action, and, being an instinctive soldier, had a better understanding of events. He pointed out to his *Morning Post* readers that the superior mobility of the Boers allowed them to concentrate their forces at any point where they were attacked, that the carefully pre-pared Boer reserve positions were out of range of British artillery, and that the ground was too broken for night operations. In excusing Buller, he glossed over the fact that the solution to the problems of British mobility lay in their own hands – but readers who were following the campaign carefully would remember that in a previous dispatch he had criticised the force's huge baggage train.

Fortunately, the army was still solidly behind its Commander-in-Chief, and even Major-General Lyttelton, who covertly criticised his commander to the press, believed that twice the number of troops available would be needed to remove the Boers from their well-prepared entrenchments which barred the way to Ladysmith.

Buller had tried everywhere along the Tugela from Colenso as far westwards as he, though not the cavalry, had thought feasible. For his fourth attempt he looked at the ground east of Colenso, where the Tugela turns northwards towards Ladysmith, isolating the Boer left flank before flowing *behind* their defences. This seems such an obvious line of attack that historians have criticised Buller for not attempting it earlier. Thirty years later, Churchill's simple but damning explanation was that 'Buller had not happened to think of it before.' And at the time no one else had suggested it either, not even the clever young correspondent. Nevertheless, Churchill's criticism is warranted. Buller, with his vast experience, should have considered this route as one of his initial options, and not waited to be driven to it.

Unsure of the best line of attack, Buller ordered a reconnaissance in force. On 12 February a composite force was ordered to secure a feature known as Hussar Hill. Taking part was the South African Light Horse, which cantered out at 8 a.m. 'We never get up early in this war,' wrote Churchill in his dispatch three days later. Was this a comment on the lack of urgency which characterised British operations, or a light-hearted quip to show that English gentlemen set whatever pace they themselves decided? Probably the former, though most London readers would have taken it as a typical example of British *sang-froid*.

At midday Buller arrived and 'made a prolonged reconnaissance of the ground with his telescope'. The reconnaissance complete, he left an hour later, and the force which had secured the hill began the difficult task of withdrawing under enemy fire.

Once again the breakfast tables in London were treated to a visual account. As Churchill rode away, 'the ground two hundred yards further back was all alive with jumping dust'. The Boer marksmen were shooting short. On reaching a ridge the regiment dismounted and, the horses having been led to the rear, the men dropped down and began to pick off the enemy: 'Not less than four hundred men on either side were firing as fast as modern rifles will allow.' Fortunately, the distance between the opposing forces prevented this becoming the bloody sort of duel seen on Spion Kop, but it was an entirely new experience for young Jack Churchill, in action for the very first time.

As Winston Churchill, walking along the line of prone riflemen, approached his brother, he 'saw him start in the quick, peculiar manner of a stricken man'. Jack had been hit in the leg. Writing to Pamela nine days later, Churchill reported: 'Here is an example of Fortune's caprice ... There was very hot fire – bullets ... in dozens. I was walking about without any cover – I who have tempted fortune so often. Jack was hit. I am glad he is out of harms way *honourably* for a month.' Jack was sent back to Durban to be treated on the *Maine*, one of his mother's first patients.

Churchill was not alone in thinking he had sublime protection. John Atkins, the *Manchester Guardian* correspondent who had shared Churchill's tent in Estcourt, writing of Jack's wound, commented: 'It seemed as though he had paid his brother's debts.'

As a result of his reconnaissance and, no doubt, the intelligence reports he received, Buller decided to outflank the Boer defences east of Colenso by capturing a thousand-foot feature called Monte

Cristo which dominated the whole Boer defensive position. The South African Light Horse was to play a major role in this operation. As usual, Buller moved methodically. On 14 February Hussar Hill was reoccupied after a short, sharp skirmish in which the South African Light Horse lost only a few horses and men. Covering the next four miles took three days, but on the seventeenth the regiment chased away some hundred Boers barring the final approach to Monte Cristo, leaving the British in possession of the tangled ridges at the foot of the mountain. The following morning the infantry secured the whole feature. From the peak of Monte Cristo, Ladysmith was plainly visible.

Churchill telegraphed the *Morning Post* two days later that 'now at last success was a distinct possibility'. Keen to see for himself, he followed close on the heels of the infantry: 'Only eight miles away stood the poor little persecuted town,' he wrote. The victory of Monte Cristo had 'revolutionised the situation in Natal', and 'laid open a practicable road to Ladysmith'.

It was to be a fortnight – the longest interval ever between his instalments – before Churchill wrote his next dispatch, from the *Maine*, on board which he was taking a few days' rest. To his readers he explained: 'We have passed through a period of ceaseless struggle ... I could not pause to record anything.' Buller's caution had prevailed, and he had concluded that the country was too broken for a further advance from Monte Cristo. Encouraged by the sight of so many fleeing Boers fearing that they had been outflanked, he decided to abandon the newly captured high ground and to revert to his original choice of approach, which had failed in December: an advance from Colenso. The little town was occupied without resistance on 19 February, and a pontoon bridge thrown across the Tugela a mile to the north. So far, so good. But many of the Boers who had streamed north now returned, and Buller was faced once more with a determined and well-organised enemy positioned on a series of hills ideally situated for defence. It was not until the twenty-second that the first two of these, Horseshoe and Wynne Hills, were in British hands.

Churchill's second dispatch from the *Maine* described in detail the attack on Hart's Hill the following day. Under Major-General Hart, it was headed by three Irish regiments which are now only names in history: the Inniskilling Fusiliers, the Connaught Rangers and Churchill's old friends the Dublin Fusiliers. 'It was a frantic scene of blood and fury . . .' wrote Churchill. 'The greater part of the front line was shot down.' Once again, though, his own guardian angel seems to have been working overtime. A shrapnel shell burst directly over his head, but he was unscathed. He turned to his companion, Captain Brooke, and 'was about to elaborate my theory that shrapnel is comparatively harmless, when I saw some stir and turmoil and no less than eight men were picked up killed or wounded'. He mentioned the incident to Pamela in a letter which ended: 'My nerves were never better and I think I care less for bullets every day.' We can only wonder about the state of Pamela's nerves – although we can say with certainty that Churchill was as careless of them as he was of bullets.

The repulse of the attack was complete. Out of 1,200 officers and men of the two leading battalions, both colonels, three majors, twenty other officers and six hundred men had been killed or wounded. 'The dead and wounded lay thickly scattered, the dead mixed with the living, the wounded unattended . . . and harassed by the fire from both sides and from our artillery.'

On 25 February an armistice was arranged for both sides to collect their wounded and bury the dead. Churchill wrote: 'The neglect and exposure for forty-eight hours had much aggravated the case of the former, and the bodies of the dead, swollen, blackened and torn by the terrible wounds of the expansive bullets, now so generally used by the enemy, were ugly things to see.'

Buller moved his artillery back to Monte Cristo and repositioned the pontoon bridge two miles downstream, planning to resume his outflanking movement and bypass Hart's Hill in order to attack Railway and Pieter's Hills, the last obstacles before Ladysmith. A day was spent in final preparations for the attacks, which began early in the morning of 27 February: 'We arose – all had slept in their boots and had no need to dress – drank some coffee and rejoiced that the day promised to be cool.' That would be welcomed

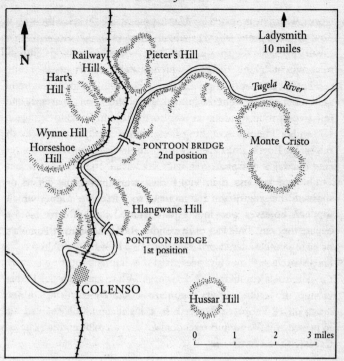

The Breakthrough to Ladysmith

by the infantry, on whom all depended. Failure on this day might well seal the fate of Ladysmith. Churchill, with his instinct for history, noted that it was Majuba Day, the anniversary of the British defeat in 1881 which had ended the First Anglo–Boer War. It was also to be the day on which Majuba was at last avenged.

By late afternoon the infantry had been successful. The way to Ladysmith was indisputably open. The South African Light Horse, which had been providing long-range supporting fire from the northern end of Hlangwane Hill, galloped down to the pontoon bridge in order to pursue the retreating enemy. But Buller would not allow them to cross. Churchill was left to chafe and fume over the General's words, which he reported as: 'Damn pursuit! Better leave them alone now they are going off.' Perhaps Buller was afraid of releasing the cavalry in the dark, but it was a timid decision, which caused Churchill to comment, 'Damn the prize which eases future struggles!'

The first intimation the defenders of Ladysmith had of their imminent relief was the sight the following morning of an apparently endless wagon train winding its way north, accompanied by groups of horsemen. There was nothing the garrison could do to impede the retreating Boers. The cavalry who might have galloped out to intercept the wagon train had no horses – they had long since been eaten.

Then came a message from Buller, announcing that his cavalry were on the way. With the cavalry, of course, was Churchill. He was not, however, positioned quite where he would have liked to be, in the van, but was riding some way back, with the cavalry brigade commander, Lord Dundonald. He was not therefore, as his dispatch was to imply, present at the dramatic meeting between the garrison's commander Sir George White and Colonel Hubert Gough, the leading cavalry regimental commander, as the sun went down on 28 February. Nevertheless, his imagination enabled him to provide his *Morning Post* readers with an account exciting enough to match the event:

> The evening was deliciously cool. My horse was strong and fresh for I had changed him at midday . . . Beyond the next ridge was Ladysmith . . . the centre of the world's attraction . . . within our reach at last. The excitement of the moment was increased by the exhilaration of the gallop . . . We raced through the thorn bushes by Intombi Spruit . . . Presently we arranged ourselves in military order . . . so that there might be no question about precedence, and with Gough, the youngest regimental commander in the army, and one of the best, at the head of the column, we forded the Klip River and rode into the town.

The siege, which had lasted for 118 days, had been lifted. During that time hopes had been raised many times, only to be disappointed as each of Buller's attempts to lift the siege had failed. Disease and hunger had brought Ladysmith to its last gasp. For the low morale,

ABOVE Buller (*left*) and his staff
watching the battle of Spion Kop
from Mount Alice.

RIGHT Colonel Thorneycroft,
who commanded his own
mounted infantry regiment of
colonials and Uitlanders.

ABOVE The author's son Alexander on Spion Kop, showing the ridge up which his great-grandfather twice climbed under fire. The reservoir in the distance now fills the gorge of the Tugela River.

BELOW The British main trench on the day after Spion Kop.

ABOVE RIGHT The same scene today.

RIGHT Churchill and Lord Basil Blackwood on Hlangwane Hill, after Spion Kop.

RIGHT Lady Randolph Churchill on board the hospital ship *Maine*, with her son Jack as a patient.

BELOW Churchill, Captain Percy Scott and Jack saying farewell to Lady Randolph and the *Maine*.

ABOVE Brigadier-
General John Brabazon,
commander of the
Imperial Yeomanry.

ABOVE RIGHT General
Ian Hamilton.

RIGHT Field Marshal
Lord Roberts.

Churchill (*seated, second from right*) returning home on board the *Dunotar Castle*. Standing fourth from the right is Abe Bailey, whose son John later married Churchill's daughter Diana.

Churchill in October 1900, as the newly elected Member of Parliament for Oldham.

General Sir George White had a good deal to answer. Hunger had been accompanied by humiliation, many of his officers believing that a garrison of twelve thousand troops should have adopted a more offensive attitude.

There had also been tensions between the garrison and the relieving force. White felt bitter towards Buller, whose communications to him had sometimes lacked tact or caused misunderstanding. One such occasion was after the repulse at Colenso, when Buller's so-called 'surrender message' seemed to be advocating capitulation: '. . . suggest your firing away as much ammunition as you can, and making the best terms you can'. For his part, Buller had always blamed White for getting himself and his men locked up in Ladysmith and forcing its relief to become the main plank of British strategy. The fact that White and the more influential of his senior officers belonged to the 'Indian' ring of the army, while Buller was an 'African', added to the mutual resentment.

With the relief, these tensions evaporated. They would return when the Indians and Africans had more time to get at each other's throats. Meanwhile General White made a speech which received a rousing cheer, and when Buller rode into town the following morning he was entertained with champagne and trek ox at White's headquarters.

Churchill may not have been at the head of the relieving force as it rode into Ladysmith, but from the moment he entered the town he was again at the centre of events.

As I followed in his footsteps I was guided by Pitch Christopher, a local historian and long-established resident of Ladysmith. We traced my grandfather's movements on that late afternoon from the brown waters of the Klip River to the Christophers' house, Budleigh, where on the night of the relief he attended a grand dinner given by General White. The colonial-style house with its wide verandahs is virtually unchanged since that day, and as we sat in the dining room where my grandfather had sat a century before we could almost hear the popping of the bottles of champagne, jealously preserved throughout the siege. I could easily visualise the warm welcome Churchill received from his old friend from the North-West Frontier, Colonel Ian Hamilton, one of those who had been cooped up in Ladysmith. 'Never before,' wrote the *Morning Post*'s correspondent, 'had I sat in such brave company.'

Mrs Audrey Tanner described for me the meeting in Ladysmith between Churchill and her father, Major Sam Mare, a guide with Buller's column, as he had related it to her: 'A short, thickset man was seen tearing about looking for someone who could give him details of the movements of the relief column.' When Major Mare had provided the information required, 'The man handed over a £10 note and tore off again.' Churchill had been anxious to discover the timetable for the parade at which Buller and White would meet.

He made good use of his information, and gave his readers a comprehensive account of the event. He had positioned himself to advantage, as I discovered from the diary of Lieutenant-Colonel B.W. Martin, which is kept in the Ladysmith Siege Museum:

> I, personally, was fortunate enough to secure standing room ... opposite the City Hall ... I therefore enjoyed an uninterrupted view of the official meeting between General Sir Redvers Buller and General Sir George White ... I stood alongside and conversed with a young man of somewhat untidy appearance ... He wore the slouch hat with Sakabula feathers ... he asked me my name and then told me he was Winston Churchill, and that he was a War Correspondent attached to the South African Light Horse.

Churchill evidently considered himself a correspondent first and a soldier second.

On 10 March, in some six thousand words written in Durban, Churchill summed up the Natal campaign for his readers. He began by recounting the immediate aftermath of the relief of Ladysmith. He questioned Buller's decision not to allow the cavalry to pursue the retreating Boers, and offered the thought that the Commander-in-Chief had been deeply moved by the recent heavy losses, and was reluctant to demand further sacrifices.

As an inquisitive journalist with access to anyone who mattered,

Churchill probed for replies to questions which few had asked, and no one had yet answered. He spent some time with General White, asking him why the British had courted disaster by crossing the Tugela and operating so far forward at the outbreak of war. White blamed General Sir Penn Symons, who had been in command before his arrival in Natal, and who had seriously underestimated the Boers' military strength. On assuming command White had sought the opinion of the Governor of Natal, Sir Walter Hely-Hutchinson, who advised that Penn Symons, having occupied northern Natal, should stay there, as a withdrawal would encourage the Boers and dishearten the loyalists.

Against his own instincts, White had followed Hely-Hutchinson's advice and not changed the plans made by Penn Symons, who he said was 'a brave fighting man, and you know how much that is worth in war'. Churchill, who had campaigned with Penn Symons, would not have disagreed with that description, though personal bravery was hardly a solution to the problems with which White had been left.

Churchill asked how White had allowed himself to become locked up in Ladysmith. To White it was not a question of being locked up: 'I considered it a place of primary importance to hold.' He said he would not act differently if he had the chance to live through the campaign again. This was an assessment with which Churchill would have disagreed, but as he came away from the interview he remembered how the relieving troops had cheered White as they marched into Ladysmith. Knowing the war was still far from won, Churchill once more opted for a morale-sustaining judgement, declaring that the troops' verdict was one 'the nation may gratefully accept'.

He was also, he wrote, anxious to discuss the campaign from the viewpoint of Buller, who had arrived in South Africa only as White was being driven back into Ladysmith. Churchill did not know to what extent Buller was responsible for the gross underestimate of the number of troops that would be required. What he did know was that everyone, from top to bottom, had miscalculated. He likened the military hierarchy to a scientist whose calculations were exact to a minute fraction, only he 'had left out a nought'. Churchill discussed the campaign with Buller, who told him that as Commander-in-Chief he could have assigned Natal to a subordinate, but had decided: 'I was the big man. I had to go.'

Having considered all the factors, the *Morning Post* correspondent concluded: 'it does not appear that the holding of Ladysmith was an unfortunate act.' The town's defence and relief would 'not make a bad page in British history'. This was hardly a ringing endorsement of the British strategy, but rather a further echo of Napoleon's dictum that in war, which is largely a succession of errors made under pressure, victory goes to he who makes the fewest mistakes.

In his assessment of the generals, Churchill wrote that Britain was most fortunate after a prolonged peace to find 'leaders of quality and courage, who were moreover honourable gentlemen'. Of their courage and honour he had no doubts, nor ever would. It was that which probably inclined him against a judgement on their quality. There was, moreover, every reason at this stage of the war to avoid making a frank assessment: they were the only leaders available. Their reputations needed bolstering.

In the last sentence of his final dispatch on the campaign, Churchill's opinion is clear: 'Whatever may be said of the generals it is certain that all will praise the enduring courage of the regimental officer and the private soldier.'

FOURTEEN

A Lull in the Storm

FOLLOWING THE RELIEF OF LADYSMITH, the Boers abandoned their campaign in Natal and retired through the Drakensberg and Biggarsberg mountain ranges into their own territories. From there they denied the British any easy advance into either the Orange Free State or the Transvaal. All was now relatively quiet, except for the occasional unimportant skirmish between outposts – unimportant, that is, to all except the few men engaged. Taking advantage of what he called a lull in the storm, Churchill turned his attention to personal matters.

He was able to digest the reviews of his novel *Savrola*, which had been published in London and New York in the first half of February 1900. The first book he had started, it had been put aside when his adventures on the North-West Frontier and in the Sudan had led to him writing *The Story of the Malakand Field Force* and *The River War*, both best-sellers stamped with the authority of an author who had been present at the scene of great events. *Savrola* could not compete at that level.

The plot of the novel is straightforward. The people of the European state of Laurania, refused the franchise by a tyrannical government, rebel. A young revolutionary, Savrola leads them against the military dictator, who uses his beautiful wife Lucile as a decoy, believing that Savrola's followers will desert him if he is seen to associate with her. Predictably, the two fall in love. Savrola sweeps away the dictatorship, but is rejected by the people he has saved because he insists on a fair trial for the prisoners they have taken. He and Lucile flee the country. However, there is a happy ending: 'After the tumults had subsided, the hearts of the people turned again to the illustrious exile who had won them their freedom.'

The reviewers, while praising the scenes of action, thought little of the romance woven into the story. In this they reflected the opinion of Churchill's grandmother, the Duchess of Marlborough, who when he had sought her comments on the novel had written: 'It is clear you have not yet attained a knowledge of Women.' Nevertheless, *Savrola* provides a fascinating insight into the young Churchillian mind. While he was writing it in Bangalore at the age of twenty-three, he had written to his mother: 'All my philosophy is put in the mouth of the hero.' What is remarkable is the maturity of that philosophy, and how it was to be accurately reflected during Churchill's long career thereafter.

The burgeoning public reputation of *Savrola*'s author ensured that the book went through several reprintings, but from the absence in Churchill's letters of any reaction to the reviews, he would seem to have agreed with the *Star*: 'Mr Churchill has travelled far in the three years since he wrote *Savrola*.' He had asked his mother to send copies of his other books to a wide circle of friends and influential people, but *Savrola* was less favoured. 'I have consistently urged my friends to abstain from reading it,' was his comment years later.

Lady Randolph, chafing aboard the *Maine* in Durban harbour, had, against her elder son's advice, visited Chieveley while Buller's troops were still battling towards Ladysmith. In her autobiography, *Reminiscences of Lady Randolph Churchill*, she described the moment when her train passed the site of her son's heroic action and capture:

> About twenty miles after leaving Frere we slowed down, and the friendly guard, knowing who I was, rushed to tell me we were passing the place of the armoured train disaster. Sure enough there was the train, lying on its side, a mangled and battered thing, and within a few yards a grave with a cross –

three sentries mounting guard – marking the place where the
poor fellows killed in it were buried.

Although a proud and loving mother, Lady Randolph could never
have been regarded as maternal; even so, her account can only be
called minimalist. This is not necessarily surprising, as in a book
of 460 pages she barely refers to her two sons at all.

She observed the Boer positions beyond Colenso through bin-
oculars, breakfasted with the 7th Fusiliers, and was shown a 4.7-inch
naval gun, mounted on a railway truck, which had been named
after her by the sailors who manned it. Unfortunately she was
unable to see her sons, who were then dashing about the country
with the South African Light Horse.

Now, with Ladysmith relieved, she went up the line again. This
time, though Jack was still convalescing aboard the *Maine*, Winston
was able to show her around. He met her at Colenso, where, in
her words, 'after viewing and kodaking the terrible ruin and devas-
tation . . . we got on a trolley, pushed by natives, and left for Ladysmith. This was an excellent way of seeing everything as the whole
of the last two months fighting had been along the line.' Her party
toured Ladysmith, where they were offered dinner and beds by
General Buller, and returned with an ambulance train the following
morning.

A week later, on 17 March, Lady Randolph and the *Maine* sailed
for England via Cape Town. Churchill, in Durban to see her off,
took the opportunity to settle an outstanding debt. Although his
finances were as precarious as ever, he sent a letter to a Mr Bucker-
idge enclosing a cheque for £78 'to cover the cost of various articles',
and 'regretted the delay in payment which had been due to the
distressed situation'.

Churchill realised that the value of his next book, *London to
Ladysmith*, based on his *Morning Post* dispatches, would be much
enhanced by his escape from Pretoria. On 21 March he wrote
to Lady Randolph, who was now back in London, asking her to
renegotiate his contract with the publishers, Longmans: 'Make sure
I get £2,000 on account of the royalties: but don't delay publication.'

The following day he again turned to her for help when an American, Major James Pond, proposed a lecture tour of the United States, where his South African exploits had made him a popular hero. She was asked to find out if Pond was the 'biggest man', and if not, who was. Churchill thought that a fee of £5,000 for three months' lecturing would not be excessive 'for such a labour and for making oneself so cheap ... we cannot afford to throw away a single shilling'. Lady Randolph was an effective agent, securing the £2,000 advance from Longmans and accurately prophesying that by a lecture tour he could 'make a fortune'.

Although Churchill was still on active service with the South African Light Horse, he now decided to write a play. He outlined his ideas in a letter to Pamela Plowden, and asked her to approach Herbert Beerbohm Tree, actor-manager of Her Majesty's Theatre in London's Haymarket: 'I will write a play: scene South Africa: time: the war ... this should be produced by Tree at H. Majesty's theatre in the autumn'. He expounded at length on how he would bring the play to life: 'I can make the people talk and act as they would in real war.' Pamela had sent him a food parcel for her brother-in-law, Major Edgar Lafone, and he concluded his letter by reporting that the Major had been 'too ill to profit by it, so I am going to eat it myself'. He had not explained how he would find time to write a play while campaigning. In the event he was spared the task, his mother pouring cold water on the idea by telling him that the British public would not 'stand any war play'.

With the Boer retreat from Natal came a popular demand by British South Africans for the punishment of the rebels, particularly the British-born naturalised burghers who, anticipating a Boer victory, had supported them. Churchill took an opposite view, advocating reconciliation rather than vengeance, and suggested an approach which combined pragmatism with magnanimity. His view, in a telegram to the *Morning Post* on 24 March 1900, was repeated and amplified in a letter published in the *Natal Witness* five days later. A policy of revenge and punishment, he believed, would lead to a long-drawn-out guerrilla campaign. 'An eye for an eye and a tooth for a tooth' were not worth 'five years of bloody partisan

warfare and the consequent impoverishment of South Africa ...
But it is not only or even mainly on these grounds that I urge
generous counsels.' He warned the people of Natal against laying
themselves open to the charge of racial animosity – meaning animosity between Boers and British, for although large numbers of
blacks were involved on both sides in the war, mainly as labourers,
there was an unspoken agreement that this was a 'white man's war'.
Churchill's letter ended with an exhortation for racial harmony
between the white combatants: 'Peace and happiness can only come
to South Africa through the fusion and concord of the Dutch and
British races ... Let no one try to make the golden days more
distant.'

His words were ill-received both in London and Natal. His own
paper, the *Morning Post*, carried his message but expressed its dis-
agreement with it, while the Natal press was unanimous in its
condemnation. Writing to Churchill, his friend Sir Walter Hely-
Hutchinson, the Governor of Natal, kept a foot in both camps by
admitting that leniency might be the best course, although it should
not be allowed to alienate loyal feeling in South Africa. The High
Commissioner, Sir Alfred Milner, would later say, as he and Churchill galloped in pursuit of jackals under Table Mountain: 'People
must forgive and forget but now passions are running too high. I
understand your feelings but it does no good to express them now.'

At the end of March Churchill obtained an indefinite leave of
absence from the South African Light Horse in order to join Field
Marshal Lord Roberts's army, which had relieved Kimberley on
15 February, occupied Bloemfontein on 13 March, and was now
poised to advance through the Orange Free State into the Transvaal. Churchill took the train for Durban, and the *Morning Post*
applied for its principal correspondent in South Africa to be
accredited to Roberts's army.

His dispatch of 31 March, written on the train, could do little
more than comment, as he passed them, on various features which
had played a significant part in the campaign. He enlivened it with
a paragraph on soldiers' language, prompted by a conversation he
overheard between a truckload of volunteer reinforcements, whose

arrival in Ladysmith delayed the train's departure, and a few sun-burned old hands who had fought their way through Natal. Churchill explained that 'the epithet which the average soldier uses so often as to make it perfectly meaningless, and which we conveniently express by a ———, is always placed before the noun it is intended to qualify.' He cited examples: under no circumstances would any soldier say, '——— Mr Kruger has pursued a ——— reactionary policy,' but rather, 'Mr ——— Kruger has pursued a reactionary ——— policy.' Having explained that five days in a boat on the Nile with a company of Grenadiers had given him the chance to become acquainted with these idiomatic constructions, he concluded: 'I insert this little note in case it may be useful to some of our national poets and minstrels.'

Pausing in his journey only to dine in Pietermaritzburg, Churchill arrived in Durban just in time to embark on a coaster, the *Guelp*, for East London. Twenty-four hours at sea and a further forty-eight by rail brought him to Cape Town. The *Morning Post*'s readers were soon made aware that he found little to like in what he described as 'imported social Capetown'. In the Mount Nelson Hotel, he wrote, he found luxury but no comfort. The dining room was spacious but overcrowded. The waiters were clean but too few. Thus the good dinner was cold before it had reached the table.

The world and his wife seemed to be staying at the hotel – 'particularly the wife'. In Cape Town there were 'more colonels to the acre than in any place outside the United States'. Intrigue, scandal, falsehood and rumour were rife. Overrun with amateur strategists, the city gave a completely misleading impression of South Africa: 'There is too much shoddy worn there at present.' Only in Government House did Churchill find an understanding of the situation – and a chance to ride and hunt in congenial company under Table Mountain.

As the days passed it became apparent that an obstacle had arisen to prevent him joining Roberts's army. In his dispatches he had always sought to present events in the best possible light, in order that the military leadership would retain the confidence of those at home. Surely, he felt, the problem could not lie in that direction.

But in fact his writing had raised hackles. Through two good friends in Lord Roberts's headquarters, Generals Ian Hamilton and William Nicholson, Churchill discovered that the obstacle was none other than the Commander-in-Chief himself. He had two principal objections to Churchill. The first was that his Chief of Staff, General Lord Kitchener, who had taken such exception to parts of *The River War*, would resent Churchill's attachment to the main army. The second was Roberts's personal anger at the dispatch in which Churchill had criticised the sermon at the military church service in the aftermath of Spion Kop.

Behind these specific irritations was no doubt the more general one of a junior officer doubling as a war correspondent – a situation which was supposed to have been forbidden – buzzing around the battlefield and even, as at Spion Kop, haranguing generals. A pen-picture in a regimental magazine was sent to Pamela Plowden, who, thinking it 'rather funny', passed it on to Lady Randolph:

> On the stricken field
> See:- With wallets
> stuffed with ointments
> Balm'd 1st field dressings
> ever accompanied by his
> faithful Vulture = gently
> chiding erring generals,
> heartening disheartened
> Brigade Majors – the
> prematurely bent figure
> of the late Candidate for
> Oldham, the one lodestone
> of hope to the weary
> soldier.

Churchill did not allow Lord Roberts's antipathy towards him to colour what he wrote. In a letter of 7 April to the Colonial Secretary, Joseph Chamberlain, after commenting on some unfortunate minor setbacks in Roberts's campaign, he expressed the hope 'that the resolve of the country will not weaken', and declared, 'We all have entire confidence in Lord Roberts.' No doubt he delighted in also reporting that the Commander-in-Chief had 'put Lord Kitchener in his place several times'.

Hamilton and Nicholson were favoured members of the Roberts 'Indian Ring', and eventually persuaded their chief to allow Churchill to accompany the forthcoming campaign. A terse note from the Military Secretary, written on 11 April, informed him that 'Lord Roberts desires me to say that he is willing to permit you to accompany this force as a correspondent – for your father's sake.' This grudging permission was all that Churchill needed, and he immediately set off for Bloemfontein. It was not until 1 May that he bothered to comment, writing to his mother, 'You will form your own opinion as to the justice of making me accept as a favour what was already mine as a right.'

The train stopped at Bethany, where Churchill stayed the night rather than arrive in Bloemfontein at midnight. There he called on Lieutenant-General Gatacre, whom he had met during the Sudan campaign. Gatacre was no longer the dashing and energetic man he remembered; months of campaigning with insufficient resources had worn him down. Nevertheless, Buller had supported him after the débâcle at Stormberg. In conversation with Churchill, Gatacre brightened up when he spoke of the immediate future, which held the prospect of action on favourable ground with his whole division available to him. 'So I left him. Early next morning he was dismissed from his command and ordered to England, broken, ruined, and disgraced.' Roberts's new broom had summarily swept Gatacre away.

Churchill did not mince his words in telling his readers that this dismissal carried quite the wrong message to the army. Initiative would die as commanders asked for detailed instructions so that they might be covered in all eventualities. He wondered who else might be arbitrarily dismissed, dressing up the thought as a remark by 'an irreverent subaltern' – a ploy he had used when criticising the army chaplain. He ended his dispatch by saying he dare not pursue the subject further. But he had already gone too far for his own good. The 'lodestone of hope to the weary soldier' was in danger of becoming a lodestone to weary generals. His forthright views on the shameful way Gatacre had been treated infuriated Roberts, coming so soon after he had allowed the young correspondent to join his army. Whenever they passed, Churchill's salute would be curtly acknowledged only as that of a stranger.

When Churchill arrived in Bloemfontein, the *Morning Post* already had Lord Cecil Manners accredited as a correspondent with Lord Roberts's column. Manners's diary records that he received a long telegram from Churchill 'informing me he has been authorised by *Morning Post* to replace me here'. Churchill softened the blow with a personal letter: 'I am exceedingly sorry to be the cause of disturbing you here ... If you think of going to Natal, I may be of some assistance to you by giving you letters to some of the Powers on that side.' Manners did not take the hint that he should go to Natal, and was later taken prisoner on the outskirts of Johannesburg.

Having thus installed himself as the senior correspondent, Churchill's first dispatch from Bloemfontein, dated 16 April, describes a town whose original population of four thousand had swollen tenfold in the previous month:

> The Market Square is crowded with officers and soldiers listening to the band of the Buffs. Every regiment in the service, every Colony in the Empire is represented ... The inhabitants – bearded burghers who have made their peace, townsfolk who never desired to make a quarrel – stand around and watch complacently ... Trade has followed hard on the flag ... the market is buoyant.

The victorious army was showing a friendly face to the Boer population. There were banquets to which Boers were invited. Fraternising was part of Lord Roberts's policy, and with pretty girls and women on hand, the army needed no encouragement. The Commander-in-Chief wrote in an optimistic vein to Queen Victoria. He considered the Orange Free State as good as conquered, and forecast that the Transvaal would follow as soon as Johannesburg and Pretoria were occupied. With the centres of government in British hands, the war would soon be over. Meanwhile, in response to his offer of amnesty, many Boers had returned to their homes and, taking an oath of neutrality, accepted defeat.

But resuming the offensive would take longer than Lord Roberts had estimated. The troops needed new clothing and boots. Their rations had to be brought up to the proper level. A Boer ambush during the advance on Bloemfontein had resulted in the loss of a large number of wagons and their contents, all of which needed to be replaced. Hard-ridden and poorly-fed horses had succumbed; the cavalry division alone had lost 1,500 during the relief of Kimberley. To this number of re-mounts had to be added the animals required for the thousands of mounted infantry which it was planned to raise. And if the new horses were to fare any better than their predecessors, their rations had to be increased. All these requirements had to come up a single line of narrow-gauge railway.

But the biggest logistic difficulty was one of Lord Roberts's own making. He and his Chief of Staff, Lord Kitchener, had centralised the army's logistical system, thinking to make it more efficient. Replacing well-tried arrangements had achieved the very opposite effect, as a result of which Kitchener became known in the army as 'K for Chaos'.

In his dispatch of 16 April Churchill describes the problems of re-equipping the troops for the next phase of operations. Criticising the rickety logistics system would not have brought improvements, as his earlier dispatch had done in the case of the army chaplains, but would only have increased Roberts's irritation with him, to his own disadvantage and that of those who had petitioned on his behalf. So, while providing a detailed explanation of the logistical problems, Churchill omitted to mention the difficulties which had given rise to Kitchener's nickname among the troops. And, suppressing whatever feelings may have arisen as a result of his own graceless treatment, he described the Commander-in-Chief as 'the Queen's greatest subject'. There is no doubt that he viewed Roberts with considerable respect.

Another large omission in his dispatch is any criticism of the army medical services, which in Bloemfontein were truly appalling. A serious typhoid epidemic which lasted from April to June was the inevitable result of the overcrowding, poor hygiene and an inadequate water ration, which had led men to drink from contaminated sources. The Surgeon General was generally thought to be out of his depth, while the sanitation officer was none other than the Colonel whom Buller had sacked for his incompetence in countering an outbreak of typhoid in Ladysmith. The epidemic in Bloemfontein brought a death rate worse than Ladysmith's had ever been, and killed many more men than did Boer bullets. Roberts's lack of interest in such matters was largely to blame. He tolerated terrible inefficiency and complacency in his senior medical officers yet often sacked his generals with little justification. Churchill must have been aware of the dreadful state of Roberts's medical services, yet nowhere in any of his accounts of the Boer War are they even mentioned.

Any frustration which may have arisen from Churchill's need to mute his criticism was short-lived. The Boers in the Orange Free State were by no means as beaten as Roberts had thought. Churchill once more moved towards the sound of gunfire, away from Bloemfontein and the irritation of being ignored by the Commander-in-Chief, the friend of his father and a household name at home. The excitement in prospect gave him 'little time to worry unduly about the displeasure even of so great a personage and so honoured a friend'.

FIFTEEN

Return to Pretoria

'I had thrown double sixes again.'
WINSTON CHURCHILL,
dispatch to the *Morning Post*, 22 April 1900

CHURCHILL'S DISPATCH of 16 April 1900 includes a passing mention of an audacious move by the Boers at the end of March: 'But while the army waited, as it was absolutely forced to wait . . . the Boers recovered from their panic, pulled themselves together, and, for the moment boldly seized the offensive. Great, though perhaps temporary, were the advantages they gained.'

This was the advance by General Christiaan de Wet, the Commandant General of the Free State, who swooped into the southeast of the Orange Free State with a mere fifteen hundred men. Churchill was uncharacteristically brief in his account of events: 'I do not intend to be drawn into a detailed description . . . For many reasons it deserves a separate and detailed consideration, chiefly because it shows the Boer at his very best: crafty in war and, above all, deadly cool.'

De Wet recognised that a guerrilla campaign was the only sensible means of engaging a British army which had overwhelming numerical superiority. His first target, the waterworks at Sannah's Post, only twenty miles east of Roberts's headquarters, brought him a haul of seven guns, over a hundred wagons and more than four hundred prisoners. Three days later he overwhelmed a British garrison at Reddersburg, fifty miles south of Bloemfontein. Churchill inclined his readers towards a tolerant view – 'Let us judge no one harshly or in ignorance' – before revealing some telling figures: 'With a loss of eight killed and thirty-one wounded, the retreating troops surrendered when relief was scarcely five miles away.' He does not mention the numbers who surrendered: 546. That would have been too damning. After Reddersburg, de Wet moved seventy-five miles to the east and laid siege to the town of Wepener. By now the British cavalry and infantry in large numbers were catching up with him, so he withdrew to safety north of Bloemfontein.

De Wet's sixteen-day rampage was a foretaste of the guerrilla war of which Churchill had warned when he advocated reconciliation at the end of the campaign in Natal. Political factors were also helping to stiffen the morale of many Boers who might otherwise have accepted Roberts's offer of amnesty. The British government's insistence that it was not prepared to acknowledge the independence of the Transvaal or the Orange Free State played directly into the hands of Kruger, who portrayed it as a threat to all that the Afrikaner held dear. 'The lately penitent rebels are stirring,' wrote Churchill as he set off to join the fighting in the south-east of the Free State, no doubt well pleased to distance himself from the headquarters of an unfriendly Commander-in-Chief.

Anticipating the need to move rapidly around the new theatre of operations, Churchill equipped himself comprehensively, with a four-horse wagon from which to live and horses on which to ride with the cavalry. This gave him the ability to move 'sometimes quite alone across wide stretches of doubtful country . . . then dart back across a landscape charged with silent menace, to keep up a continuous stream of letters and telegrams to my newspaper'. No doubt the editor of the *Morning Post* thought it money well spent.

Accompanied by his wagon and horses, Churchill took the train to Edenburg, fifty miles south of Bloemfontein. He then trekked for two days through the pouring rain until he caught up with the 8th Division, commanded by Major General Sir Leslie Rundle – known as Sir Leisurely Trundle – whom he had known during the Omdurman campaign.

Having enjoyed Rundle's hospitality, he hurried on next day to join Brigadier-General John Brabazon's brigade, which was scouting ahead. As always, Churchill wanted to be part of the action, but in this case there was an added incentive: Brabazon was 'a man of striking character and presence', the sort of soldier he admired. A friend of Lord and Lady Randolph, he had played an influential part in Churchill's early military career, for it was the regiment which Brabazon commanded, the 4th Hussars, to which Churchill had gravitated when he was commissioned. Thereafter the two men became lifelong friends.

An impoverished Irish landlord, Brabazon had earlier, because of straitened finances, resigned his commission in the Grenadier Guards to become a gentleman volunteer in the Ashanti campaign of 1874. Here he so distinguished himself that his commission was restored, a virtually unprecedented occurrence. The portrait of him in *My Early Life* illustrates aspects of his character which attracted Churchill. Brabazon had 'an inability real or affected to pronounce the letter "R" ... His military career had been long and varied ... To the question, "What do you belong to now, Brab?" he replied, "I never can wemember, but they have gween facings [their uniform lapels] and you get at 'em from Waterloo." Of the stationmaster at Aldershot he inquired ... "Where is the London twain?" "It has gone Colonel." "Gone! Bwing another."'

The Boer War had not been kind to Brabazon. He had arrived in South Africa at the head of a regular cavalry brigade but had fallen out with General Sir John French, his divisional commander, a younger man who was more able to adapt to the changing nature of war. Twenty years before, French had been a subaltern in Afghanistan and junior to Brabazon, whose amusing stories about those days were often at French's expense, as were his jaunty comments on current tactics. As a result, Brabazon, said to be 'to be too old for real work' and 'too fond of comfort', found himself commanding the Imperial Yeomanry, a hastily raised force organised by a committee of fox-hunting gentlemen at home. This setback notwithstanding, he was still a debonair commander pursuing the war more vigorously than most. With Brabazon, Churchill was once more in his element.

As Sir Leslie Rundle's force approached the Boer stronghold of Dewetsdorp, 'Brabazon was all for battle.' The pace was being set by more cautious commanders, but to appease him the cavalry were allowed to probe the enemy defences. Churchill was with Brabazon when Angus McNeill, commanding the locally-raised Montmorency's Scouts since Montmorency himself had been killed, rode up and asked permission to cut off a party of two hundred mounted Boers by taking possession of a small hill. Permission granted, McNeill ordered his fifty scouts to mount, and, turning to Churchill, shouted, 'Come with us, we'll give you a show now – first class.'

Writing his dispatch that same evening, Churchill recorded: 'So, in the interests of the *Morning Post*, I got on my horse and we all started . . . as fast as we could.' It was a race. The Boers were ahead, but for them the going was uphill, and they were probably worse mounted. However, a few, with better horses than their comrades, began to forge ahead. Then the Scouts were forced to dismount, some hundred yards from the hilltop, to cut a wire fence barring their way.

The delay was fatal to their venture, and very nearly fatal for the *Morning Post*'s correspondent. The heads of a dozen Boers appeared above the rocks, 'grim, hairy and terrible'. There were obviously many more behind them. 'Too late,' McNeill called, 'back to the other kopje [hill]. Gallop!'

'Then the musketry crashed out, and the "swish" and "whirr" of bullets filled the air. I put my foot in the stirrup. The horse, terrified at the firing, plunged wildly.' When Churchill tried to spring into the saddle it slipped and his horse, breaking away, galloped after the fast-disappearing Scouts: 'I was alone, dismounted, within the closest range, and a mile at least from cover of any kind.' For the second time in South Africa, Churchill had to run for his life from Boer riflemen. Then a lone rider appeared ahead of him. From his cap badge he was a member of Montmorency's Scouts, 'a tall man, with a skull and crossbones badge, and on a pale horse. Death in Revelation, but life to me.' Churchill called for a stirrup, and when, to his surprise, the man stopped, mounted behind him.

I called on Trooper Clement Roberts's daughter, Mrs Doris Maud, in Durban. She showed me the letter which my grandfather had sent to her father, expressing his 'great admiration' for Roberts's 'coolness and courage'. He continued: 'I have always felt that unless you had taken me up on your saddle I should myself certainly have been killed or captured.'

As they raced away with bullets whistling past, Churchill grasped the horse's mane and found his hand soaked with blood from where the horse had been hit by an expanding bullet. 'Oh, my poor horse,' exclaimed Roberts. It was his own horse, Rajah, which he had bred and broken on his farm before joining the Scouts.

'Never mind,' said Churchill, 'you've saved my life.'

'Ah, but it's the horse I'm thinking about,' replied Roberts.

That, Churchill reported to his readers, was the total of their conversation. He characteristically summed up this latest adventure as if it had been no more than a game of backgammon: 'I had thrown double sixes again.'

All the officers who witnessed what had happened agreed that Roberts was worthy of some honour – even the Victoria Cross was mentioned. Six years later, on hearing from the British High Commission in Johannesburg that no award had been made to Roberts, Churchill had the case reopened. Doris Maud proudly showed me the Distinguished Conduct Medal which her father had then received as a result.

By the time Lord Roberts had assembled the twenty-five thousand men and seventy guns he thought necessary to capture Dewetsdorp, the 2,500 Boer defenders, who had given the impression of much greater strength, had slipped away. With them went the prisoners and guns they had captured at Sannah's Post and Wepener. Churchill's report that the episode could not be 'contemplated with feelings of wild enthusiasm' foreshadowed, in the muted terms he thought appropriate at the time, his comments thirty years later when he described the events around Dewetsdorp as 'the most comical operations I have ever witnessed'. No doubt this impression was coloured by Brabazon's droll commentary on the daily shilly-shallying of the high command.

When Brabazon was left to mop up after the capture of Dewetsdorp, Churchill attached himself to General French's cavalry division, which was advancing northwards. He found the atmosphere in the headquarters strained. His simultaneous use of sword and pen had earned French's disapproval, and his friendship with Brabazon was a further irritant. Fortunately he had one ally in French's headquarters. Jack Milbanke, the closest of the few friends he had made at Harrow, had recently recovered from wounds, was newly decorated with the Victoria Cross, and was French's ADC. Yet even he was unable to ease the tension. French ignored Churchill's presence to such an extent that the two men, who would later become friends and colleagues, exchanged not a single word during the Boer War.

In a long letter to Lady Randolph from Bloemfontein on 1 May, Churchill assessed the impact on his reputation of his activities in South Africa. He thought that on the whole he had gained, although there was an undercurrent of hostile criticism. He touched on his political future. As long ago as 14 January the Conservatives of Southport had wanted to adopt him as their candidate for the forthcoming general election. In the hectic days before Spion Kop he had wired back hastily, 'Impossible decide here.' They persisted in their attempts to persuade him, but without success. In April, in a letter to Joseph Chamberlain mainly about the course of the war, Churchill wrote that he hoped to find a seat before the dissolution of Parliament, which was already in the air. Having virtually made up his mind to stand again for the Conservatives in Oldham, he sent his mother a cheque for £50 for registration expenses. It was intended that she should forward it after she had determined that he had sufficient funds in his bank account to meet it.

Money remained a constant concern. In his letter he aired his concern over the expense of a political career, and asked Lady

Randolph to find out from leading politicians whether appearing as a paid lecturer in order to bolster his finances would weaken his political position. Pamela received a brief mention. She wrote long letters, but although he avowed that they were very interesting to him, they did not make him any wiser 'as concerns the general situation at Home'. Lady Randolph, who remained his closest confidante, should therefore write and tell him everything.

The letter was posted as Churchill joined General Ian Hamilton, who had been given the task of protecting the right flank of Lord Roberts's advance on Johannesburg. Hamilton was another of Churchill's heroes. When Churchill's Boer War dispatches were published later in 1900 as *Ian Hamilton's March*, he inserted a chapter devoted entirely to Hamilton's career, a tribute to a soldier with the same instincts for active service as himself. The admiration was mutual, as Lady Hamilton noted in her diary on 20 June 1902: 'I can't bear him [Churchill], which is rather a pity as Ian thinks such a lot of him and says he is bound to be a Commander-in-Chief or a Prime Minister – which ever line he cares to cultivate.' However, within nine months she had also taken an admiring view, writing 'terrific Winston' in her entry for 24 March 1903.

For the advance with Hamilton, Churchill was joined by his cousin 'Sunny', the 9th Duke of Marlborough. The close friendship between the two cousins had started in childhood when they had played together at Blenheim Palace under the strict eye of their grandmother, the Duchess. Three years older than Churchill, Marlborough had succeeded to the title in 1892, and had married Consuelo Vanderbilt, an American heiress, three years later. He would later hold a number of government posts, including Under-Secretary of State for the Colonies.

He had gone out to South Africa with the Imperial Yeomanry, and had become an Assistant Military Secretary, one of a considerable number of the aristocracy on Roberts's staff. Because of the pointed criticism this had occasioned in the radical press, Roberts began to dispense with some of their undoubtedly superfluous services. Marlborough, on being told he would remain in Bloemfontein when the refreshed and replenished forces advanced north, appealed

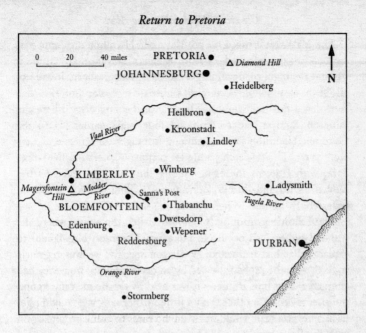

Bloemfontein to Diamond Hill

to Churchill, who persuaded Hamilton to take them both with his column.

The cousins set off in Churchill's wagon, which had a 'raised floor of deal boards beneath which reposed two feet of the best tinned provisions and alcoholic stimulants London could supply'. They caught up with Hamilton at Winburg, having come through 'the Boer infested countryside defenceless but safely'.

Churchill's dispatches over the next fortnight, from Winburg, Kroonstadt and Heilbron, describe a series of actions as the British advanced rapidly to the Vaal. As usual his London readers are given the flavour of life in the field. At 'the pretty little town of Lindley' he sought to replenish his wagon and found a store where: 'You may buy a piano, a kitchen range, a slouch hat, a bottle of hair wash, or a box of sardines over the same counter . . . Personally I sought potatoes.'

The Vaal was crossed on 26 May, and Hamilton's column was switched to the left flank of Lord Roberts's advance. By 2 June it had cut the main road running west from Johannesburg. It had not all been easy going. Churchill's dispatch of the previous day recorded a final stiff fight at Doornkop, the very place where the Jameson Raiders had surrendered four years earlier. Here the Gordons, Hamilton's own regiment, lost eight officers and eighty-eight men. The dispatch painted a picture of the battlefield after dark, with lanterns flickering among the rocks as search parties moved hither and thither, occasionally calling out for stretcher-bearers.

The following morning, Churchill visited the slopes where the worst slaughter had occurred. He asked a Gordon Highlander to explain what had happened. 'Well you see, sir, we was regularly tricked,' was the reply, followed by an explanation of how they had charged a crest line, thinking it was held by the Boers, only to find the enemy lining another crest a little further on. 'We couldn't get back – never a man would ha' lived to cross the black ground again with the fire where it was.' The Gordons carried on 'soon as we'd got our breath. It had to be done.' As had often been the case before, the Boers flinched from close combat with the bayonet, and the day was won.

Having recounted this conversation, Churchill told his readers that the 'melancholy spectacle' of eighteen dead Highlanders lined in a row, their faces covered with blankets, caused him and a fellow officer a moment of 'illogical anger, and we found ourselves scowling at the tall chimneys of the Rand'. Their rage was illogical, he wrote, because the war was not being fought to win the goldmines. If he had privately begun to doubt the political motives behind the unfolding military strategy, he did not intend to disillusion his readers.

With the Boers still holding Johannesburg, Hamilton, to the west of the town, was not in communication with Lord Roberts's main force to the south. He had sent two mounted men with dispatches, but as they would have to make a wide detour through broken country overrun with Boers, it would be many hours before they arrived, if they ever got through at all. Meanwhile, Churchill was pondering on his own communications. An important action had been fought, and he was anxious to get the news to London before any other correspondent. His problem was that the telegraph terminal was on the other side of Johannesburg. Perhaps he could manage to slip through the town itself.

While he was considering how he might do this, two cyclists arrived from the direction of Johannesburg. One of them, a Monsieur Lautré, a Frenchman connected with the mining industry, said he would guide Churchill through the town, while the other offered the loan of his bicycle. Hamilton produced more dispatches for Lord Roberts, and with these in their pockets the two cyclists pedalled off, with the sun setting behind them.

Well might Churchill write: 'As we passed our farthest outpost line I experienced a distinct sensation of adventure.' Having changed his uniform and slouch hat for a civilian suit and soft cap, he was, in effect, an officer operating in plain clothes behind enemy lines. If he were captured, he would most likely be shot out of hand.

Soon after starting, the cyclists came across a scout from the Rimington Tigers* moving cautiously forward. He was unsure of the military situation, and only knew for certain that the *Times* correspondent from Hamilton's headquarters had passed that way on a horse. Lautré, fired with enthusiasm, declared that they would get through before *The Times*. Cycling on, they were soon in Johannesburg.

In his dispatch of 2 June, Churchill described houses with boarded-up windows, and groups of people chatting at the street corners. Two cyclists raised no undue suspicion, but there was one moment of alarm when a mounted Boer with full campaigning kit, wearing a slouch hat with a white feather, reined into a walk alongside them. Lautré and Churchill conversed in French, and after a while the Boer spurred his horse into a trot and drew away.

Eventually, as the streets turned again to country roads, three British soldiers came into view. They were scavenging for food to

---

* Two hundred colonial guides raised by Major Mike Rimington, one of the special service officers sent out in July 1899.

supplement their rations. They turned back when Churchill warned them that they would be shot or taken prisoner if they proceeded further, and, followed by the cyclists, the three men returned to their bivouac area. Here Churchill learned the whereabouts of Lord Roberts's headquarters, still some seven miles distant. Striking across country, pushing their bicycles for an hour, he and Lautré came across another bivouac area, which turned out to be the headquarters of General Tucker, yet another acquaintance of Churchill's from his days in India. He provided whisky and clear directions to Lord Roberts.

On a good road again, the cyclists spun along at ten miles an hour, until, passing a hotel, Churchill decided the time had come for dinner. Inside he found Lionel James, the principal correspondent of *The Times*, who was awaiting the arrival of his subordinate from Hamilton's headquarters. Then, having 'dined hastily and none too well' and 'secured the reversion of half the billiard table, should all other couches fail', Churchill and Lautré pedalled on. At half past ten, after a further two miles, they reached Lord Roberts's headquarters, in the local magistrate's house. The dispatches were taken in by an orderly, and in a few minutes Lord Kerry, an aide-de-camp, appeared with a summons from the Commander-in-Chief. Hospitably entertained, and with the offer of a comfortable bed for the night – 'the first for a month' – Churchill gave an account of Hamilton's achievements 'to my father's old friend and now once again my own'.

The following day, 3 June, under arrangements agreed between British and Boers, Johannesburg surrendered. The war appeared to be nearly over. The Rand and its untold wealth was virtually within the British grasp, as was the vision of a British Federation of South Africa. There seemed no point in fighting for a prize which was being offered on a plate. In return for surrendering without a fight and a guarantee that the mines would be left in working order, the Boers were allowed an armistice of twenty-four hours in which to withdraw their army.

The breathing-space allowed General Botha to withdraw all his heavy guns. Jan Smuts, the young Attorney-General who, on that damp veldt back in November, had resisted requests for Churchill's release as a non-combatant, also put the twenty-four hours to good use. He removed to safety the contents of the mint and the Standard Bank, the last boxes of gold from the Rand, and all the reserve ammunition from the magazine. Thus the armistice, which had seemed a good idea at the time, would enable Botha, with Smuts as his Assistant Commandant General, to prolong the war.

As the Boers trundled away to fight another day there was a ceremonial parade in Johannesburg at which the *Vierkleur* was hauled down and the Union Jack hoist in its place. While the occupying army were celebrating, the correspondent of the *Morning Post* was hurrying back to Hamilton. As he returned by what had become a safe route he could reflect that, while no one could claim to have captured it, he had been the first British soldier to enter Johannesburg

Two days later, in the early morning of 5 June, Churchill was among the first to enter Pretoria, and the first to reach the British prisoners of war. They had been moved in the six months since he had fled the States Model School, but a mounted Boer directed him to the camp where they were now being held. Lieutenant Thomas Frankland recorded: 'At about half past eight two figures in khaki came round the corner, crossed the little brook and galloped towards us. Who should I see on reaching the gate but Churchill, who, with his cousin, the Duke of Marlborough, had galloped in front of the army to bring us the good tidings.' Another prisoner, Augustus Goodacre, described in his diary how 'Suddenly Winston Churchill came galloping over the hill and tore down the Boer flag, and hoisted ours amid cheers.' An officer in the Dublin Fusiliers named Grimshaw produced the Union Jack, which he had made from rearranged pieces of a Boer *Vierkleur*. It was the first British flag to fly over Pretoria since 1881. Churchill's dispatch of 8 June gives the time as 8.47 a.m.

During May the war had been going badly for the Boers. They had made little effort to defend Johannesburg and Pretoria, and their siege of Mafeking had been lifted on 17 May. Lord Roberts hoped that they would now be inclined to treat for peace. An armistice was agreed and a meeting between the Commander-in-Chief and the Boer generals arranged for 9 June. Meanwhile the British force in Pretoria had been reduced to sixteen thousand men, camped in convenient places around the city. But Botha had merely been stalling for time while he regrouped his forces, and when he called off the meeting just as it was about to begin, 'the imperious necessities of war demanded fresh efforts'. Reading Churchill's dispatch of 14 June, it is clear that the Boers had humbugged the British, who now had to do something about the threat posed by Botha's seven thousand Transvaal burgers and twenty-five pieces of artillery assembled some fifteen miles to the east of Pretoria.

After the fall of Pretoria, Churchill had written to his mother on 9 June: 'I propose to come home ... Politics, Pamela, finances and books all need my attention.' All the key Boer centres were now in British hands, and there were no longer any besieged British garrisons. Churchill could see that the war would soon turn into the guerrilla campaign of which he had warned. His adventures to date had been to the mutual benefit of his country and himself, and there was little point in him staying any longer in South Africa. However, Lord Roberts was about to launch his army against Botha's force to the east, and Churchill would not leave until that action was over. He told his mother: 'should I come through all right I will seriously turn my face towards home.'

Having, against all normal odds, been preserved thus far, it would have been only human for Churchill not to have pushed his luck any further. He was well aware of the 'indiscriminating bullet', about which he had written in *The Story of the Malakand Field Force*, where he pointed out that no matter how bright a future is forecast for a rising soldier, each time he goes into action 'his chances of being killed are as great as, perhaps greater, than those of the youngest subaltern whose luck is fresh'. However, in this final action, which became known as Diamond Hill, Churchill's bravery and initiative rose to new heights. It was as if he realised this was his last opportunity to chance his arm and demonstrate the sense of destiny of which he had so often written and spoken.

The Boers were deployed along a line of hills astride the railway line to Delagoa Bay. It was the very country through which Churchill had ridden among the coal sacks six months earlier. Lord Roberts's plan was to use his cavalry to turn the flanks of the Boer position while pressing their centre with his infantry. His aim was modest: to clear any threat to Pretoria. But it was hoped that the Boers would be forced to abandon many of their heavy guns. Against an enemy of seven thousand Roberts's force numbered some fifteen thousand, not an overwhelming superiority against a strongly entrenched position.

The operation began on 11 June. The turning movements were not as successful as had been hoped, and the battle continued throughout the twelfth, by the end of which Hamilton's force had captured sufficient of the centre ground to be confident of a successful conclusion the following day. However, as day broke on the thirteenth it was seen that the Boers had withdrawn in good order. Hamilton immediately advanced, but the exhausted British cavalry and mounted infantry were in no condition to continue the pursuit.

In *My Early Life*, Diamond Hill is covered in a single sentence: 'I had one more adventure in South Africa.' Churchill's dispatch to the *Morning Post* of 14 June gives a detailed eye-witness account of the three-day action, but omits any mention of his own part. This was left for Ian Hamilton to fill in many years later in his memoirs, *Listening for the Drums*:

> Winston gave the embattled hosts at Diamond Hill an exhibition of conspicuous gallantry . . . The key to the battlefield lay on the summit but nobody knew it until Winston managed to give me the slip and climb this mountain. He ensconced himself in a niche not much more than a pistol shot directly below the Boer commandos . . . they could have knocked him off his perch with a volley of stones. Thus it was from his lofty perch Winston had the nerve to signal me, if I remember right, with his handkerchief on a stick, that if I could only manage to gallop up at the head of my mounted infantry we ought to be able to rush this summit.

No doubt Hamilton used the term 'conspicuous gallantry' because it was the language of citations for the Victoria Cross, and after the battle he made persistent efforts to achieve some recognition of Churchill's 'initiative and daring and of how he had grasped the whole layout of the battlefield'. Hamilton later explained his failure to secure a medal for Churchill: 'He had two dislikes against him – those of Bobs and K [Lords Roberts and Kitchener]. And he had only been a Press Correspondent they declared – so nothing had happened.' The military establishment were unlikely to give a medal to a bumptious young subaltern who had so often outsmarted and outperformed them.

At Diamond Hill Roberts had achieved his limited aim. Botha had achieved rather more. By his successful withdrawal he had inspired the Boers to continue the fight, so that six weeks later it was clear that the war was far from over. The Boer generals de Wet and de la Rey were rampaging across the veldt, while Botha still had a well-organised army at large not much more than a hundred miles east of Pretoria. In late August General Sir Redvers Buller, advancing north from Natal, defeated this army, but the remnants melted into the precipitous country of north-eastern Transvaal to continue a guerrilla campaign.

On 10 December Lord Roberts sailed for England, Field Marshal Lord Kitchener having succeeded him as Commander-in-Chief on 29 November. Buller had departed on 24 October, five days after President Kruger had fled to Europe to continue pleading the Boer cause, aboard a Dutch warship.

Kitchener now pursued a scorched-earth campaign, denying the guerrillas anything which might sustain them: horses, families, sympathisers and farm animals. Boer women and children were concentrated in two dozen camps which became notorious for epidemics of dysentery and typhoid. Farms were burnt and a system of blockhouses and barbed wire was built to limit the mobility of the enemy.

Meanwhile, the 'Indians' and 'Africans' continued their feud in London. Buller was given his old job, the training command in Aldershot, while Roberts was made Commander-in-Chief of the Army, received an earldom and an award of £100,000. The 'Indians' sealed their victory in October 1901 with Buller's shameful dismissal from the army on a trumped-up charge of indiscipline. In self-defence against an 'Indian' campaign orchestrated through Leo Amery and *The Times* he had made public, against the government's wishes, the so-called 'surrender telegram' which he had sent to General White in Ladysmith. Others had a more favourable opinion of him: a monument to him in Exeter was inscribed 'He saved Natal.'

The war dragged on until May 1902, when Botha declared to the other Boer leaders that they had no option but to accept Kitchener's terms. On 31 May, with Smuts eloquently advocating peace, a meeting of Boer delegates at Vereeniging voted to accept the terms of surrender. They were signed that night in Pretoria; the two republics ceased to exist, were absorbed into the British Empire and together were paid £3 million to help rebuild their shattered economies.

Paul Kruger died in exile in Switzerland in 1904. Louis Botha became Premier of the Transvaal in 1907, and was the first Prime Minister of a united South Africa from 1910 until his death in 1919. Jan Smuts followed Botha as Prime Minister from 1919 to 1924, and again from 1939 to 1948, and was instrumental in the formation of the United Nations. Botha and Smuts became statesmen on the world stage, where they often acted in concert with Winston Churchill.

All this was in the future when, in June 1900, a few days after the battle of Diamond Hill, Churchill resumed his 'full civilian status and took the train for Cape Town'. He would never return to Pretoria, but he never entirely lost touch with it, sending a message on 16 November 1955, the occasion of its centenary: 'It is my privilege, as one not unacquainted with Pretoria's hospitality, to offer the city my heartiest congratulations.'

En route to Cape Town, the train stopped with a jolt a hundred miles south of Johannesburg while Churchill was breakfasting. He descended to the track, and at that moment a small shell burst on the embankment close by. A hundred yards ahead was a wooden bridge in flames. The train was crowded with soldiers, but as far as Churchill could see, there were no officers. In their absence, he once again took charge of a train, as he had done eight months previously (one wonders if the presence of officers would have made any difference). Not wishing to repeat his experience of the previous November, he ran along the line, climbed into the cab and directed the driver to reverse until the sanctuary of a fortified camp three miles back was reached. In the process some Boers appeared and, his full civilian status notwithstanding, Churchill fitted the wooden stock to his Mauser and scattered them with a few rounds.

At the time he thought this would be the last occasion on which he would see shells and bullets fired in anger. Thirty years later he was to write: 'This expectation, however, proved unfounded.'

EPILOGUE

A Triumphal Progress

THE *Dunotar Castle*, with Churchill aboard, docked at Southampton on 20 July 1900. The conquering hero could not have failed to make the comparison between the rapturous welcome he had received in Durban and his low-key return to his native land.

Lady Randolph, who would normally have turned out for such an event, was busy preparing for her wedding to George Cornwallis-West, 'the most handsome man in the Army'. It was an unsuitable marriage, destined for the rocks although it lasted on and off for thirteen years. Churchill took the imminent arrival of a stepfather of his own age in his stride. He was in any case completely absorbed with his own affairs. He had achieved everything he had aimed for when he had set sail for South Africa nine months before, and more. He knew where he was going, and he intended to get there as quickly as possible.

He had demonstrated beyond doubt that he could make his living with the pen. His first collection of dispatches, *London to Ladysmith*, published in May, had already sold thirteen thousand copies and the second collection, *Ian Hamilton's March*, had been prepared for the publisher while he was still at sea. *The River War* was about to be reprinted, and *The Malakand Field Force* was still selling. 'I have about £4,000 altogether,' he told his brother Jack. 'With judicious economy, I shall hope to make that carry me through the lean years.'

In South Africa Churchill had also established a reputation within the army, and had made friends in high places. Many of the officers with whom he had mixed would rise to high command in the First World War, when Churchill would be a member of the war cabinet. There were some members of the high command, like Kitchener, who thought him too hot to handle, but as he climbed the political ladder he would win them over. In the wider world his dispatches, written without fear or favour, had confirmed that he was his own man, and had established him as one whose views demanded respect. He had been courted by such powerful men as Sir Alfred Milner, the High Commissioner at the Cape, who following their discussion three weeks earlier had written to Churchill: 'I spoke very freely of my ideas as to the future, because I see your interest and *want your help.*'

The one thing he had not achieved was the decoration for bravery he so earnestly desired. George Wyndham, the Under-Secretary of State for War, told him that the War Office had received a dispatch dealing with the armoured train incident. Mentioning this to his brother, Churchill wrote: 'I do not expect I shall get anything out of it, not at any rate the one thing that I want. I have, however, had a very good puff.' He coveted a medal as proof of his courage, which he regarded as the characteristic which underwrote all others. But his very actions had provided proof in plenty, and a medal would have been no more than the icing on a cake.

Churchill returned to England greatly matured. He was secure in the knowledge that he had achieved fame and recognition at home, and that he had placed his feet firmly on the international stage. Even so, he was doubtful if he would immediately succeed in entering Parliament, for he was standing in the forthcoming general election – which because of the overtly jingoistic tone of much of the campaign became known as the 'Khaki Election' – as a Conservative, for the predominantly Liberal constituency of Oldham. The Conservatives, who were in power, were determined to appeal to the country before the enthusiasm engendered by the recent military victories in South Africa had waned.

Churchill wasted no time in starting his election campaign.

Parliament was dissolved on 17 September, and on the eighteenth he wrote to Lord Rosebery, a prominent politician who had been a friend of Lord Randolph, and Prime Minister from 1894 to 1895: 'Tomorrow we begin our campaign in Oldham . . . I prepare myself for defeat but cannot quite exclude the hope of victory.'

His hopes must have been bolstered by the reception he received the following day when he entered Oldham in a procession of ten landaus and spoke to an overflowing house at the Theatre Royal. Describing his adventure in Witbank, he mentioned Daniel Dewsnap, who had predicted: 'They will all vote for you next time.' The audience shrieked: 'His wife's in the gallery!' This gave rise to general jubilation, during which the mill girls burst forth with a new music-hall ditty of the day:

> You've heard of Winston Churchill
> This is all I need to say –
> He's the latest and the greatest
> Correspondent of the day.

The election was energetically contested on the sole issue of the war in South Africa. The Liberals, while supporting the war, alleged gross Conservative misconduct in its prosecution, and argued that they would have avoided the conflict, while achieving the same ends by more skilful diplomacy. As a result, even those Liberals who had supported the war measures found themselves condemned by the Conservatives as pro-Boer. Churchill fought on the platform that the war, being a just one, should be fought to an indisputable conclusion, and followed by a generous settlement.

Under the electoral system in force at that time, the Oldham constituency elected two Members of Parliament, and four candidates – two Liberal and two Conservative – were vying for the two seats. Churchill had pleaded with his mother to help him with his campaign, but she remained in Scotland on an extended honeymoon, and for feminine presence the Conservatives had to rely on the wife of Churchill's running mate, Charles Crisp. In a turnout of fifty thousand voters on 1 October, Churchill took the second seat. Splitting the Liberal vote, he was sixteen votes behind the leading Liberal, Alfred Emmott, and 222 votes ahead of the Liberal who came third, Walter Runciman. Crisp trailed Runciman by 177 votes. It had been such a close-run thing that, in rushing to print, *The Times* of 2 October announced Churchill's defeat. The record was set straight the following day, with an apology and a leading article welcoming his election to Parliament.

Oldham had been one of the first constituencies to vote in an election which would be spread over six weeks. As a result of his victory, Churchill found himself a star turn, in demand to speak in support of Conservative candidates still campaigning. Arthur Balfour, the Leader of the House of Commons and soon to become Prime Minister, begged Churchill to speak for him in Manchester. 'After this,' Churchill wrote, 'I never addressed any but the greatest meetings . . . Five or six thousand electors . . . with venerated pillars of the party and many-a-year members of Parliament sitting as supporters on the platform!'

Winston Churchill had arrived. Still two months short of his twenty-sixth birthday, it seemed to him that he was enjoying 'a triumphal progress through the country'.

This triumphal progress had really started with his adventures in South Africa. Had there been no Anglo–Boer War, Churchill's ambition would still, no doubt, have rapidly propelled him onwards and upwards. But in the event he was able to use the war as his launching pad. What, I wondered, were his later feelings about the causes of that conflict into which he had entered with such enthusiasm.

In his election campaign he had described the war as just and necessary. It would have been surprising, given his recent experience and the political climate in Britain, if he had held any other view. It was a view he reiterated during November 1900 to capacity audiences during the twenty-nine lectures which Christie's lecture agency arranged throughout the country. But whereas the British provided sympathetic listeners, audiences in America, where Churchill lectured in ten cities during December, proved very different. In a letter to Lady Randolph he described the atmosphere: 'There is a strong pro-Boer feeling which has been fomented against me.'

In Chicago he was heckled by Irish-Americans, and although he turned their abuse to cheers by describing the Dublin Fusiliers in action – 'trumpeters sounded the charge and the enemy were swept from the field' – he did not enjoy the experience. In Boston the chair was taken by Mark Twain, whose introductory speech, although very complimentary to Churchill himself, included the words: 'I think that England sinned when she got herself into a war in South Africa which she could have avoided.' Churchill's retort, 'My country right or wrong,' drew the reply, 'When the poor country is fighting for its life, I agree. But this was not your case.'

Churchill stuck to his guns and saw the tour through, when speakers of lesser calibre would have abandoned it. But there is no doubt he was surprised by the depth of pro-Boer feeling.

It had, however, not affected his views when he made his maiden speech in the House of Commons on 18 February 1901. He ridiculed the sympathy which some Members of Parliament professed for the Boer cause: 'If I were a Boer fighting in the field – and if I were a Boer I hope I should be fighting in the field – I would not allow myself to be taken in by any message of sympathy.' He continued by welcoming the recent decision to send reinforcements to South Africa, but, advocating a strategy of stick and carrot, appealed for leniency towards those Boers who surrendered, saying that they should be guaranteed their security, religion and 'all the honours of war'. In answer to those Members who had 'seen fit to stigmatise [the war] as a war of greed', he said: 'This war from beginning to end has only been a war of duty.'

He had evidently put behind him that fleeting moment of the previous June when, as he had told his *Morning Post* readers, he and a fellow officer had 'scowled at the tall chimneys of the Rand'. From his election speeches onwards he spoke of nothing but 'a just war'. It would be thirty years before he hinted at second thoughts, when, describing the arguments he advanced during the election of 1900, he wrote: 'This at the time was my sincere belief.'

I turned to *A History of the English Speaking Peoples*. As it was written largely in the 1930s but was revised before its publication in the 1950s, I thought it would reveal whether Churchill had undergone any change of mind on the events which led to the Anglo–Boer War. In it he points to the Jameson Raid, which 'ended in the failure it deserved', as the turning point at which 'the entire course of South African history was ... violently diverted from peaceful channels'. Beyond that, he simply records accurately the catalogue of misunderstandings and the course of events which led to war.

It was while reading his short story 'The Dream' that I stumbled on some of his further thoughts. In this short account he relates how, one foggy November afternoon in 1947 while he was in his studio copying a portrait of his father that had been painted in Ulster in 1886: 'I turned ... and there, sitting in my red leather upright armchair, was my father. He looked just as I had seen him in his prime.' There followed a conversation, in the course of which Churchill related the history of the last half-century, while his father commented on what he heard.

Lord Randolph enquired how his son earned his living, and was told that he wrote books and articles for the press. Up to his death the father had held no high opinion of his son's abilities, and his reply faintly echoes that: 'Ah, a reporter. There is nothing discreditable in that.' Churchill made no mention of the many other roles he had played (and was still playing – ahead were four more years in his second term as Prime Minister) during the past fifty turbulent years. As Churchill's *tour de force* drew to an end, his father expressed surprise that his son had 'developed so far and so fully'. He observed that Churchill seemed to know a great deal about world events, and might have done a lot to help and even made a name for himself had he gone into politics. With that the dream ended.

But 'The Dream' is more than an ironic little fantasy. Throughout it I sensed Churchill's own political philosophy in his father's words. It was Lord Randolph's reference to the Anglo–Boer War which caught my keenest attention: 'England should never have done that. To strike down two independent republics must have lowered our whole position in the world.'

Had there been a change of heart, as he grew older, in the young man who had so readily pursued the Boer in what he had called 'a just war'? Had half a century of wars, in which he had always been centre stage, caused him to revise his views? Had the mature statesman, half American by birth and recently intimately involved with America during the titanic struggle of World War Two, been influenced by the memory of his audiences in Chicago and Boston nearly fifty years before?

I cannot say for what reason, but I do believe that in the course of that half-century Churchill's innermost thoughts on the Anglo–Boer War underwent a considerable change. His way of expressing them was through the ghost of his father: 'England should never have done that.'

REFERENCE NOTES

ABBREVIATIONS

AHD   Aylmer Haldane, diary, Haldane papers

CAC   Churchill Archives Centre

DMP   WSC's dispatches to the *Morning Post*. Dated as printed in *London to Ladysmith* and *Ian Hamilton's March*

EL   Winston S. Churchill, *My Early Life*

NAR   National Archives Repository, Pretoria

RSC   Randolph S. Churchill, *Winston S. Churchill*, Vol. I: *Youth*

WSC   Winston Spencer Churchill

ONE: *Gateway*

2 'He was my' RSC, p.283
2 'endless forests' EL, p.89
3 'a mere social' Sandys, *From Winston with Love and Kisses*, p.182
3 'to scenes of' CAC
4 'the desire for' EL, p.118
4 'She is the' CAC
5 'I should advise' CAC
5 'When I think' CAC
6 'I rode forward' CAC
6 'I have faith' CAC
6 'I rode my' CAC
6 'Bullets are not' CAC
6 'We were to' EL, p.158
7 'I saw the' ibid.
7 'in our path' ibid., p.189
7 'like a race' ibid., p.190
7 Battle of Omdurman: ibid., p.201
8 'Had the army' CAC

TWO: *Preparing for War*

9 'Please understand' *History of the English Speaking Peoples Vol IV*, p.296

10 'Our Account with' RSC, p.499
11 'a practical political' EL, p.240
11 'He is a' ibid.
12 'able to write' ibid., p.241
12 'inhuman slaughter' CAC
12 'passed from hand' Churchill, *The River War*, Vol. II, p.212
12 'a bit of' EL, p.241
13 'Harmsworth telegraphed me' CAC
13 Boer War correspondents: Read, *The Power of News*, p.106
14 'most happy to' CAC
14 'He would have' EL, p.244
15 'I fear the' CAC
15 'It is definitely . . .' CAC
16 'About the Cinematograph' CAC
16 'My dear Winston' CAC
16 'a very clever' Manchester, *The Last Lion*, p.242
16 Randolph Payne & Sons: CAC
17 'I saw Winston' CAC
18 'I send you' CAC
18 'I see no earthly' Halle, *The Irrepressible Churchill*, p.29
18 'I see the American' CAC
18 'Dear Sandys' collection of Steve Forbes, New York

THREE: *Cruising to a Catastrophe*

21 'Redvers Buller has' *Black and White Budget*, 30 December 1899
22 'acquired no reverence' *Incidents and Reflections*, Atkins, p.122
22 'We have had' CAC
23 'Buller was a' EL, p.247
24 'I am very' CAC
24 'What an odious' DMP, 26 October 1899
25 'This morning we' DMP, 29 October 1899
26 'It looks as' EL, p.250
26 'I dare say' ibid.
27 'It is a long' and subsequent WSC quotations, DMP, 1 November 1899
29 'a cat' CAC
29 'I write you' CAC
30 'misgivings were dispelled' EL, p.254

FOUR: *The Station Yard*

33 'They have never' DMP, 6 November 1899
34 'quite ready to' Menpes, *War Impressions*, pp.124–7
35 'Go to hell' Hurst, *Winston Churchill: War Correspondent South African War*, p.46
36 'He wanted to' *Estcourt Gazette*, 14 December 1940
36 'Mark my words' Derek Clegg to the author
36 'We had found' Chaplin, *Winston Churchill and Harrow*, p.66
37 'How many more' DMP, 9 November 1899
38 'We soon reached' ibid.
39 '*I did that*' Atkins, *Incidents and Reflections*, p.127
39 'bought the ground' DMP, 10 November 1899
39 'the State may' CAC
41 'It is a great' Magnus, *Kitchener: Portrait of an Imperialist*, p.287
41 'When I left' Churchill, *The World Crisis* (abridged edition 1931), p.140
42 'a lonely, young' Stevenson, 'Correspondence with Colonel W.

Park Gray', unpublished manuscript
42 Norgate: Liz Burrow (great-granddaughter), letter to the author

FIVE: *Knight Errant*

45 'Wilson's death trap' DMP, 20 November 1899
46 'We started at' ibid.
46 'I do not' Haldane, *A Soldier's Saga*, p.142
46 WSC's admission: WSC, conversation with Major-General Hilyard, quoted in Pakenham, *The Boer War*, p.278
47 'As the train' DMP, 20 November 1899
47 'Keep cool' Atkins, *The Relief of Ladysmith*, p.75
47 'The Boers held' DMP, 20 November 1899
48 'quick witted and' Haldane, *A Soldier's Saga* 143
48 'Mr Winston Churchill' CAC
50 'A very brave' Martin, *The Durban Light Infantry*, p.73
50 'All the time' *Contemporary Review*, December 1901, p.872
50 'I have had' DMP, 20 November 1899
50 Botha and artillery: Martin, *The Durban Light Infantry*, p.73
51 'The Boers maintained' CAC
51 'There was a' DMP, 20 November 1899
52 'As many wounded' ibid.
52 'The armoured engine' *Natal Advertiser*, 15 November 1899
52 'Seeing the engine' DMP, 20 November 1899
53 'I can't leave' R.E. Clegg, *Escourt Gazette*, 14 December 1940
53 'My mind retains' EL, p.264
54 'When one is' ibid., p.265
55 'What have you' ibid., p.266
56 'Not many, perhaps' DMP, 24 November 1899
56 'like cattle' Atkins, *The Relief of Ladysmith*, p.193
57 'very young, unshaven' *Outspan*, 26 May 1944

57 'We don't catch' DMP, 24 November 1899

SIX: *The Botha Legend*

59 'He also refused' NAR
59 'Who may my' Mrs Yvonne Knowles to the author
59 'We talked of' EL, p.267
60 'Publish this' *No Charge for Delivery*, C.W.L. de Souza, p.88
60 'I was captured' RSC, p.474
61 'Few men that' EL, p.267
62 'something interesting' RSC, p.209
62 Muriel Wilson to Churchill: ibid., p.210
62 'It was so' *Sunday Express*, 22 October 1967

SEVEN: *Into Captivity*

64 'the only war' Extra edition of *Natal Advertiser*, 15 November 1899
64 'in the most' *Natal Advertiser*, 17 November 1899
65 'I had a' Leslie papers
65 'Churchill is a' CAC
65 'gave glowing details' *Cornhill Magazine*, July 1900
65 'Mr Churchill is' *Truth*, 23 November 1899
66 'I came down' RSC, p.467
67 'He has received' CAC
69 'I would point' CAC
69 'It has occurred' CAC
71 'two strangely long' and subsequent WSC quotations, DMP, 24 and 30 November 1899
75 'a small young' Karl Kohler, letter to the author
79 'Morning Post, London' de Souza papers

EIGHT: *The States Model School*

80 Details of States Model School: C.W.L. de Souza, unpublished manuscript, Chapter 2
80 Layout of school: NAR
81 'Cox's should be' CAC
82 'a far seeing' DMP, 3 December 1899

82 'He is no' Marie de Souza's diary, de Souza papers
82 Godfray's unpopularity: Haldane, *How we Escaped from Pretoria*, p.60
82 'rather a poor' DMP, 3 December 1899
83 'I do not imagine' CAC
83 'I expect to' CAC
83 'Mr Winston Churchill' NAR
84 'skilful pious soldiers' NAR
84 'persistent jingoistic attitudes' de Souza papers
86 'blessed with less' Haldane, *A Soldier's Saga*, p.161
86 'One is reminded' EL, p.281
86 'In my view' NAR
86 Question of *parole*: NAR
88 'The Government does' NAR
88 'courtesy, courage and' CAC
89 'I am 25' CAC
89 'a kind hearted' DMP, 3 December 1899
91 'received them sitting' ibid.
92 'Unless I am' CAC
93 'He suggested coming' Haldane, *How we Escaped from Pretoria*, p.53
94 'any parole that' NAR
94 'I do not' de Souza papers
95 'if I accept' NAR
97 'You're afraid' AHD, note 29 October 1935
97 'That damned fool' ibid.

NINE: *Controversy*

99 'Great excitement' Hofmeyr, *The Story of my Captivity*, p.132
99 'Wednesday 13th' Marie de Souza diary, de Souza papers
100 'In my view' NAR
100 Stephan Schotel's version of WSC's escape: Pamela Holst, letter to the author
101 'Escape not due' NAR
101 Godfray and Haldane: Haldane, *How we Escaped from Pretoria*, p.60
103 'Englishman, 25 years' NAR
103 de Haas reward: Ambassador du Buisson to the author
103 'I enclose a' CAC
104 Formal inquiry: Davy, *Churchill and Pretoria*; NAR

105 'A man gives' Hofmeyr, *The Story of my Captivity*, p.136
105 'I think I' RSC, p.498
106 'I wonder whether' NAD
106 'He was not' CAC
106 'threw quite an' AHD, Chapter X
108 ' "Twice Captured" ' *Morning Post*, 26 October 1900
108 '[I] contradict absolutely' CAC
108 'The enclosed correspondence' CAC
109 'believing him to' AHD, Chapter X
109 'I see by' ibid.
110 'what I honestly' quoted in *Sunday Times*, 1 June 1997
110 'I have a lot' CAC
111 'I must allow' AHD, Chapter X
111 'Had Churchill only' ibid.
113 'sneering allusions' ibid., Chapter IX
114 'I think you' ibid.
114 'slipped off without' and subsequent quotations, *Sunday Times*, 1 June 1997

TEN: *Wanted Dead or Alive*

116 'Just received the' CAC
117 'The night was' and subsequent WSC quotations, DMP, 22 December 1899
121 'I just felt' EL, p.294
122 'Still the odds' ibid., p.295
122 *'Wie is daar?'* ibid.
123 'like a drowning' ibid., p.297
124 'They'll all vote' ibid., p.298
125 'My four friends' ibid., p.299
125 'The patter of' ibid., p.301
126 'shot into the' ibid., p.298
126 Mineworker and cigar: *Johannesburg Star*, 11 December 1923
126 Ada Blunden and Ellen David: Mrs Mary Swan to the author
127 Burnham and escape plan: Mr John Burnham to the author
127 'The hazards of' EL, p.304
128 'Now, Dan, I' *Oldham Chronicle*, 22 October 1961
128 'And again, after' EL, p.307
128 'I well remember' *Johannesburg Star*, 2 September 1907
129 Haldane's amazement: Haldane,

How we Escaped from Pretoria*, p.186
131 'the excitement of' EL, pp.308–11
131 'We drove to' *Johannesburg Star*, 22 December 1923; EL, pp.310–11
131 Telegram to *Standard and Diggers News*, 23 December 1899
132 'nearly a dozen' DMP, 22 December 1899

ELEVEN: *A Soldier Again*

134 'Why weren't we' Black Watch Museum
136 'Your gallant son' Pakenham, *The Boer War*, p.241
137 'We are in' *Natal Mercury*, 25 December 1899
138 'He said we' *Natal Witness*, 30 December 1899
138 'From the Town' ibid.
139 'all this pruning' DMP, 24 December 1899
140 'Glory to God' DMP, 4 January 1900
140 'I will do' Brenthurst Library
140 'I am sending' Durban Municipal Library
141 WSC note to secretary: CAC
141 'When my dad' note in the possession of J. McLachlan
142 Letters to WSC from Howard, Burnham, McKenna and Addams: CAC
142 'after the heroic': CAC
143 'The Buck and' EL, p.317
143 'Winston Churchill turned' CAC
144 'A commission, please' and subsequent conversation EL, p.319
145 'I stitched my', ibid.
145 'the long plume' ibid., p.320
145 'Alas dearest we' CAC
146 'Sir Redvers Buller' DMP, 13 January 1900
146 'Boom. Thud, thud' and subsequent WSC quotations, DMP, 8 January 1900

TWELVE: *A General on Spion Kop*

150 'I have never' DMP, 13 January 1900
152 'Very few of' DMP, 25 January 1900

153 'aroused the most' DMP, 22 January 1900

153 'The stony face' ibid.

154 'Old and grey' DMP, 25 January 1900

158 'that acre of' Atkins, *The Relief of Ladysmith*, p.237

159 'We appear to' Pakenham, *The Boer War*, p.299

160 'one self-appointed' ibid., p.303

161 'perhaps the reader' and subsequent WSC quotations, DMP, 25 January 1900

163 Captain Levita's account: Pemberton, *Battles of the Boer War*, p.194

164 'fully believing', Reitz, *Commando*, p.78

165 'the soldiers lay' ibid., p.79

165 'We Boers would' Atkins, *The Relief of Ladysmith*, p.245

165 'five very dangerous' CAC

THIRTEEN: *Into Ladysmith*

167 'free from all' and subsequent WSC quotations, DMP, 4 February 1900

169 'My Mother and' CAC

170 'I did not' *The Reminiscences of Lady Randolph Churchill*, p.423

170 'You must not' letter in the possession of Winston S. Churchill

171 'Buller had not' EL, p.336

171 'We never get' DMP, 15 February 1900

172 'Here is an' CAC

172 'It seemed as' *Relief of Ladysmith*, Atkins, p.270

173 'Now at last' DMP, 19 February 1900

173 'We have passed' DMP, 4 March 1900

174 'It was a' DMP, 5 March 1900

174 'was about to' ibid.

174 'My nerves were' CAC

174 'The neglect and' DMP, 5 March 1900

174 'We arose' DMP, 6 March 1900

176 'Damn pursuit' EL, p.340

176 'Damn the prize' ibid.

176 'The evening was' DMP, 6 March 1900

177 'suggest your firing' Pakenham, *The Boer War*, p.239

178 'Never before had' ibid.

178 'I, personally, was' Martin, *Diary of the Siege of Ladysmith*

179 'a brave fighting' and subsequent WSC quotations, DMP, 10 March 1900

FOURTEEN: *A Lull in the Storm*

182 'After the tumults' WSC, *Savrola*, p.211

182 'It is clear' CAC

182 'All my philosophy' CAC

182 'I have consistently' EL, p.165

182 'About twenty miles' Cornwallis-West, *The Reminiscences of Lady Randolph Churchill*, p.438

183 'after viewing and' ibid., p.446

183 'to cover the' letter in the possession of Elliott H. Costas

183 'Make sure I' CAC

184 'for such a' CAC

184 'I will write' CAC

184 'stand any war' CAC

184 'five years of' CAC

185 'People must forgive' EL, p.345

186 'imported social Capetown' and subsequent WSC quotations, DMP, 13 April 1900

187 'rather funny' CAC

187 'that the resolve' CAC

188 'Lord Roberts desires' CAC

188 'You will form' CAC

188 'So I left' DMP, 13 April 1900

188 'an irreverent subaltern' ibid.

189 'I am exceedingly ' letter in the possession of Mr W.H. Mackay

189 'The Market Square' DMP, 16 April 1900

190 'the Queen's greatest' ibid.

191 'little time to' EL, p.349

FIFTEEN: *Return to Pretoria*

192 'But while the' and subsequent WSC quotations, DMP, 16 April 1900

193 'sometimes quite alone' EL, p.350

194 'a man of' EL, p.70

194 'an inability real' ibid., p.76

194 'to be too' Pakenham, *The Boer War*, p.318

195 'So, in the', and subsequent WSC quotations, DMP, 22 April 1900

196 'great admiration' letter in the possession of Mrs Doris Maud

196 'Oh, my poor' DMP, 22 April 1900

196 'contemplated with feelings' DMP, 1 May 1900

197 'the most comical' EL, p.352

197 'Impossible decide here' CAC

198 'as concerns the' CAC

199 'raised floor of' EL, p.360

199 'the pretty little' DMP, 22 May 1900

200 'Well, you see' and subsequent WSC quotations, DMP, 2 June 1900

201 'As we passed' EL, p.363

202 'dined hastily and' and subsequent WSC quotations, DMP, 2 June 1900

203 'At about half' Frankland's diary, quoted in RSC, p.628

203 'Suddenly Winston Churchill' Goodacre's diary, quoted ibid., p.529

204 'the imperious necessities' DMP, 14 June 1900

204 'I propose to' CAC

204 'his chances of' Churchill, *The Story of the Malakand Field Force*, p.170

205 'I had one' EL, p.367

207 'full civilian status' ibid.

207 'It is my' NAR

208 'This expectation, however' EL, p.368

EPILOGUE: *A Triumphal Progress*

209 'I have about', CAC

210 'I do not' CAC

211 'Tomorrow we begin' CAC

212 'After this, I' EL, p.374

212 'A triumphal progress' ibid., p.375

212 'There is a' CAC

213 'trumpeters sounded the' Halle, *The Irrepressible Churchill*, p.33

213 'I think that' EL, p.376

213 'If I were' and subsequent quotations, Randolph S. Churchill, *Winston S. Churchill*, Vol. II, pp.7–9

213 'scowled at the' DMP, 2 June 1900

213 'This at the' EL, p.373

214 'ended in the' *A History of the English Speaking Peoples*, Vol IV, p.294

214 'I turned' Churchill, 'The Dream', p.12

214 'Ah, a reporter' ibid., p.22

214 'developed so far' ibid., p.28

214 'England should never' ibid., p.24

BIBLIOGRAPHY

PUBLISHED SOURCES

Amery, L.S. (ed.), *The Times History of the War in South Africa* (seven vols), Sampson Low, Marston & Co, 1905

Atkins, J.B., *Incidents and Reflections*, Christophers, 1947

Atkins, J.B., *The Relief of Ladysmith*, Methuen, 1900

Brendon, Piers, *Winston Churchill, A Brief Life*, Secker & Warburg, 1984

Bonham Carter, Violet, *Winston Churchill as I Knew Him*, Eyre & Spottiswoode and Collins, 1965

Chadwick, *The Anglo–Boer War in Natal*

Chaplin, E.D.W., *Winston Churchill and Harrow*, Harrow School Bookshop, 1941

Churchill, Randolph S., *Winston S. Churchill*, Vol. I: *Youth*, Heinemann, 1966

Churchill, Randolph S., *Winston S. Churchill*, Vol. II: *Young Statesman*, Heinemann, 1967

Churchill, Randolph S., *Companion*, Vol. I, Heinemann, 1967

Churchill, Winston S., *The Malakand Field Force*, Longmans, 1898

Churchill, Winston S., *The River War*, Longmans, 1899

Churchill, Winston S., *Savrola*, Longmans, 1899

Churchill, Winston S., *Ian Hamilton's March*, Longmans, 1900

Churchill, Winston S., *London to Ladysmith*, Longmans, 1900

Churchill, Winston S., *The World Crisis*, Thornton Butterworth, 1923

Churchill, Winston S., *My Early Life*, Macmillan, 1930

Churchill, Winston S., *A History of the English Speaking Peoples*, Vol. IV, Cassell, 1958

Churchill, Winston S., *The Dream: Collected Essays of Sir Winston Churchill*, Library of Imperial History, 1976

Cornwallis-West, Mrs George, *The Reminiscences of Lady Randolph Churchill*, The Century Co., 1907

de Souza, C.W.L., *No Charge for Delivery*, Books of Africa, Cape Town, 1969

Gilbert, Martin, *Churchill: A Life*, Heinemann, 1991

Gilbert, Martin, *In Search of Churchill*, HarperCollins, 1994

Graham, Alexander J.P., *The Capture and Escape of Winston Churchill*, Edinburgh Press, Salisbury, Rhodesia, 1965

Guedalla, Philip, *Mr Churchill: A Portrait*, Hodder & Stoughton, 1941

Haldane, Aylmer, *How we Escaped from Pretoria*, Blackwood, 1900

Haldane, Aylmer, *A Soldier's Saga*, Blackwood, 1948

Halle, Kay (ed.), *The Irrepressible Churchill*, Facts on File Publications, 1966

Hofmeyr, Adrian, *The Story of my Captivity*, Edward Arnold, 1900

Hurst, H.H., *Winston Churchill: War Correspondent South African War*, Knox Printing & Publishing Company, Durban, 1944

James, Robert Rhodes, *Churchill: A Study in Failure*, Weidenfeld & Nicolson, 1970

Leslie, Anita, *The Life of Lady Randolph Churchill*, Hutchinson, 1969

Magnus, P., *Kitchener: Portrait of an Imperialist*, John Murray, 1958

Manchester, William, *The Last Lion*, Michael Joseph, 1983

Martin, A.C., *The Durban Light Infantry*, Vol. I, HQ Durban Light Infantry, 1961

Martin, B.W., *Diary of the Siege of Ladysmith*, Ladysmith Historical Society, 1970

Menpes, Mortimer, *War Impressions*, A. & C. Black, 1901

Pakenham, Thomas, *The Boer War*, Weidenfeld & Nicolson, 1979

Pemberton, W.B., *Battles of the Boer War*, Batsford, 1964

Ponting, Clive, *Churchill*, Sinclair-Stevenson, 1994

Pretorius, F., *The Anglo–Boer War 1899–1902*, Don Nelson, Cape Town, 1985

Read, Donald, *The Power of News*, Oxford University Press, 1992

Reitz, Deneys, *Commando*, Faber & Faber, 1929

Roberts, Brian, *Churchills in Africa*, Hamish Hamilton, 1970

Sandys, Celia, *From Winston with Love and Kisses*, Sinclair-Stevenson, 1994

Spies, S.B. and Nattrass, Gail (eds), *Jan Smuts' Memoirs of the Boer War*, Jonathan Ball, 1994

UNPUBLISHED SOURCES

Black Watch Museum
de Souza, C.W.L., unpublished manuscript, de Souza papers, Pretoria
de Souza, Marie, diary, de Souza papers, Pretoria

Bibliography

Haldane, Aylmer, diary, Haldane papers, National Library of Scotland
Stevenson, R.E., 'Correspondence with Colonel W. Park Gray',
    unpublished manuscript
Tanner, A.D., 'John Densham Mare 1881–1966'

NEWSPAPERS

British

Contemporary Review
Cornhill Magazine
Morning Post
Oldham Chronicle
Sunday Express
Sunday Times

South African

Durban Daily News
Estcourt Gazette
Johannesburg Star
Natal Advertiser
Natal Mercury
Natal Witness
Outspan
Standard and Diggers News

INDEX

Index

Index